Windows NT Domain
Architecture

Gregg Branham

D1279291

International Standard Book Number: 1-57870-112-0

Library of Congress Catalog Card Number: 98-89281

02   01   00   99   4   3   2   1

Interpretation of the printing code: The rightmost double-digit number is the year of the book's printing; the rightmost single-digit, the number of the book's printing. For example, the printing code 99-1 shows that the first printing of the book occurred in 1999.

Composed in QuarkXpress and MCPdigital by Macmillan Computer Publishing

Printed in the United States of America

Trademark Acknowledgments

Warning and Disclaimer

Publisher *Don Fowley*

Executive Editor *Linda Ratts Engelman*

Managing Editor *Patrick Kanouse*

Acquisitions Editor
Karen Wachs

Development Editor
Lisa M. Thibault

Project Editor*
Jennifer Nuckles

Copy Editor
Greg Pearson

Indexer
Tim Wright

Acquisitions Coordinator
Jennifer Garrett

Manufacturing Coordinator
Brook Farling

Book Designer
Gary Adair

Cover Designer
Aren Howell

Proofreader
Megan Wade

Production Team Supervisor
Daniela Raderstorf

Layout Technician
Jeannette McKay

About the Author

Gregg Branham has been working with Windows NT since its first release. Currently, he is the president of Altus Network Solutions, Inc. (www.altusnet.com). Altus provides comprehensive consulting services for Windows NT and other BackOffice® products. Greg has completed several domain design and implementation projects for a wide range of clients. He has been an instructor for Learning Tree International for more than two years, teaching courses that involve Windows NT domain setup and establishment of trust relationships. As part of his work within Learning Tree, Gregg has taught hundreds of consultants, engineers, and administrators the skills necessary to design and manage multiple domain environments. Gregg is a Microsoft® Certified Systems Engineer (MCSE), a Microsoft Certified Trainer (MCT), and a Cisco Certified Network Associate (CCNA). He received his electrical engineering degree from the Georgia Institute of Technology.

About the Technical Reviewers

These reviewers contributed their considerable practical, hands-on expertise to the entire development process of *Windows NT Domain Architecture*. As the book was being written, these folks reviewed all the material for technical content, organization, and flow. Their feedback was critical to ensuring that *Windows NT Domain Architecture* fits our readers' need for the highest quality technical information.

Marc Charney has 12 years of experience in the computer industry. Upon receiving his degree from the University of California, Berkeley, in 1987, Marc went to work for the Federal Reserve Bank of San Francisco. At the Federal Reserve, he was involved in the design of computer models of the United States economy. After that, Marc moved on to Sybase, where he helped develop its sales-office integration, automation, and networking strategy. While at Sybase, Marc concentrated his efforts on networking and integration of systems, including PCs, Macintoshes, UNIX, and VAX. Following Sybase, Marc went to work for Delta Life & Annuity, where he managed a complete overhaul of its network and systems infrastructure. This process involved a large network redesign effort as well as a method for seamlessly integrating Windows NT, Novell NetWare, AS400s, and UNIX systems. Marc is currently working at First Tennessee Bank as an Internet security and intranet development manager. His current efforts are focused on Web integration of current bank systems.

Darshan Doshi, a senior systems architect, is the president of C J Technologies USA, Inc., a consulting firm specializing in Microsoft Windows NT and Microsoft BackOffice technologies. He is an MCSE who specializes in Microsoft SMS and Windows NT. He obtained his master's degree in electrical engineering from the University of Texas at Arlington in 1992 and has been working with Windows NT since then. His consulting assignments have included Fortune 500 companies such as Merrill Lynch and Merck & Co. He lives with his wife in North Brunswick, New Jersey. They both love the outdoors and have traveled extensively in Europe, Asia, and the United States. They are celebrating the birth of their first child, Ronak.

Dedication

This work is dedicated to my father, whose hard work and determination are unmatched by anyone I have ever encountered.

Acknowledgments

I would like to thank everyone at Macmillan for making this project a pleasant experience. Special thanks go to Linda Ratts Engelman for helping me achieve the correct focus, to Lisa Thibault for enduring my slaying of the Queen's English, and to Karen Wachs and Jennifer Garrett for keeping me on schedule and offering encouragement during the tough times.

Deserving praise also goes to Darshan Doshi and Marc Charney, who suffered through the technical review of the material. Thank you for your helpful commentary and commitment to producing a high-quality text.

I would like to thank Jon McDonald for contributing many helpful suggestions and parting with some of his favorite KiXtart scripts.

Many thanks go to my fellow instructors at Learning Tree International, who were kind enough to review the table of contents and offer many helpful suggestions.

Thanks also go to Susan for enduring my occasional crabbiness and offering support and understanding throughout the project.

Finally, I must extend thanks to Mom and Dad for being great friends as well as great parents and for offering support and encouragement in all that I do.

Feedback Information

At Macmillan Technical Publishing, our goal is to create in-depth technical books of the highest quality and value. Each book is crafted with care and precision, undergoing rigorous development that involves the unique expertise of members from the professional technical community.

Readers' feedback is a natural continuation of this process. If you have any comments regarding how we could improve the quality of this book, or otherwise alter it to better suit your needs, you can contact us at networktech@mcp.com. Please make sure to include the book title and ISBN in your message.

We greatly appreciate your assistance.

Contents at a Glance

Table of Contents

Introduction

Windows NT Domain Architecture is intended to assist you in the process of planning, designing, and implementing your domain architecture. It is also intended to provide you with strategies for organizing users and groups, sharing resources, and implementing enterprise services. The driving goal behind this book is to fill a gap in your Windows NT toolbox with a resource that covers Windows NT domains from the ground up. Although it would be helpful, you do not need to have experience with multiple domain networks. However, you should have some experience with basic NT system administration; the early chapters of the book establish domain concepts and build the foundation for working with multiple domains.

Although there are many texts that present the steps for basic administrative tasks, there are few, if any, that discuss the strategic guidelines you must follow to design and support an enterprise NT network. In this book you will find detailed information on how to best set up and configure your Windows NT computing infrastructure—from the design of your domain model all the way through to your organization of users and configuration of enterprise services such as DHCP and WINS.

The motivation for writing the book stems from my instructional and consulting experience. In both the classroom and at the client site, I have watched companies struggle with poorly designed Windows NT networks. The reasons for a poor design vary. In most cases, the company did not devote the proper amount of time and resources to the planning stage. Those who influence the design often do not fully understand how Windows NT operates and interacts at the domain level. As a result, they cannot fully weigh the advantages and disadvantages of a particular design, and they do not foresee the impact of a design on the end users or administrative staff.

This book is designed to bring focus to the important issues you need to consider regarding your domain architecture. Whether you are a consultant designing a Windows NT enterprise network or an administrator of a multiple domain environment, I am confident you will find this book to be a valuable resource and an important addition to your Windows NT knowledge base.

The Contents

Chapter 1, "Workgroups Versus Domains," introduces both the workgroup and the domain model. The chapter focuses on the problems associated with using Windows NT machines in a workgroup. In the final section of the chapter, you are presented with an introduction to the domain model, which is compared to the workgroup model to emphasize the solutions it provides.

Chapter 2, "Domain Concepts," explains the boundary of a domain and the relationship between primary and backup domain controllers. The chapter also explores the process of joining Windows NT machines to the domain and provides an in-depth look into the process of domain authentication.

Chapter 3, "The SAM Database," discusses the properties of the SAM database. The SAM database stores user, group, and computer accounts along with properties for each account. In this chapter you will learn about the structure of the SAM, how to calculate its size, and how it is synchronized among domain controllers.

Chapter 4, "Connecting Domains with Trust Relationships," explains trusts and strategies for using trust relationships. A trust relationship allows users of one domain to access resources of another domain. Consequently, a trust impacts the logon process, file system permissions, and resource sharing. The chapter ends with information on troubleshooting trusts.

Chapter 5, "Domain Models," introduces the four domain models advocated by Microsoft. The chapter presents the advantages and disadvantages of each model along with valuable information on how each can be applied to different business structures.

Chapter 6, "Domain Planning," covers the issues that affect domain design. The chapter starts with common goals that you must define for your business. You are then presented with information required to analyze your needs on an enterprise scale and on a site-by-site basis. The final section of the chapter illustrates many common approaches to organizing domain structures for medium and large networks.

Chapter 7, "Domain Reconfiguration," examines the perils and pitfalls of changing your domain architecture. The chapter starts by explaining the details of moving users and computers to a new domain. Then, three common domain reconfigurations are presented with a detailed outline of how each one is successfully completed.

Chapter 8, "Domain Security," discusses security from a domain perspective. A domain is a security boundary that is extended by trust relationships. In this chapter you will find a list of security measures you can follow to protect your

NT systems. The chapter also presents information on how to properly configure account and audit policies and how to enforce strong passwords. The
chapter ends with a brief discussion of firewalls and how they are commonly
used in a Windows NT environment.

Chapter 9, "Organizing Users," focuses on the organization of users and
groups in a multiple domain environment. The chapter begins with an introduction to the different types of users and groups on the system and an explanation of rights and abilities. The chapter offers detailed information on how
global and local groups are best used to grant access to domain users and
trusted domain users. In addition, the chapter discusses the arrangement of
users into groups for the purpose of granting administrative capabilities on the
system.

Chapter 10, "Logon Scripts, Profiles, and Policies," provides useful information on how to effectively use logon scripts, profiles, and policies to control the
user environment. In this chapter you will learn how to use KiXtart to create
powerful logon scripts and how to set up and configure server-based profiles.
Later in the chapter, policies are introduced and strategies for their design and
implementation are presented. The chapter ends with details related to the
setup and configuration of the directory replication service used to replicate
logon scripts and policies in the domain.

Chapter 11, "Controlling Access to Domain Resources," explains NT file system security. In this chapter you will be presented with guidelines for configuring resource permissions in multiple domain environments. Utilities for the
inspection and setting of folder and file permissions are also discussed.

Chapter 12, "The Browser," focuses on the operation and tuning of the
browser. The browser is the gateway to network resources and, on most enterprise networks, it proves to be problematic. The chapter begins with a detailed
look at how browsing works and how machines are elected to maintain the
browse list. Following that is information on how to modify machines to
weigh the election criteria and force machines to become master browsers.
Finally, utilities are introduced to assist you in troubleshooting browser problems.

Chapter 13, "Enterprise Services: DHCP, WINS, and DNS," provides configuration strategies for DHCP, WINS, and DNS in multiple domain environments.
DHCP is used for the automated assignment of IP addresses on TCP/IP networks. The operation of DHCP and implementation strategies are discussed in
the chapter. For name resolution, WINS and DNS are used. WINS is used to
resolve NetBIOS names and is needed for file and print sharing across subnets,
whereas DNS is used to resolve domain names and is needed by most socket-
based applications.

In addition to the chapters, there are four appendices that offer specific help with particular tools or processes. Included are Appendix A, "Working with Performance Monitor;" Appendix B, "Working with Network Monitor;" Appendix C, "Changing IP Addressing Schemes;" and Appendix D, "Changing Naming Conventions."

Conventions Used in This Book

The following conventions are used in this book:

Tip

Tips provide you with helpful troubleshooting information as well as advice on how to approach common problems.

Author's Note

Author notes are used to convey personal experiences and real-world applications of a particular strategy.

Troubleshooting Tip

Troubleshooting tips provide resolutions for some problems you may encounter during deployment.

Warning

Warnings provide you with information you need to know to avoid damage to data, hardware, or software, or to avoid error messages that tell you that you are unable to complete a task.

Chapter 1

Workgroups Versus Domains

This chapter will review:

- **The Workgroup Model**
  A workgroup is a low-cost peer networking solution that allows machines to be logically grouped for the purpose of sharing resources.

- **Windows NT Workgroups**
  The security capabilities of Windows NT challenge its ability to function well as a workgroup client.

- **Introduction to Microsoft Domains**
  A Microsoft domain offers a robust arrangement of machines that share a common user accounts database. Benefits of the Microsoft domain include centralized administration and enhanced security.

The Workgroup Model

Microsoft provides two possible ways to organize your computers: a *workgroup* and a *domain*. The workgroup model, which originated with Windows for Workgroups, was designed as a low-cost, easy-to-use peer networking solution. Because the workgroup model is based on peer networking, a server is not required—so the cost of the solution is lowered.

Without a server, all resources in the workgroup model must be shared from individual client machines. Users are typically responsible for establishing the shares and setting their security. As a result, the security for resources is often neglected or minimal at best.

Author's Note

The share-level security of a workgroup forces users to remember too many passwords. Imagine a network of 10 machines with two shared resources each. If a separate password were used to connect to each resource, you would have to remember 20 passwords.

continues

Continued

> *You can avoid this problem if you have Windows 95 clients and an NT or NetWare server. Windows 95 supports both share-level and user-level security; however, for user-level security the Windows 95 machines require an NT server or NetWare server for authenticating access to its shared resources.*

Workgroups do not impose any restrictions on the users' ability to browse and connect to resources. They can browse resources in any workgroup and connect to resources for which they have a password. If the resource has a blank password, connection to the resource is automatic.

Workgroup Organization

The organization of a workgroup is simple: Machines that share similar functionality are placed into a workgroup. In most organizations, the workgroups are arranged based on departments or company divisions. For example, a typical workgroup might consist of all machines in the sales or engineering department (see Figure 1.1).

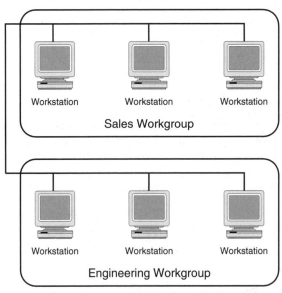

Figure 1.1   *Workgroups are a way of organizing machines and resources commonly shared by a group of users.*

By organizing machines into a workgroup, you can organize the presentation of resources in the browse list, displaying each workgroup separately. You can expand each workgroup in the list to expose the machines in that workgroup and ultimately reach resources on a particular machine. This makes it easy for users in the same workgroup to share resources and exchange data.

Problems of the Workgroup Model

The workgroup model presents the following problems:

- Workgroups lack security.

- Resource administration is performed by users.

- Share-level security forces users to memorize too many passwords.

- Resources are not backed up unless each individual workstation is backed up.

- Connectivity to resources is unpredictable because clients may not leave their machines powered on.

- Resources are decentralized and located on multiple computers.

A workgroup is nothing more than a logical grouping of machines and has no effect on the administration of users and groups or the control of resources. The machines in a workgroup do not share their security with other workgroup members, nor do they share a common list of users and groups who can access the workgroup's resources. Furthermore, the workgroup model advocates peer-to-peer networking, which leads to many problems on an enterprise network.

Windows NT Workgroups

Windows NT workgroups are complicated by the existence of a local Security Accounts Manager (SAM) database on each NT machine. The *SAM database* is used to authenticate both interactive and network logons. Before you can browse resources on a remote NT machine in a workgroup, you must be authenticated by the remote machine. Although this remote authentication increases network security, it turns the workgroup model into an administrative nightmare.

To better understand the interaction of NT machines in a workgroup configuration, consider the network in Figure 1.2.

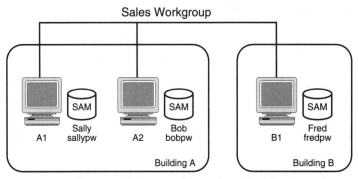

Figure 1.2   *An NT workgroup of three machines. Note that the SAM also contains an administrator account and a disabled Guest account.*

When Sally logs on interactively to A1, her credentials (that is, username and password) are checked against those found in the local SAM database on the A1 machine. Notice there is no Sally account on A2 or B1. As a result, Sally cannot log on interactively from either of those two machines.

The Need for Multiple Accounts

Suppose Sally needs to log on interactively to machine A2 in Figure 1.2. To give a user the ability to log on to more than one machine in an NT workgroup, you must define an account for her on each NT machine. In Figure 1.3, an account for Sally has been added to A2. Now Sally can log on interactively from A1 or A2.

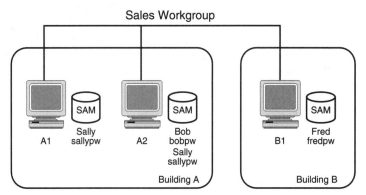

Figure 1.3   *An NT workgroup in which Sally has an account on two machines.*

Suppose Fred needs to grant Sally access to files on his machine. With Windows 95, Fred would simply share the folder containing the files, assigning a read-only or full-access password to the share. Because of its enhanced security, NT is more complicated than that. Before a remote user can list the shares of an NT workgroup machine, the user must be authenticated by the local SAM. Fred must first grant Sally access to the machine by creating an account for her in the local SAM or by enabling the Guest account.

The Impact of NT Abilities

The next step in granting Sally access to the files is for Fred to share the folder containing the files. This is where you encounter another problem with Windows NT and the workgroup model. If Fred were a member of only the Users group, he would lack the ability to share or stop sharing folders and printers. Abilities under Windows NT are predefined for built-in local groups and cannot be changed directly. (For more information on these abilities, see Chapter 9, "Organizing Users.")

The only way to give Fred the ability to share a folder is to give his account membership in the Power Users or Administrators group. If Fred shares the data folder on his machine and creates a Sally account, we have the configuration shown in Figure 1.4. Note that Sally now has three separate accounts, but the same password is used for all three. This makes it easier for Sally to access remote resources without being prompted for a separate username and password.

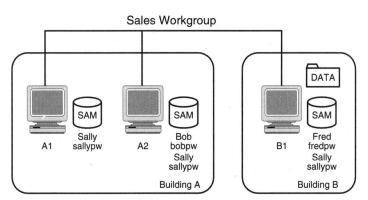

Figure 1.4   *Sally can access the shared Data folder on Fred's NT workstation.*

When you browse the resources on a remote NT machine, the credentials are sent across the wire, and the remote machine checks them against those listed in its SAM database. There are three possible outcomes of this search:

- There is a username and password that matches your local credentials in the SAM database on the remote machine. In this case you are authenticated, and you are able to list the shares.

- You do not have a valid account in the SAM database on the remote machine, but the Guest account on the remote machine is enabled with a blank password. In this case you are connected under the context of the Guest account, and you are able to view the shares.

- You do not have a matching username and password in the local SAM database, and you are prompted with an Enter Network Password dialog box (see Figure 1.5).

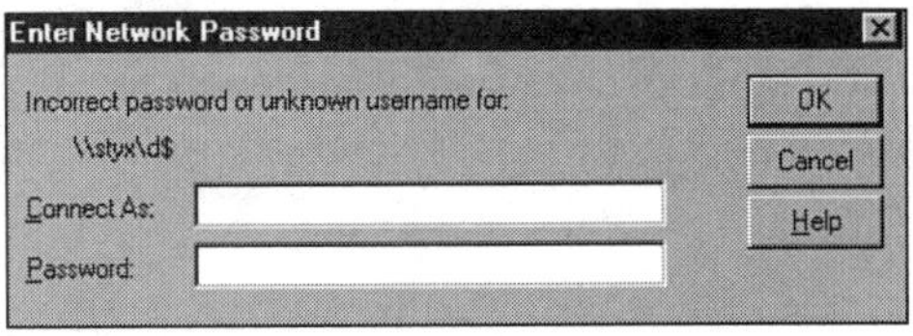

Figure 1.5   *The Enter Network Password dialog box appears when your current credentials cannot be found on the remote machine.*

The notion of separate accounts with different passwords is interesting. While utilities such as Explorer prompt you with an Enter Network Password dialog box, others such as User Manager for Domains and Server Manager provide no way of connecting to a remote machine under the context of a different account.

Troubleshooting Tip

Suppose you are an administrator, and you have an Administrator account on a remote machine but with a different password. The only way to administrate the remote machine with tools such as User Manager for Domains and Server Manager is to generate a Security Access Token on the remote machine. You can issue the following command to generate a Security Access Token:

```
net use \\<remote machine name>\IPC$ /user:<remote username>
```

You are then prompted to enter your password for the remote machine. After doing so, a Security Access Token is generated on the remote machine, and you can use utilities such as Server Manager to view its properties, shares, and so on. The Security Access Token is good for about 15 minutes; after it expires, you must issue the net use *command again.*

Consider once again the small network in Figure 1.4, in which Sally needed access to resources on three separate machines that required a username and password. Now consider a larger network with 50 users who need access to at least 10 machines each. Don't forget that everyone also needs to print to the same printer. You now have many accounts to create on each machine. To avoid this work, many administrators enable the Guest account on each machine. However, this is a huge security hazard, and it cancels out the added security you can achieve with Windows NT.

In Figure 1.6, Fred enables the Guest account to give Sally access to the Data folder. By doing so, Fred also gives Bob access to the Data folder (either intentionally or inadvertently). What if Bob were to view or delete files in the shared Data folder? Under most circumstances, you can use the auditing capabilities of NT to track a user's access to files. However, because Bob and Sally (and everyone else) can connect to the Data folder using the Guest account, Windows NT cannot distinguish a remote user who deletes the files!

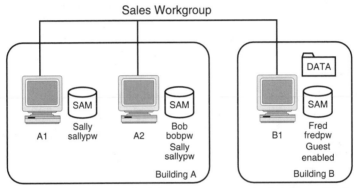

Figure 1.6 *Because Fred has enabled the Guest account, both Sally and Bob can access Fred's machine.*

No Common Security Policy

You must consider the security policy of the NT workgroup model. Not all machines share a common security policy; for example, one machine may be configured to require a six-character password, whereas another may be configured to require an eight-character password. Global security is nearly impossible with the NT workgroup model. On any network in which security is a concern, users should be forced to change their passwords periodically; Windows NT has the capability of enforcing such a policy.

Let's suppose you set all machines *individually* to the same security policy settings, requiring users to change their passwords on a regular basis. How can users remotely change their passwords on another workgroup NT machine? They can't! The users must physically go to the machine and log on to change their password.

Consider the example in Figure 1.4, in which Sally needed to access files on Fred's machine in a different building. If Sally had to change her password on Fred's machine, she would have had to travel to Building B and log on from the console of Fred's machine to do so.

The Perils of Peer Networking

To further explore the NT workgroup model, let us consider the idea of peer-to-peer networking. Peer-to-peer networking makes sense on small networks without a server. However, it is not a good idea on large networks because it promotes the sharing of folders and printers from each individual workstation, which makes backing up the data nearly impossible. Unless you have a tape drive in each workstation, you must back up the machines over the network. Backing up each hard disk would take too long, so users must adopt a convention of saving their work in a particular directory captured by the backup software. Furthermore, you must configure the backup software to capture the data from each machine. What a lot of extra work compared to saving data in one central location that is backed up on a regular basis!

In most cases, people using an NT workgroup attempt to centralize resources by locating them on a single Windows NT Workstation. However, they are also faced with a maximum limit of 10 user connections. This can be verified by typing the following at the command window:

```
net config server
```

This means that if 10 users are accessing a share on an NT workstation, the 11th user is rejected because there are too many user connections. From this perspective, Windows 95 is a better workgroup "server" than Windows NT Workstation because it places no restriction on the number of user connections.

Introduction to Microsoft Domains

A *domain* is similar to a workgroup in the sense that it is a grouping of machines. However, a domain is an administrative unit that shares a common database of users and groups and the same security policy. By sharing a single database of users and groups, you avoid the workgroup's problem of multiple isolated SAM databases on each workstation.

A *domain controller* is responsible for storing the domain SAM database. The domain controller must be an NT server. All domain workstations use the domain SAM to authenticate both interactive and network logons.

Figure 1.7 illustrates a domain similar to the workgroup used in the previous examples. Because Bob, Sally, and Fred have accounts defined on the domain controller, they can log on to any workstation in the domain. When Sally logs on, her credentials are sent to the domain controller for authentication. Then, when Sally attempts to browse resources on a remote domain workstation or server, her credentials are passed back to the domain controller for authentication.

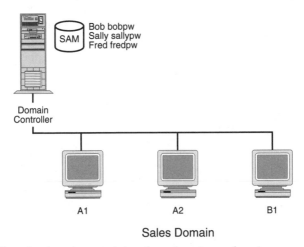

Figure 1.7   *The sales domain containing three domain workstations.*

Benefits of a Domain

A domain offers many benefits that workgroups do not. Some of the benefits include

- Centralized administration
- Security
- Ease of use

Centralized Administration

By locating all user and group accounts in a single database, you gain the benefit of conducting all administration in a single location. No longer is there a need to define an account for each user requiring access to a machine or its resources. With a domain, you simply define an account once on the domain controller. This eliminates 90% of the problems of the workgroup model.

The domain SAM can be leveraged by any workstation or server in the domain for the purpose of granting domain users and groups access to resources. Thus, if Fred is a user on Workstation B1 (refer to Figure 1.7) and needs to grant

Sally access to a folder on that machine, he can select the Sally account from the domain SAM and place it on the Directory Permissions for the folder. The list of permissions for files, folders, and printers is commonly referred to as an access control list (ACL).

Centralized authentication by the domain controller gives domain administrators the ability to leverage features such as logon scripts, policies, and profiles much more easily than in the workgroup model. In fact, you can define a single logon script for everyone in the entire domain. You can also define Windows NT and Windows 95 policies that can be implemented based on username, group membership, or machine name. See Chapter 10, "Logon Scripts, Profiles, and Policies," for information on system policies.

Security

In addition to providing a unit of administration, a domain is also a security boundary. Everyone outside the domain is considered untrusted, and they are not granted access to domain resources (unless they are from a trusted domain, as described in Chapter 4, "Connecting Domains with Trust Relationships"). The security policy you define on the domain controller applies to all accounts in the domain. Thus, you can easily implement and modify a password policy that applies globally to all users and machines in the domain.

In a domain, users can change their password from their workstation and have that change propagated to the domain SAM. This eliminates another problem of the workgroup, which doesn't allow users to change passwords remotely.

Ease of Use

One of the driving concepts behind a domain is that users need to remember only one username and password to access domain resources. Separate passwords for each remote share or machine are no longer required. Of course, this does not mean that all user accounts automatically have access to all domain resources. Access to domain resources should be controlled by the administrator, who can deny an individual user or a group access to specific domain resources.

Users also gain mobility with a domain; they are able to log on to any domain workstation. No matter which domain workstation users log on to, their credentials are sent to the domain controller for authentication.

Chapter *2*

Domain Concepts

This chapter will review:

- **Domain Controllers**
  Domain controllers maintain the user accounts database and provide authentication services.

- **PDCs and BDCs**
  A Microsoft domain can have only one primary domain controller. Backup domain controllers are used for fault tolerance and load balancing.

- **Domain Troubleshooting**
  The PDC is the most critical machine in the domain. Understanding the effects of a PDC crash and the process of promoting a BDC is crucial for planning a good domain architecture.

- **PDC/BDC Loading**
  Knowing how to measure and gauge domain controller performance allows you to do a much more effective job of capacity planning.

- **The Authentication Process**
  A detailed understanding of the authentication process helps you effectively place domain controllers and lower WAN authentication traffic.

- **Windows 2000 and Active Directory**
  Active Directory, the Windows 2000 directory service, overcomes many NT 4 limitations and has a significant impact on domain design.

Domain Controllers

A *domain* is an administrative grouping of machines that share a single user accounts database and a common security policy. A domain requires one primary domain controller (PDC) and can have one or more backup domain controllers (BDCs). Domain controllers play a critical role in the domain because they maintain the Security Accounts Manager (SAM) database, which is the database of user accounts. The SAM database must be used to authenticate access to all domain resources. BDCs maintain a copy of the SAM database and may be used for fault tolerance and load balancing.

There are three ways to configure an NT server's role in the domain:

- PDC

- BDC

- Member Server

Member Servers do not store copies of the domain SAM, nor do they provide domain authentication services. Consequently, Member Servers are excellent choices for file, print, and application servers (FPAs). Isolating enterprise applications such as SQL Server and Microsoft Exchange give you a greater ability to tune and optimize the server for the application.

You can reverse the roles of a PDC and BDC using Server Manager. However, you cannot change a machine from a Member Server to a domain controller (PDC or BDC), or vice versa. For example, suppose you want to replace your SQL server with a newer machine and use the older machine as a BDC. You must reinstall Windows NT on the older machine and configure the new installation as a BDC.

Author's Note

Windows 2000 will allow you to change a machine's role from a Member Server to a domain controller without reinstalling Windows NT.

PDCs and BDCs

Primary and backup domain controllers store the domain SAM database. The SAM database contains information such as username, password, and group membership. The contents of the SAM and its synchronization among domain controllers are discussed at length in Chapter 3, "The SAM Database."

The only changeable copy of the SAM database is on the PDC; BDCs maintain a read-only copy of the SAM (see Figure 2.1). Because the SAM is changeable only on the PDC, no conflicting changes can be made to the database, which ensures its integrity. Despite having a read-only SAM, BDCs are still able to authenticate users and fulfill requests for logon scripts, policies, and so on.

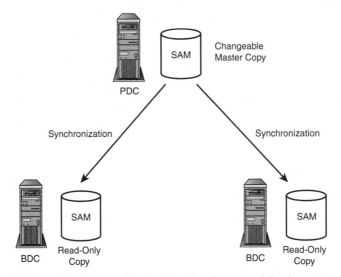

Figure 2.1   *BDCs maintain a synchronized read-only copy of the domain SAM.*

Domain administration tools such as User Manager for Domains and Server Manager must have access to the PDC. If the PDC is unavailable, you cannot use the tools to administer the database. By placing the master copy of the SAM on the PDC and allowing only one PDC per domain, Microsoft has created a single point of failure for the administration of users, groups, and workstations in the domain. Consequently, the location of the PDC is an important part of domain architecture.

The synchronization of the SAM database from the PDC to BDCs occurs automatically. Any change made via User Manager for Domains or Server Manager is committed to the PDC SAM and distributed to the BDCs based on the synchronization interval set in the Registry. A listing of Registry parameters for SAM replication is presented in Chapter 3.

Because domain controllers store the SAM database, they are responsible for authenticating all domain users. Authentication involves more than simply verifying a user's credentials upon logon. Windows NT also performs *pass-through authentication*. When a user requests access to a resource on a Member Server, the Member Server accepts the user's credentials and passes them to the domain controller for authentication. Thus, domain controllers perform authentication throughout the day as people use resources.

BDCs are often used to load-balance authentication traffic at a remote site. Suppose you have a single domain that spans two geographic areas connected with a leased line. In Figure 2.2, when users log on in New York, their authentication requests are processed by the BDC in New York. Placing a BDC in New York alleviates the authentication traffic forwarded to the Atlanta PDC. This not only speeds up access to resources for New York users, but it also relieves the WAN link of unnecessary congestion.

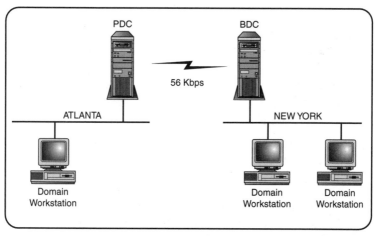

Figure 2.2   *Placing a BDC in New York eliminates the authentication traffic directed to the Atlanta PDC.*

Tip

Imagine you are working on a large corporate network with 5,000 users and an 8MB SAM. Suppose you must change a person's group membership, but the PDC is located across a 56Kbps network link. Upon opening User Manager for Domains, the PDC would pull the users and groups across the wire. At 56Kbps, you would be looking at a wait of over two minutes. To alleviate this problem, you could choose Low Speed Connection from the Options menu in User Manager for Domains (see Figure 2.3).

Importance of PDC

The PDC is critical to the operation of the domain because it contains the only SAM database in the entire domain that can be modified. When you use tools such as User Manager for Domains or Server Manager—even from the console of a BDC or a domain workstation—you are viewing the SAM database on the PDC.

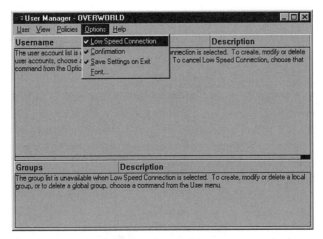

Figure 2.3   *Selecting Low Speed Connection enables you to manipulate user and group properties without downloading a list of users and groups from the PDC over a slow network link.*

Without the PDC, the following occurs:

- You cannot set permissions on domain resources. Adding domain users or groups to the ACL requires connectivity to a functional PDC.

- You cannot reset passwords, change group memberships, modify profile paths, or perform other actions with User Manager for Domains.

- A portion of Server Manager's functionality is disabled (see Figure 2.4).

Figure 2.4   *When the PDC is unavailable, some functionality of Server Manager is lost.*

Effects of a PDC Crash

By design, a domain can have only one functioning PDC. When the PDC fails or network connectivity to the PDC is lost, you must decide whether you need to promote a BDC. Here are some factors to consider if the PDC fails:

- How long do you expect the PDC to be unavailable?

- Do you need User Manager for Domains during this time?

- Do you need to add any computer accounts in Server Manager during this time?

- Do you need to set permissions on any domain resources during this time?

- How are users authenticated now that the PDC is unavailable? In other words, can users reach a BDC, or are they logged on using cached account information?

In many cases, it is not necessary to immediately promote a BDC to a PDC when you discover the PDC is unavailable. For instance, if you plan to take the PDC offline for a network card upgrade, you do not need to promote a BDC. As a courtesy to users, however, you should inform everyone in the domain that they will be unable to change passwords during the time the PDC is down for scheduled maintenance.

Changing a BDC to a PDC

Promoting a BDC to a PDC is a multistep process that occurs between a selected BDC and the currently active PDC. (Note that the active PDC is demoted as a part of the process.) Under normal operating conditions, you are not given the option to change a PDC to a BDC but only the option to promote a BDC. The special case in which you can explicitly demote a PDC is investigated at the end of this section.

The promotion operation is composed of the following steps:

1. Full synchronization of the SAM database occurs between the BDC and PDC. This ensures that the BDC contains a completely up-to-date copy of the SAM.

2. NetLogon Service is stopped on both machines. This does not mean the machines drop connections—they just cannot perform any authentication during the time the promotion process takes place.

3. The active PDC is demoted to a BDC.

4. The BDC is promoted to a PDC.

5. NetLogon Service restarts on both machines. Now both machines are ready to perform their authentication responsibilities.

Note the order of the demotion/promotion. This way, if the process should fail there won't be two functioning PDCs on the network.

Author's Note

You should be aware that Remote Access Service (RAS) stops and restarts as part of the BDC promotion process. The RAS stops immediately after the NetLogon service stops (step 2) and restarts after the NetLogon service restarts (step 5). Unlike NetLogon, however, RAS drops user connections when it stops. Consequently, it is not a good idea to dial into a PDC or BDC to change its role in the domain.

> *Tip*
>
> *In step 1 of the BDC promotion process, a full synchronization of the SAM occurs. A* full synchronization *means the entire SAM is copied from the PDC to the BDC. If the SAM is large or the network link between the machines is slow, this can take a considerable amount of time. For this reason, it is a good idea to maintain at least one BDC on the same LAN as the PDC. This makes for a fast full synchronization of the SAM and enables you to get a new PDC up and running very quickly should the original PDC crash.*
>
> *It is also a wise idea to put the PDC and BDC on separate circuit breakers. All too often people place the PDC/BDC pair side-by-side and even plug both into the same UPS.*

The steps listed for the BDC promotion process are simple, and they work well when the PDC is available. But what happens if you need to promote a BDC when the PDC is unavailable (if it crashes, for example)? If you attempt to promote a BDC while the PDC is unreachable, Server Manager prompts for confirmation before continuing (see Figure 2.5). Because the BDC cannot contact the PDC, a full synchronization does not occur. The BDC then removes the read-only flag on its SAM database and opens it for modification. This poses no problem while the original PDC is offline.

Figure 2.5   *If the PDC is unavailable, Server Manager prompts you with a warning before allowing you to promote the BDC to a PDC.*

However, when you boot the original PDC, a peculiar situation arises. Each time a PDC boots, it checks to see if there is another PDC for its domain. If the BDC has been promoted to a PDC and you boot the original PDC, it discovers an active PDC for the domain and stops its NetLogon service. In this special situation, you are given the option to demote the original PDC to a BDC (see Figure 2.6). If you demote the original PDC to a BDC, it performs a full synchronization of its SAM, overwriting its current database with the newer, more up-to-date copy on the newly functional PDC (the promoted BDC).

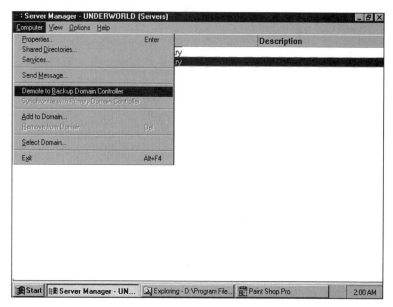

Figure 2.6   *The Demote to Backup Domain Controller option is available only when a PDC detects another PDC during the boot process.*

Author's Note

Consider the failure of a network link connecting two remote sites that are part of the same domain. Because only one site can contain the PDC, the other site is likely to have a BDC. In such a case, you may be compelled to promote the BDC at the remote site if the network link will be down for an extended period of time.

When the network link comes back up, you will have two functioning PDCs on the network. The original PDC will recognize the promoted BDC when it attempts to replicate its SAM, and errors will be registered with the Event Log (see Figure 2.7). However, neither PDC will present the option of demoting to a BDC. To solve the problem, you must reboot one of the PDCs. As it boots, it will detect the other PDC, stop its NetLogon service, and then present the option of demoting to a BDC. When the machine is demoted to a BDC, changes to its SAM will be lost forever. For more details on how to demote to a BDC when two PDCs are functioning on the same domain, please see Microsoft Knowledge Base article Q167248.

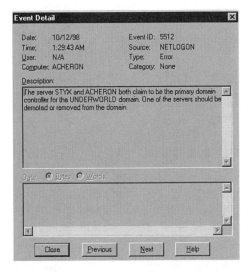

Figure 2.7 *If a network link is restored and two functional PDCs are on the network, errors indicating a conflict are registered on the Event Viewer.*

PDC/BDC Loading

Domain controllers generally require less memory and processing power than an FPA server. However, in many cases people use PDCs and BDCs as much more than simply domain controllers. These machines often contain services such as DHCP and WINS, and in many cases BDCs are used for file and print sharing or applications such as Microsoft's Systems Management Server (SMS).

The number of users supported by a domain controller can vary greatly. In large organizations it is not uncommon for hundreds of users to authenticate against a single domain controller. Following are some factors that affect domain controller performance:

- Size of the SAM database

- Number of authentication requests

- Frequency of authentication requests

To explore the performance of the domain controllers on your network, you need to learn to use Performance Monitor and Network Monitor. Performance Monitor enables you to chart, log, and report metrics on your NT system; Network Monitor is a troubleshooting tool that captures network traffic to and from the server. See Appendix A, "Working with Performance Monitor," and Appendix B, "Working with Network Monitor," for more information about these tools.

The following list contains Performance Monitor objects and counters relevant to domain controllers:

Memory	Pages/sec
	Available Bytes
Physical Disk	% Disk Time
	Avg. Disk Queue Length
Processor	% Processor Time
Server	Server Sessions
	Logon/sec
	Logon Total
Server Work Queues	Queue Length
System	Context Switches/sec
	System Calls/sec
	System Up Time

Author's Note

The Logon Total is a summation of all logons since the boot of the machine; you must use the System Up Time counter to see how many seconds the machine has been on. Be sure to account for the time that people are generally out of the office. In other words, the average logons per second is a diluted value because most users are at work only eight hours per day.

Tip

If the number of logons per second is around six or seven, you should consider choosing the Maximize Throughput for Network Applications option for the Server service. This will likely increase the number of simultaneous logons permitted to 20 per second. To modify the properties of the Server service, right-click on Network Neighborhood and select Properties. In the tabbed dialog box, select the Services tab, highlight Server in the Network Services list box, and click the Properties button.

Domain Clients

After installing domain controllers, you must add client machines to the group by configuring them to use the domain. A Windows 95 machine simply needs to be configured to log on to the domain. You must go through a different process to join an NT machine to the domain.

Joining the Domain

Windows NT uses *security identifiers (SIDs)* to identify users, groups, and NT domain workstations. All NT machines in the domain must have a computer account in the domain SAM. When the computer account is created, a unique SID is used to identify that machine to the domain controllers. The account can be created using Server Manager before joining an NT machine to the domain, or it can be created during the process of joining the domain (see Figure 2.8).

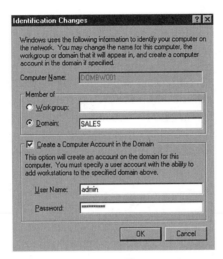

Figure 2.8 *A computer account can be created during the process of joining the domain. Creating a computer account requires a Domain Admin username and password.*

When an NT machine joins the domain, four important things happen:

- A computer account in the domain SAM is created.

- The domain controller assigns a password to the NT workstation. This password is used by the NetLogon Service to set up an encrypted authentication channel to a domain controller.

- The NetLogon Service starts. Workgroup machines do not use the NetLogon service, but domain workstations and servers use it to set up the encrypted authentication channel.

- The Domain Admins global group is placed into the Administrators local group. This allows anyone who is a member of the Domain Admins global group to administer the workstation. In addition, the Domain Users global group is added to the Users local group.

> **Tip**
>
> *To join a domain across a WAN link, the client workstation must use WINS or LMHosts to resolve the IP address and NetBIOS information for the PDC. If it uses LMHosts, you must use the #DOM directive to indicate that the machine is a domain controller.*

Domain Authentication

For an NT workstation, the authentication process has two parts:

- Machine ID authentication

- User ID authentication

The authentication process relies on NetBIOS and can vary depending on the protocols used by the domain workstation and server. For our purposes, we will assume the network uses TCP/IP and WINS.

Author's Note

For years, NetBIOS has been the basis for communication on Microsoft networks. The original NetBIOS command set was used by IBM. Microsoft turned the command set into an API that can be called over any protocol. Thus, you commonly hear people refer to "NetBIOS over TCP/IP."

NetBIOS uses special suffixes to describe the workstation, its group membership, and its services. NetBIOS names (such as your computer name) are limited to 15 characters, and a 16th character can contain a NetBIOS suffix. To see the NetBIOS information your NT machine uses, open a command window and type nbtstat -n.

For a complete listing of NetBIOS suffixes, see Microsoft Knowledge Base article Q163409.

Machine ID Authentication

There are three steps for machine ID authentication:

1. The NT domain workstation begins by querying WINS for a <1C> NetBIOS record matching the domain name, and WINS returns a list of IP addresses and domain controllers. The PDC is always first in the list of domain controllers, which is limited to a maximum of 25 entries and organized in the order that the domain controllers have refreshed their WINs entries. Entries not owned by the queried WINS server are moved to the bottom of the list. If the WINS query fails, the client sends out a broadcast name query request for the <1C> record.

2. The machine sends a locally broadcast NetLogon request for the domain <1C>. At the same time, it sends unicast NetLogon requests to all domain controllers returned in the WINS response in step 1.

3. The machine's ID is authenticated by the domain controller that responds first.

This process of setting up a session to a domain controller is called *NetLogon discovery*. If the first NetLogon discovery fails, it is repeated two additional times at five-minute intervals and subsequently at 15-minute intervals. The Registry parameters related to the NetLogon service can be found in the following location:

SYSTEM\CurrentControlSet\Services\Netlogon\Parameters

User ID Authentication

The *user ID authentication* depends on where the user account has been defined. If the user account has been defined in the same domain as the computer account, the established NetLogon channel is used for user ID authentication.

Logging on to trusted domains (which is discussed in Chapter 4, "Connecting Domains with Trust Relationships") is more complicated. To explore the process for a multiple domain environment, we'll call the domain storing the computer accounts the *Resource domain* and the domain storing the user accounts the *Accounts domain*. The following steps outline the process of logging on to a trusted domain:

1. The NT domain workstation sends a pass-through validation request to the Resource domain controller that it already has a session established with.

2. The Resource domain controller issues a NetLogon broadcast locally and sends the pass-through authentication to the Account domain controller it established a session with during its boot process.

3. The Resource domain controller passes the validation response and the name of the Account domain controller that validated the request to the NT client.

4. The NT client makes a connection to the Account domain controller to run a logon script, download a policy, or perform some other action.

If a domain controller containing your account information cannot be reached, it is possible for you to log on with cached account information. NT normally stores account information for the previous 10 interactive users, but you can change the number of cached logons via the following Registry key:

HKLM\Software\Microsoft\Windows NT\Current Version\Winlogon\

ValueName: CachedLogonsCount

Data Type: REG_SZ

Values: 0 – 50

> **Tip**
>
> *To determine your logon server, go to Start, Programs, Administrative Tools, Windows NT Diagnostics. From the Network tab you can view the Logon Server and Logon Domain (see Figure 2.9).*

Figure 2.9   *Windows NT Diagnostics can be used to see the server that authenticated your logon request.*

> **Author's Note**
>
> *The problem of authenticating across a WAN plagues many enterprise NT installations. With knowledge of the authentication process and a good domain design, the problem can be prevented. A good design involves a network topology that allows NT clients to reach a domain controller via broadcast rather than going through a routed network. For multiple domains, the design should involve the placement of an Accounts domain BDC on the same LAN segment as the Resource domain controller.*

Windows 2000 and Active Directory

Windows 2000 uses the Active Directory service to overcome many limitations of the NT 4 domain implementation. You can think of the Active Directory as the "Yellow Pages" for the network. It will contain information on all objects in the domain, including users, groups, and network resources. The Active Directory can store up to 1 million objects, overcoming NT 4's limitations on SAM size.

The *schema* describes all objects and attributes in the directory. Similar to a C++ data structure, the schema resembles an object class, whereas the directory resembles an object instance. By design, the schema is extensible and allows for the addition and modification of directory objects.

Active Directory Services Interface (ADSI) allows you to write programs that modify the directory objects and attributes in C++, Visual Basic, Java, JavaScript, and VB Script. For example, you may want to add an attribute to the user object to store a home address or phone extension. The flexibility of the system will open many doors for third-party vendors to create directory-aware applications.

Users will be able to search the Active Directory by querying the global catalog. The *global catalog* is a partial replica of objects in the Active Directory; it does not contain all attributes for each object in the directory. Administrators can control the information published in the global catalog, which supports two query protocols:

- LDAP v.2 and v.3

- MAPI-RPC

In summary, the schema describes the objects and attributes in the Active Directory, the directory stores all objects and attributes, and the global catalog makes specific objects and attributes available to users.

Active Directory is a distributed database using multi-master replication. Consequently, the concept of a PDC (from NT 4) is eliminated because all domain controllers maintain a changeable copy of the database. To prevent corruption and control replication, an *Update Sequence Number (USN)* is applied to each change.

Author's Note

Any distributed system that allows the same information to be updated in multiple locations must provide a lockout mechanism to control the order in which changes are applied. In other words, if two domain administrators attempt to modify the same account property in different locations, one of the changes must take precedence over the other. Unless the system applies a timestamp or version-tracking information to the changes, the potential exists for changes to be applied in the wrong order and corrupt the user accounts database.

Novell Directory Services overcomes the lockout problem by timestamping changes and forcing servers to maintain perfect time synchronization. Windows 2000 takes a different approach through its use of USNs.

Chapter 3

The SAM Database

This chapter will review:

- **SAM Contents**
  The SAM database is stored as part of the Registry on domain controllers. It stores user, group, and computer account information for the entire domain.

- **SAM Size**
  The size of the SAM database is a key factor in every domain design. Knowing the size calculations related to the SAM will help you optimize your domain design strategy.

- **SAM Synchronization**
  The NetLogon service is responsible for SAM synchronization. The traffic associated with synchronization greatly affects your placement of domain controllers for load balancing and fault tolerance.

SAM Contents

The SAM database is the heart of the domain model. The user and group information stored in the SAM is used for authentication and controlling access to resources. The SAM stores the following information:

- User accounts

- Group accounts

- Computer accounts (for NT servers and workstations only)

- Trust relationship accounts

Windows 95 machines do not have computer accounts in the domain SAM and fail to utilize many of the advanced security features supported by Windows NT. Only Windows NT machines have computer accounts in the SAM. Unknown to many, each NT machine changes its computer account password every seven days. New passwords are randomly generated, and the change is initiated by the client machine.

Several security features are employed to protect the SAM information. The user, group, and computer accounts are distinguished using security identifiers (SIDs), and each account has a corresponding password. User passwords are not stored in clear text; they are hashed using the RSA MD4 hashing algorithm. The SAM database is stored using triple DES encryption. The latest service pack uses a strong system key to further protect the SAM database; see Microsoft Knowledge Base article Q143475 for more information.

SAM Storage

The SAM database is a part of the NT Registry. The files that compose the Registry, called *hive files*, can be found in the WINNT\SYSTEM32\CONFIG directory. Two files make up the SAM database:

WINNT\SYSTEM32\CONFIG\SAM
WINNT\SYSTEM32\CONFIG\SECURITY

In the WINNT\SYTEM32\CONFIG directory are a SAM.LOG and a SECURITY.LOG file, which are used in a manner similar to a transaction log for a database. These transaction logs help maintain the integrity of the Registry when changes are made.

A copy of the Registry hive files can be found in the WINNT\REPAIR directory. This directory is used during the initial installation to back up the initial Registry. Files in the REPAIR directory are updated when you create an Emergency Repair Disk (ERD).

Upon startup, the Registry files are loaded and exclusively locked by NT (that is, they can be directly accessed only by the NT system). The entire SAM database is loaded into RAM and cannot be paged out to the hard disk. Locating the SAM in fast, volatile memory should speed up the logon validation process.

The Registry editor can be used to view the structure of the SAM. However, before you can do this, you must change the default Registry permissions. The SAM is stored in two Registry keys:

HKEY_LOCAL_MACHINE\SAM
HKEY_LOCAL_MACHINE\SECURITY

The default Registry permissions for these keys are illustrated in Figure 3.1.

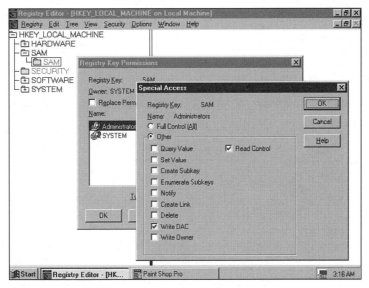

Figure 3.1 *The default permissions must be changed for you to see the structure of the SAM and SECURITY portions of the Registry.*

To view the structure of the SAM database you must modify permissions for the SAM and SECURITY registry subkeys. You modify the permissions by adding your user account with Full Control to each subkey. After doing so, you can expand the SAM and SECURITY keys to expose the structure of the SAM (see Figure 3.2).

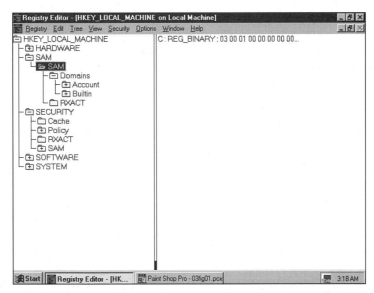

Figure 3.2 *After changing the permissions, you can expose the structure of the SAM.*

SAM Structure

The SAM is composed of three separate sections:

- *SAM Accounts database.* Contains user, group, and computer accounts created by the administrator.

- *SAM Built-in database.* Contains built-in user and group accounts.

- *LSA database.* Contains the LSA (Local Security Authority) secrets used in trusts and domain controller account passwords. This also includes account policy settings.

SAM Size

The size of the SAM database is extremely important in enterprise environments because it must be synchronized among all domain controllers. Ideally, the SAM would store user, group, and computer accounts for the largest organization and mirror changes in real time. Realistically, you must live with the fact that much of the synchronization occurs over slower WAN links (instead of LAN links) and that the SAM has size limitations.

Author's Note

When you run RDISK.EXE to create an ERD, the utility does not update the SAM and SECURITY files. Because the SAM database can grow to a size of several megabytes, RDISK.EXE is not designed to capture the SAM. However, if the SAM and SECURITY files are small enough to fit on the ERD, you can run RDISK -S *to update them.*

The theoretical size limitation of the SAM database is 40MB, although a more practical size is around 20MB. You can calculate the size of the SAM based on the user and group structure of your NT domain, as follows:

User Account	1024 bytes
Computer Account	512 bytes
Global Group Account	512 bytes for the group plus 12 bytes per member
Local Group Account	512 bytes for the group plus 36 bytes per user

Tip

Windows Terminal Server increases the size of each user account in the SAM from 1KB to 2KB per user. The extra 1KB is used to store information describing the user's last terminal session and the user's terminal session configuration. For large organizations, the introduction of Windows Terminal Server can dramatically increase the size of the SAM. Consult the Windows Terminal Server documentation for more information.

Calculating the SAM Size

XYZ Corporation has a domain with 4,000 global domain users, 2,000 NT Workstations, and 100 NT servers. There are 500 global groups with an average of 120 users each. There are only 20 local groups with an average of 8 members. What is the estimated size of the domain SAM?

Number of user accounts	(A)	4000
Number of global groups	(B)	500
Average number of global group members	(C)	120
Number of local groups	(D)	20
Average number of local group members	(E)	8
NT Workstation and server domain members	(F)	2000 + 100
Domain SAM Size =	A×1024 +	
	B×512 +	
	C×B × 12 +	
	D×512 +	
	E×D×36 +	
	F×512	
	=6,162,200 bytes, or	
	approximately 6.16MB	

Author's Note

If you delete a large number of users or groups from the SAM, it does not shrink in size. Although Windows NT provides no mechanism to compress the size of the SAM, it does reclaim the space when users and groups are added. Microsoft proposes three recommended solutions to the problem. To obtain further information on the problem and the solutions, see Microsoft Knowledge Base Article Q140380.

SAM Synchronization

The primary domain controller (PDC) contains a master copy of the SAM database, and all backup domain controllers (BDCs) synchronize their SAM with the PDC. The SAM on the PDC is the only one that can be modified; the BDC SAM is read-only. When you make a change to the SAM database, it is committed to the master SAM on the PDC and replicated to all BDCs.

Changes to the SAM are recorded in a *change log*. The default size of the change log in Windows NT is 64K. Because each change entry is approximately 32 bytes, the log typically holds about 2,000 changes. The PDC checks for changes to its SAM on a regular interval (every five minutes). When the PDC discovers one or more changes, it informs all BDCs of the change. However, not all BDCs are informed at the same time; this prevents overloading the PDC with numerous simultaneous requests for changes.

When a BDC requests changes from the PDC, it informs the PDC of the last change it received. Thus, the PDC is able to track which BDCs have been updated. The synchronization process uses UDP port 138 (NetBIOS Datagram Service), and communication takes place using mailslot messages. The sequence of events is outlined in the following list:

1. The PDC discovers a change to its SAM.

2. The PDC announces the change to a BDC.

3. The BDC connects to IPC$ of the PDC.

4. The BDC establishes a secure channel to the PDC and uses the NetLogon service to verify the SAM.

5. The BDC uses server message blocks (SMB) or Remote Procedure Calls (RPC) to transfer the updated data (depending on the size of the update).

Author's Note

When you add a user account or reset a password, the change is made to the master copy of the SAM located on the PDC. Because the PDC checks for changes every five minutes, this change can take as much as five minutes to replicate to a BDC.

Tip

You can use the ADDUSERS.EXE utility from the NT Resource Kit to export the user and group information from the SAM to a text file. You can also use the utility to add a large number of accounts to the SAM. This is best done by listing all the new accounts in a spreadsheet, exporting the spreadsheet to a comma-delimited text file, and importing the file into the SAM using the ADDUSERS utility.

You can extract user and group information from the SAM by issuing the following command:

```
addusers \\computername /d <filename>
```

By default, the command creates a comma-separated text file that can be easily imported into spreadsheet programs. For more information on ADDUSERS.EXE, consult the documentation included with the NT Resource Kit.

You should be very cautious of adding a large number of accounts at once. If replication of the SAM occurs over a WAN link, you might saturate the link with a large number of changes.

Synchronization Overview

There are two types of SAM synchronization:

- *Partial synchronization.* The timed replication in which all BDCs are notified of SAM changes that have occurred since the last synchronization.

- *Full synchronization.* Copying the entire SAM to a BDC. Full synchronization events are dangerous because they can saturate slow network links. According to Microsoft, on a 56Kbps point-to-point circuit it would take about 24 hours to replicate a 30,000-user SAM.

A full synchronization typically occurs when

- A new BDC is installed

- The change log fills

- An error occurs during a partial synchronization event

When you install a BDC, you must be sure it has network connectivity to the PDC. During the installation, the BDC performs a full synchronization with the PDC to establish its initial copy of the SAM. It is also possible for a BDC to do a full synchronization if it has been offline for an extended period and the change log has filled during that time; the change log simply wraps to overwrite older changes with newer ones. When this happens, the only way for the BDC to get an up-to-date copy is to pull the entire SAM from the PDC. This is a good reason to be cautious if you are using tools that add a large number of user accounts to the SAM instantaneously.

> *Tip*
>
> *Suppose you must distribute a BDC to a remote site. If possible, you should connect the machine to the same LAN as the PDC, install Windows NT, and then distribute the machine to its remote location. Installing on the same LAN as the PDC enables a fast, full synchronization of the domain SAM, which is unlike pulling a large SAM database across a slow WAN link.*

Calculating SAM Replication Traffic

XYZ Corporation has a domain with 4,000 global domain users, 2,000 NT workstations, and 100 NT servers. The password expiration policy states that passwords expire every 60 days.

Number of user accounts	(A)	4000
Password expires in how many days	(B)	60
Number of machine accounts	(C)	2100
*How many user accounts will you add per month?	(D)	200
*How many computer accounts will you add per month?	(E)	200

*Estimate five percent of A if unknown.

Number of changes to SAM
per day =
$$A / B +$$
$$C / 7 +$$
$$D / 30 +$$
$$E / 30$$
$$=380 \text{ changes per day}$$

NOTE: This formula assumes there are 30 days per month.

Author's Note

This formula gives a good estimate but assumes that user password changes are spread over the 60-day period. In reality, most users do not change their password until Windows NT sends a warning to them stating that there are 14 days left until expiration. In most cases, user accounts on the NT system are all added at about the same time. This means that all the user account passwords will expire at nearly the same time, so there will be a large number of changes after the warnings are sent.

Synchronization Registry Parameters

The synchronization process is controlled via several Registry parameters found in the following location:

\HKEY_LOCAL_MACHINE\SYSTEM\CurrentControlSet\Services\
Netlogon\Parameters

The following sections describe each of the parameters you will find there.

Pulse

Pulse defines the pulse frequency, in seconds. All changes made to the user account database since the last pulse are collected. Then, after the Pulse time expires, a pulse is sent to each BDC needing the changes (no pulse is sent to a BDC that is up-to-date). Default value: 300 (5 minutes); value range: 60 (1 minute)–3,600 (1 hour).

PulseConcurrency

`PulseConcurrency` defines the maximum number of BDCs that the PDC will notify at one time. The NetLogon Service sends pulses to individual BDCs, which causes the BDCs to respond by requesting any database changes. To control the maximum load these responses place on the PDC, the PDC must simultaneously handle only the same number of responses as the number of pulses specified under `PulseConcurrency`. Increasing `PulseConcurrency` increases the load on the PDC; decreasing `PulseConcurrency` increases the time it takes for a domain with a large number of BDCs to send a change to all of them. Default value: 20; value range: 1–500.

PulseMaximum

`PulseMaximum` defines the maximum time between pulses, in seconds. Every BDC will be sent at least one pulse this often, regardless of whether its user account database is up-to-date. Default value: 7,200 (2 hours); value range: 60 (1 minute)–86,400 (1 day).

PulseTimeout1

`PulseTimeout1` defines how long, in seconds, the PDC will wait for a non-responsive BDC. When a BDC is sent a pulse, it must respond within this time period; if it does not, it is considered to be nonresponsive. A nonresponsive BDC is not counted against the `PulseConcurrency` limit, thereby allowing the PDC to send a pulse to another BDC in the domain.

If this number is too large, a domain with a large number of nonresponsive BDCs will take a long time to complete a partial synchronization. If this number is too small, a slow BDC might be falsely accused of being non-responsive. When the BDC finally does respond, it receives a partial synchro-nization from the PDC, which can increase the load on the PDC. Default value: 5 (5 seconds); value range: 1 (1 second)–120 (2 minutes).

PulseTimeout2

`PulseTimeout2` defines how long, in seconds, a PDC will wait for a BDC to complete partial synchronization. Even after a BDC initially responds to a pulse (as required by `PulseTimeout1`), it must continue the synchronization process or else it will be considered nonresponsive. Each time the BDC calls the PDC, the BDC again must respond in the amount of time defined by `PulseTimeout2`.

If this number is too large, a slow BDC (or one that has its `ReplicationGovernor` rate artificially governed) will consume one of the `PulseConcurrency` slots. If this number is too small, the load on the PDC will be unduly increased because of the large number of BDCs doing a partial sync. Default value: 300 (5 minutes); value range: 60 (1 minute)–3,600 (1 hour).

Randomize

Randomize specifies the BDC backoff period, in seconds. When the BDC receives a pulse, it backs off between zero and the number of Randomize seconds before calling the PDC. Randomize should always be smaller than the PulseTimeout1. Default value: 1 (1 second); value range: 0–120 (2 minutes).

Consider that the time needed to synchronize a change to all the BDCs in a domain will be greater than the following:

((Randomize/2)×Number of BDCs in domain) / PulseConcurrency

The Replication Governor

Windows NT uses a 128KB buffer for the synchronization process. You can throttle the replication process by decreasing the size of this buffer. The buffer size is changed by adding the following Registry value:

HKEY_LOCAL_MACHINE\SYSTEM\CurrentControlSet\Services\
Netlogon\Parameters
Value Name: ReplicationGovernor
Date Type: REG_DWORD
Value: 0–100

The ReplicationGovernor can be set to a value between 0 and 100, which describes a percentage of the buffer used. For example, a value of 50 causes the BDC to use a 64KB buffer. A setting of 0 prevents replication; any setting below 25 is highly discouraged.

Forcing Synchronization

Rather than waiting for the PDC to check its SAM database for changes, you can force a synchronization of the SAM database. To synchronize a single BDC, open Server Manager, highlight the BDC, and select Synchronize with Primary Domain Controller from the Computer menu (see Figure 3.3). If you want to immediately propagate the SAM changes to all BDCs in the domain, highlight the PDC and select Synchronize Entire Domain from the Computer menu.

In Windows NT 3.51, synchronizing a single BDC in Server Manager forces a full synchronization; in Windows NT 4.0, it is possible only to trigger a partial synchronization. To force a full synchronization of a BDC, you have two choices:

- Open a command window on the BDC and type

    net accounts /sync

- Use NLTEST from the NT Resource Kit as follows:

    nltest /sync /server:<name of BD

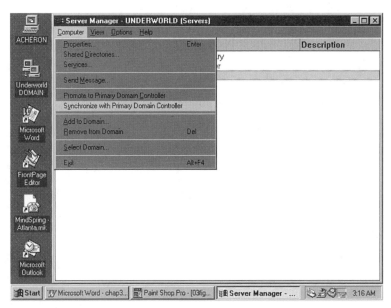

Figure 3.3 *You can force a single BDC to synchronize its SAM with the PDC.*

Chapter 4

Connecting Domains with Trust Relationships

This chapter will review:

- **The Purpose of Trusts**
  Trusts allow users from one domain to access resources in another domain without the need for more than one account.

- **Establishing a Trust**
  Establishing a trust is easy as soon as you are familiar with the terminology and multiple-step process.

- **Trust Fundamentals**
  A trust relationship affects the logon process, resource permissions, resource sharing, and group membership.

- **Trusted User Validation**
  The user authentication process becomes more complex in domains that have trusts. Understanding the validation of trusted users helps you troubleshoot authentication problems and develop strategies for the placement of trusted domain controllers.

- **Trust Strategies**
  In any multiple-domain environment, you must develop a strategy for effectively using trust relationships.

- **Troubleshooting Trusts**
  NLTEST.EXE and NLMON.EXE from the Resource Kit are excellent utilities for troubleshooting and testing trusts.

The Purpose of Trusts

Consider an organization with two domains (see Figure 4.1). In such an organization, you are faced with issues of resource sharing and user mobility. How do you grant users from DomainA access to resources in DomainB? What if some users from DomainB visit the DomainA site and need to use the DomainA workstations? These are practical issues that affect many organizations and greatly affect enterprise domain design.

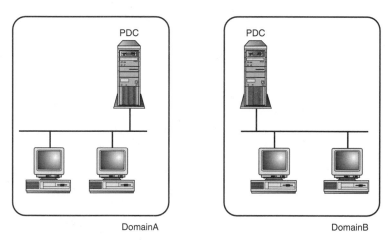

Figure 4.1 *Without trusts, domains are completely isolated.*

A domain is a security boundary: DomainA does not share user and group information with DomainB. Because you cannot see the DomainA users and groups when using DomainB, you cannot grant DomainA users access to resources in DomainB. There are only a few possible resolutions to this problem:

- *Enable the DomainB Guest account to grant Guest access to the resources.* This is a terrible solution. Enabling the Guest account gives everyone the capability of logging on to DomainB as Guest with Guest privileges. It gives access not only to DomainA users, but also any users who can reach the network of DomainB (this includes people entering the system over the Internet!). And because the system cannot distinguish the actual users or groups entering the system from DomainA, you cannot give resource access to one DomainA group while denying resource access to another DomainA group.

- *Give each DomainA user a separate username and password for DomainB.* Once again, this is a poor solution. Giving each DomainA user a username and password in DomainB does allow you to assign resource access based on the new accounts. However, if DomainA users cannot physically log on to a workstation in DomainB, they cannot change their passwords. Furthermore, if the DomainA users have a different password for their account in DomainB, they are prompted with a Connect As dialog box when attempting to access DomainB resources.

• *Establish a trust relationship.* A trust relationship allows DomainA to share its user and group information with DomainB. By establishing a trust, you give DomainB the capability of seeing the DomainA users and groups. Thus, you can set resource permissions in DomainB for DomainA users and groups.

The problems associated with multiple domains are similar to problems experienced with the NT workgroup model. With the workgroup model, you must combat the problems created by isolated SAM databases on each workstation and figure out how to best give other users access to each workstation's resources. Likewise, with multiple domains, you must resolve the problems of isolated domain SAM databases and figure out how to best give other users access to resources in each domain. Both problems are similar in nature, and so are the solutions.

To solve the NT workgroup problem, you can organize the machines into an administrative unit called a *domain*. The solution to the multiple domain problem is to establish a *trust relationship*, which provides a secure communications channel between two domains.

Establishing a Trust

Perhaps the most challenging aspect of establishing a trust is the terminology. In a trust relationship, one domain is *trusted* while the other is *trusting*. This relationship is usually illustrated with an arrow pointing from the trusting domain to the trusted domain (see Figure 4.2).

Characteristics of a trust relationship include the following:

• *Trust relationships are one-way.* If DomainA trusts DomainB, users from DomainB can be granted access to resources in DomainA. However, the opposite is not true—DomainA users cannot be granted access to DomainB resources unless you explicitly establish a second one-way trust between them.

• *Trust relationships are not transitive.* If DomainA trusts DomainB and DomainB trusts DomainC, DomainA does not automatically trust DomainC (see Figure 4.3).

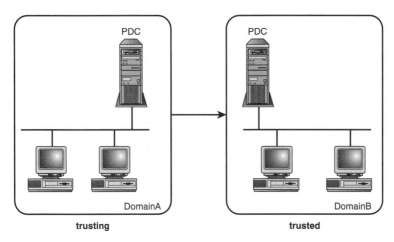

Figure 4.2 *A trust relationship is illustrated with an arrow pointing from the trusting domain to the trusted domain.*

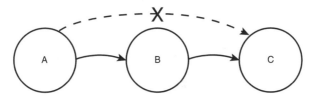

Figure 4.3 *If DomainA trusts DomainB and DomainB trusts DomainC, DomainA does not automatically trust DomainC.*

Author's Note

Windows 2000 supports one-way and two-way transitive trusts. The two-way transitive trusts use the Kerberos authentication protocol for enhanced security.

Creating a trust relationship is a multiple-step process that must be performed by the administrator of each domain involved in the relationship.

The following sequence describes the process of establishing a one-way trust between DomainA and DomainB:

1. *Determine the relationship between the domains.* For this example, we know DomainA trusts DomainB. You could also describe the relationship by saying DomainA is trusting of DomainB. It helps if you list each domain and its role in the trust relationship:

   Trusting Domain: DomainA
   Trusted Domain: DomainB

2. *Add DomainA to the list of trusting domains.* This step must be completed by an administrator of DomainB. First, open User Manager for Domains. From the Policies menu, select Trust Relationships to open the Trust Relationships dialog box (see Figure 4.4). In the Trust Relationships dialog box, add DomainA to the list of Trusting Domains.

Author's Note

When you add a trusting domain, the system prompts you for a password and a password confirmation. This password is used to establish the first connection, and it is changed by the domain controllers on a periodic basis.

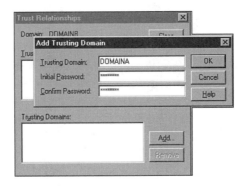

Figure 4.4 *DomainB's User Manager for Domains is used to add DomainA to the list of trusting domains.*

After the addition is complete, call the administrator of DomainA and give him or her the password you defined in this step. The administrator of DomainA then uses the password to complete the relationship.

3. *Add DomainB to the list of trusted domains.* This step must be completed by an administrator of DomainA. As described in the previous step, open User Manager for Domains, and from the Policies menu select Trust Relationships to open the Trust Relationships dialog box. Use the password from the previous step to add DomainA to the list of trusted domains. If all goes well, you will receive a dialog box indicating the trust relationship has been successfully established.

Storing Trust Information

The trust relationship information is stored in the SAM database, so you can view the information within the registry editor. As a reminder, you must change the Registry permissions on the SAM and SECURITY subkeys to give yourself permission to view the SAM information. By default, the SYSTEM is the only user with access to these subkeys.

When you establish a trust relationship, a trusted-domain object is created in the LSA of the trusting domain, and a secret object is created in the LSA of the trusted domain. On each domain controller in the trusting domain, an LSA secret object stores the password for the trust relationship. The object is stored in

HKLM\Security\Policy\Secrets\G$$<*TRUSTED DOMAIN NAME*>

The password is stored in a SAM user account on each domain controller in the trusted domain. The account is similar to other global user accounts with only one exception: A bit is set in the control field to represent an interdomain trust account. The account is not visible in User Manager for Domains, but it can be viewed via the following key in the registry editor:

HKLM\SAM\SAM\Domains\Account\Users\Names\<*TRUSTING DOMAIN NAME*>$

The primary domain controller (PDC) of the trusting domain automatically changes the password of the trusted domain object every seven days. Initiating the password change requires a secure channel. The trusting PDC keeps the old and the new password in case the update process fails on the remote PDC of the trusted domain. All domain controllers in each domain receive the trust account objects through normal synchronization.

Trust Fundamentals

A trust relationship between two domains changes the following aspects of the system:

- The logon process

- Resource permissions

- Resource sharing

- Group membership

Let's consider how each part of the system is affected by the trust relationship. For the discussion, let's consider the example that was presented in Figure 4.2: DomainA trusts DomainB, giving DomainB users access to resources in DomainA.

The Logon Process

Because users from DomainB are trusted, they can log on to any workstation in DomainA. However, the opposite is not true—users from DomainA are not trusted by DomainB and cannot log on to DomainB workstations or use DomainB resources.

On a DomainA workstation, there are three choices in the Domain drop-down list box: You can validate against the local SAM, against the DomainA SAM, or the trusted DomainB SAM. How the workstation processes your logon and performs the authentication process depends on your selection. As a DomainB user, you would select DomainB from the drop-down list box to indicate to the workstation that your account is defined in the DomainB SAM. The details of authentication related to trusted users are discussed in the "Trusted User Validation" section of this chapter.

Resource Permissions

You cannot grant users from another domain access to resources (such as files, folders, and printers) in your domain without establishing a trust. In our example, DomainB users are trusted and can access DomainA resources. However, permission to view DomainA resources is not automatically given to DomainB users.

The administrator of DomainA must set the access control lists (ACLs) on DomainA resources such that DomainB users can access them. When setting permissions for a directory in DomainA, you are presented with a drop-down list box in which you can select DomainB (see Figure 4.5). Selecting DomainB fills the list with global users (if you click Show Users) and global groups from DomainB.

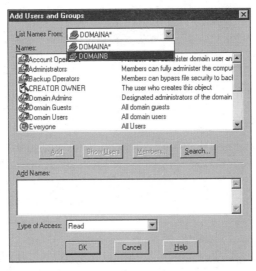

Figure 4.5 *In DomainA (the trusting domain), you can grant resource permissions to DomainB users (the trusted domain).*

From DomainA you can add the following account types to ACLs:

- DomainA—Local Users
- DomainA—Local Groups
- DomainA—Global Users
- DomainA—Global Groups
- DomainB—Global Users
- DomainB—Global Groups

From DomainB you can add the following account types to ACLs:

- DomainB—Local Users
- DomainB—Local Groups
- DomainB—Global Users
- DomainB—Global Groups

Tip

The default file system permissions are much too relaxed. For most directories, "Everyone" is listed on the ACL with Full Control. This is very dangerous and goes unnoticed on many systems. What if your domain administrator were to establish other trusted domains? In such a case, users from other domains would be able to connect to any of your shares and delete the resources! I would suggest using a command such as CACLS.EXE or XCACLS.EXE (covered in Chapter 11, "Controlling Access to Domain Resources") to remove the Everyone group and set the proper security on your file system structure.

Resource Sharing

Suppose both domains have shared resources: DomainA users can see only the shared resources in DomainA, but DomainB users can see shared resources in both domains because they are trusted by DomainA. Of course, a DomainB user's access to shared resources in DomainA depends on the permissions he or she is given to use the resources.

Group Memberships

In the trusting domain you *can*

- Add trusted global users to a local group
- Add trusted global groups to a local group

In the trusting domain you *cannot*

- Add trusted global users to a global group

- Add trusted global groups to a global group

So why would you want to add a trusted global group to a local group? Suppose there is only one domain administrator of DomainA, and that person is going away for two weeks. Who will manage the domain? Why not allow the administrators of DomainB to administer DomainA as well? To accomplish such a task, you would add the DomainB\Domain Admins global group to the local Administrators group of DomainA.

Trusted User Validation

It is important to understand trusted user validation because it affects the placement of domain controllers in an enterprise network. A common problem of enterprise networks involves trusted users validating with a distant trusted domain controller. The problem usually results from domain controller placement or the WINS client configuration. Before proceeding into an example, you need to understand how domain controllers and WINS interact.

WINS and Domain Controllers

WINS maps NetBIOS machine names and NetBIOS services to IP addresses (NetBIOS is the basis for Microsoft file and print sharing). NetBIOS records are also used to store information related to domain controllers and domain services such as browsing.

All domain controllers register a NetBIOS <1C> record with WINS. When a client queries for a list of domain controllers, WINS returns the list to the client. The list, limited to a maximum of 25 entries, is organized in the following order:

1. The PDC

2. All domain controllers registered with the WINS server, organized in the order of when they were refreshed (most recently to the least recently)

3. Domain controller entries obtained via replication partners

Figure 4.6 illustrates a network of two domains with a single one-way trust between them. The network is a TCP/IP network, and all machines use WINS. To understand the trusted user validation process, you must examine a trusted user logon.

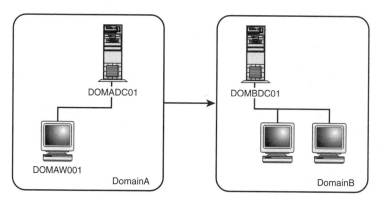

Figure 4.6 *A TCP/IP network of two domains has a single one-way trust between them.*

Assume DOMADC01 has established a secure channel to DOMBDC01 to verify the trust relationship.

Machine ID Authentication

Before a user can log on to an NT domain workstation, the workstation's machine ID must be authenticated against the domain SAM. The machine ID authentication occurs during the boot process and proceeds according to the following steps:

1. DOMAW001 queries WINS for DomainA <1C>. WINS returns a list of IP addresses for the domain controllers in the trusting domain. If the WINS query fails, the machine issues a broadcast query for DomainA <1C>.

2. DOMAW001 sends a broadcast NetLogon request for DomainA <1C> and unicast NetLogon requests simultaneously to all domain controllers in the WINS response from step 1.

3. DOMAW001's machine ID is authenticated by the DomainA domain controller that responds first. (Let's suppose this machine is DOMADC01.) At this time the setup of a secure channel to a domain controller is established.

4. DOMAW001 requests a list of trusted domains for DOMADC01. This list is displayed to the user in the Domain drop-down list box on DOMAW001.

User ID Authentication

After the machine ID authentication, the NT domain workstation is ready for user logon. The following steps outline the authentication process performed when a trusted domain user logs on to a workstation in DomainA:

1. DOMAW001 sends a NetLogon pass-through validation request to DOMADC01.

2. DOMADC01 sends a NetLogon logon request to

   - Broadcast for DomainB <1C>

   - Unicast for DOMBDC01 (because DOMBDC01 was used by DOMADC01 to verify the trust relationship between the domains)

3. DOMBDC01 authenticates the user (assuming the user is valid).

4. DOMADC01 sends the following to DOMAW001:

   - The validation response

   - The name of the DomainB domain controller that validated the user

5. DOMAW001 contacts DOMBDC01 to run the logon script or download the policy file for DomainB.

> **Tip**
>
> *For access to files and printers, the NetBIOS name cache is used to resolve a NetBIOS server name to an IP address. However, the NetBIOS name cache cannot be used by the logon process. You can view the NetBIOS name cache of an NT machine by typing* nbtstat -n *in a command window.*

Figure 4.7 depicts a typical network design involving two domains with a one-way trust. The NY (New York) domain is trusted by the LA (Los Angeles) domain, and a BDC from the NY domain has been placed on the LA LAN. This is done to eliminate validating and pulling logon scripts, policies, and so on across the WAN link. Ideally, you would want the NY user in the LA domain to validate using the LAN-attached BDC from the NY domain. However, if certain guidelines are not followed, the user may actually validate with a NY domain controller in New York.

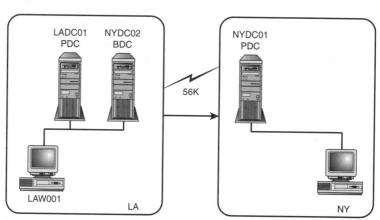

Figure 4.7   *A BDC from the trusted NY domain is placed on the LAN of the LA domain to help process the logons of trusted NY domain users.*

Here are some guidelines to force validation with NYDCO2:

- *LADC01 and NYDC02 should be on the same TCP/IP subnet.* If not, the broadcast issued by LADC01 to verify the trust relationship would fail and the WINS response would be used. LADC01 would then send unicast packets to all domain controllers listed in the WINS response. It is unlikely that NYDC01 would be used for the trust verification.

- *LAW001 and LADC01 should be on the same segment.* With this configuration, these machines are in the same broadcast domain, and the NetLogon broadcast for the LA domain <1c> is answered by LACD01. If the LA domain is large, there may be several Ethernet segments separated by a router. If this is the case, an LA domain controller and a NY BDC should be placed on each segment to ensure that NetBIOS broadcast queries for domain controllers are answered.

  A better solution is to use switched Ethernet instead of routing between each segment. A switch forwards broadcasts to each port and increases the chances of getting a response from the NetLogon broadcasts.

  Another possible solution involves opening UDP ports 137 and 138 and TCP port 139 between the LAN segments. These ports are used for NetBIOS session and datagram services; opening them allows the NetLogon broadcasts to pass through the router to adjacent LAN segments, where the query may be answered by a domain controller.

- *All machines on the LA LAN should use the same WINS server.* Configuring NYDC02 to use the same WINS server as LADC01 affects its order in the WINS response returned to LADC01 when it issues a query for NY domain <1c> records.

Trust Strategies

Now that you have seen the theory behind trust relationships and how they work, it is time to develop a strategy for using trusts. Let's start by considering two domains within an organization: Sales and Marketing.

Recall that a trust relationship allows trusted users to access resources in the trusting domain but does not allow users in the trusting domain to access resources in the trusted domain. But suppose the users of the Sales domain need access to resources in the Marketing domain and users of the Marketing domain need access to resources in the Sales domain. For situations like this, two-way trusts—actually composed of two one-way trusts—have been established (see Figure 4.8).

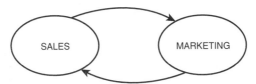

Figure 4.8 *The two one-way trusts in this arrangement allow decentralized administration, in which each department can control its own users and groups.*

With two domains, it is not much work to set up two one-way trusts. But imagine the problem this poses for an organization with several departments such as engineering, research, accounting, and manufacturing. If your organization had 20 domains and required users from each domain to access resources in all other domains, you would have to set up 380 trust relationships!

> **Tip**
>
> *If you have n domains and plan to set up trusts between every combination of two domains, you can calculate the number of trusts required with the following formula:*
>
> *n(n-1)=number of trusts*

Notice that the two domains in Figure 4.8 are very independent of each other and exhibit decentralized administration. Each domain contains user and group accounts for that domain and requires its own domain administrator. The only way to gain centralized administration is to change the domain architecture. In Figure 4.9, a separate domain has been established to store user and group information.

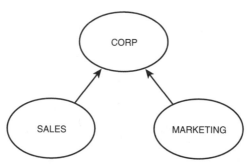

Figure 4.9   *This arrangement of trusts supports centralized administration without restricting a user to resources in a single domain.*

Notice that the Corp domain is trusted by the Sales and Marketing domains. All user and group accounts are defined in the Corp domain. Because Corp is trusted, users of the Corp domain can log on to any workstation in the Sales or Marketing domains. This design achieves several objectives:

- *Centralized administration.* All user and group accounts are administered from a single location, resulting in less administrative overhead.

- *Fewer trusts for large organizations.* Recall the organization with 20 domains. With the centralized administration, the organization would require only 20 trusts: one trust from each departmental domain to the Corp domain.

- *Small SAM databases.* Computer accounts aren't a part of the same SAM database that stores user and group accounts. Note that the machines in the Sales domain have computer accounts in the Sales domain SAM. Smaller SAM databases result in more efficient authentication and replication.

Author's Note

Chapter 5, "Domain Models," will offer greater coverage of this and many other designs. Chapter 6, "Domain Planning," will provide a methodical approach to achieving the best design for an enterprise organization.

Troubleshooting Trusts

Sometimes trusts are broken when a network link fails. Broken trusts are often related to the password for the trust relationship being changed periodically. To reset the trust password, you must reset the entire trust. You must then delete the current trust relationship and create a new one. This trust must be removed on a domain controller in each domain before it can be re-created.

Two helpful tools for troubleshooting trust relationships can be found in the Windows NT Resource Kit. NLTEST.EXE is great for testing and troubleshooting trust relationships and domain controller replication. NLMON.EXE is less powerful, but it offers the capability of monitoring trusts and synchronization. The following sections describe the switches available for each command.

NLTEST.EXE

Usage:

```
nltest [/OPTIONS]
```

`/SERVER:<ServerName>`	Specify `<ServerName>`
`/QUERY`	Query `<ServerName>` NetLogon service
`/REPL`	Force replication on the `<ServerName>` BDC
`/SYNC`	Force `SYNC` on `<ServerName>` BDC
`/PDC_REPL`	Force UAS to change message from `<ServerName>` PDC
`/SC_QUERY:<DomainName>`	Query secure channel for `<Domain>` on `<ServerName>`
`/SC_RESET:<DomainName>`	Reset secure channel for `<Domain>` on `<ServerName>`
`/DCLIST:<DomainName>`	Get a list of domain controllers for `<DomainName>`
`/DCNAME:<DomainName>`	Get the PDC name for `<DomainName>`
`/DCTRUST:<DomainName>`	Get the name of the domain controller used for trust of `<DomainName>`
`/WHOWILL:<Domain>* <User> [<Iteration>]`	See if `<Domain>` will log on `<User>`
`/FINDUSER:<User>`	See which trusted `<Domain>` will log on `<User>`
`/TRANSPORT_NOTIFY`	Notify NetLogon of new transport
`/RID:<HexRid>`	`RID` to encrypt password with
`/USER:<UserName>`	Query user information on `<ServerName>`
`/TIME:<Hex LSL> <Hex MSL>`	Convert NT GMT time to ASCII
`/LOGON_QUERY`	Query number of cumulative logon attempts
`/TRUSTED_DOMAINS`	Query names of domains trusted by workstation
`/BDC_QUERY:<DomainName>`	Query replication status of BDCs for `<DomainName>`

continues

Continued

/SIM_SYNC:<DomainName>	Simulate full sync replication <MachineName>
/LIST_DELTAS:*<FileName>*	Display the content of given change log file
/LIST_REDO:*<FileName>*	Display the content of given redo log file

NLMON.EXE

Usage:

```
nlmon /DOMAINLIST:<DomainList> /MONTRUST:<Yes/No> /UPDATE:<Mins>
/DEBUG:<HexValue>
```

/DOMAINLIST:*<DomainList>*	Specify comma-separated domain list to monitor (default is Primary/Account Domain)
/MONTRUST:<Yes/No>	Specify to monitor trusted domains also (default is NO)
/UPDATE:*<Mins>*	Specify refresh time
/DEBUG:*<HexValue>*	Debug out level

Tip

For a more elaborate description of each switch, see the Resource Kit documentation.

Using NLTEST.EXE

Suppose you suspect that LADC01 is using NYDC01 for trusted user valida-tion (refer to Figure 4.7). You can use NLTEST.EXE to determine the secure channel LADC01 is using for trusted user authentication. Here is sample output:

```
H:\>nltest /sc_query:NewYork
Flags: 0
Connection Status = 0 0x0 NERR_Success
Trusted DC Name \\NYDC01
Trusted DC Connection Status Status = 0 0x0 NERR_Success
The command completed successfully
```

This is just as you expected. Perhaps the NYDC01 was down when the trust was verified. Now you are faced with the problem of forcing the LADC01 to use NYDC02 for trusted user validation. Actually, you cannot force a LADC01 to use a particular machine for authentication. However, you can reset the secure channel, and LADC01 should use NYDC02 if it responds to LADC01's

NetLogon broadcast for a New York <1C> record before LADC01 resolves the
<1C> record via a WINS query.

```
H:\>nltest /sc_reset:NewYork
Flags: 0
Connection Status = 0 0x0 NERR_Success
Trusted DC Name \\NYDC02
Trusted DC Connection Status Status = 0 0x0 NERR_Success
The command completed successfully
```

Author's Note

*This sample use of NLTEST.EXE is just one of its many powerful
features. I strongly suggest consulting the Resource Kit documentation
to find out more about this tool and how you use it to troubleshoot
enterprise problems.*

Chapter **5**

Domain Models

This chapter will review:

- **Connecting Domains**
  If the proper amount of time is not allocated to domain planning and design, a cumbersome, monolithic network architecture can result.

- **Single Domain Model**
  A single domain model is the simplest of all domain models and ideal for smaller companies that have very few locations.

- **Complete Trust Domain Model**
  The complete trust domain model allows each location to perform separate administration while allowing users access to resources in all locations. Although the model offers many advantages, it is impaired by its inability to scale effectively for larger organizations.

- **Master Domain Model**
  The master domain model is a great selection for most businesses. It offers the benefits of centralized administration and a logical grouping of resources into separate domains.

- **Multiple Master Domain Model**
  For those companies that exceed the SAM size limitations of the master domain model, the multiple master domain model provides the ultimate in scalability.

- **Variations in Design**
  Most organizations must implement modifications to even the best design. Common exceptions include separate domains for vendors, human resources, and so on.

- **Drawbacks of Domains and Domain Models**
  Although domains and domain models solve many problems, there are many drawbacks to the solutions they provide.

- **The Impact of Windows 2000 on Domain Architecture**
  Windows 2000 introduces major changes to the operation of trust relationships and interaction among domains.

Connecting Domains

Most companies have more than one domain that they must connect through trust relationships. Companies are motivated to establish multiple domain structures for performance and/or organizational reasons.

Unfortunately, many companies do not devote the proper amount of time to planning and designing their computing infrastructure. Consequently, they usually end up with many costly mistakes and a painful transition to a Windows NT enterprise network.

Consider the following example:

January 1997	XYZ Corp. decides to change its computing infrastructure to Windows NT.
February 1997	The Atlanta sales, marketing, and engineering divisions install Windows NT on their departmental file servers. The Chicago research and manufacturing divisions follow them by installing NT file servers as well. All copies of NT are installed as PDCs (which turns out to be a big mistake).
April 1997	The company now has 20 NT domains in six cities. Help desk support staff receive a higher volume of calls concerning problems with sharing files and information across domains.
June 1997	XYZ wants to eliminate some of the domains. However, most departments refuse to relinquish control of their servers to a centralized authority. Political turmoil ensues.
July 1997	Some problems between locations are eliminated through the use of trust relationships. However, political issues abound because some departments do not want to trust other domains.
August 1997	XYZ realizes the NT domain infrastructure is poorly designed and decides to bring in a consulting team to provide a solution. The consulting team is given a network diagram illustrating the sites and trust relationships. The diagram indicates no strategy or planning behind the domains, and the team informs XYZ that the transition to a good infrastructure will take several months.
December 1997	The network now consists of six resource domains and one master domain for centralized control and administration. Help desk calls are reduced and users no longer experience logon or security problems when visiting other sites.

Although this example is entirely fictitious, it is very common. All too often, organizations rush the deployment of Windows NT without giving consideration to the big picture. In such situations, the companies usually suffer for a period of time before reaching the conclusion that they must change their domain infrastructure.

The key to achieving good domain interoperability is to look at the entire enterprise network and consider how each location factors into the network infrastructure. Chapter 6, "Domain Planning," will offer a formal approach to all the issues involved. But for now, it is important to gain a solid understanding of common domain models and how they work.

Microsoft advocates four domain models:

- Single domain
- Complete trust domain
- Master domain
- Multiple master domain

Of course, each model offers different benefits, and although these models are advocated by Microsoft, you are not forced to use a particular model. In fact, many companies, including Microsoft, organize a domain structure that is a variation of one of the models. Variations are usually established for security or performance reasons. For instance, you may establish a separate untrusted domain for your Internet servers and external DNS.

Author's Note

The majority of the businesses I have seen and consulted with use a master domain model or a variation thereof. The master domain model is great for small- to medium-sized businesses. For larger businesses, a multiple master domain model is better; Microsoft uses a variation of this domain model.

The following sections will describe each model and present examples and implementation details. Although this chapter covers all the domain models and some variations, it does not tell you how to select the best domain model for your organization. Chapter 6 discusses the issues involved in domain planning and design.

Single Domain Model

A *single domain model* has the following characteristics:

- It holds all user and computer accounts in a single SAM database.

- It supports up to 12,000 users.

- It requires no trusts.

- It is the least complex domain model, providing easier administration and a lower cost of ownership.

- It uses no logical grouping of resources.

- It uses one or more BDCs to provide fault tolerance and load balancing.

- It is the best selection for small companies with a single geographic location.

A single domain model is not always restricted to a single geographic location. In many cases, a small number of geographic sites may be part of the one domain (see Figure 5.1). However, you should generally try to avoid spanning a single domain across multiple geographic locations. Such networks usually experience poor performance and are better suited to separate domains (one domain at each location).

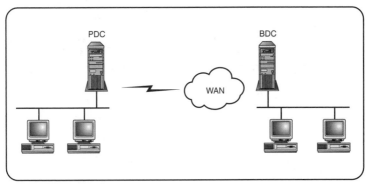

Figure 5.1   *A single domain model can extend beyond a single location and incorporate two or more smaller offices connected via a WAN.*

When a single domain spans multiple locations, the speed of the network link between the locations is crucial. Although certain Microsoft Knowledge Base articles cover implementing RAS-connected BDCs, I strongly recommend against using such ideas. If you do not have a dedicated network link between the two locations, you should consider separate domains. If you do have a dedicated network link between two locations and still want to implement a single domain across multiple locations, you should place BDCs at each location to balance authentication traffic.

Complete Trust Model

A *complete trust model* has the following characteristics:

- It is a combination of all the two-way trusts between each domain and all other domains.

- It is a good choice for companies that do not want centralized administration.

- It allows each domain to have its own administrative staff.

- It requires smaller SAM databases because the number of user accounts is divided among all domains.

- It has no PDC to hold all the user accounts, so there is no single point of failure for the enterprise. (However, there is still a single point of failure per domain.)

- It does not scale well (so it should be considered only by companies with a small number of domains).

Figure 5.2 illustrates a complete trust model with three domains. The most notable characteristics of a complete trust model are its decentralized administration and inability to scale well.

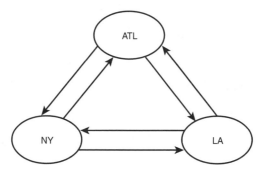

Figure 5.2 *A complete trust model is created by establishing two-way trusts between each domain.*

In a complete trust domain model, both workstation logon and resource access are made possible by the trust relationships. Users have the mobility to log on to a workstation in any domain. Likewise, users can access resources in any of the domains, assuming the administrator of the other domain grants them access to the resources. When a user logs on to a workstation in a domain other than their home domain, the user is authenticated using pass-through authentication, as discussed in Chapter 4.

The complete trust domain model does not scale well and should be used only with a small number of domains. As you add domains, the number of trust relationships does *not* grow linearly (see Table 5.1). If you have *n* domains, the number of trust relationships required is

$$n \times (n-1)$$

Due to the difficulty associated with managing and troubleshooting a large number of trusts, this model is discouraged for organizations with a large number of domains.

Table 5.1   Number of Trust Relationships in a Complete Trust Domain Model

Number of Domains	Number of Trusts Required
2	2
3	6
4	12
5	20
20	380

As the number of domains increases, there is a nonlinear growth in the number of trust relationships. For an organization with many domains, the large number of trusts required is too difficult to manage and troubleshoot.

The complete trust domain model supports decentralized administration, allowing each domain to be independently controlled. For some organizations with semiautonomous operating units, this may be a desirable feature. Consider a company with three sites: two manufacturing facilities and a corporate site. If the manufacturing facilities have qualified MIS staff and do not want to be completely controlled by the corporate site, you could arrange the domains in a complete trust. The MIS staff at each location would be responsible for such tasks as the addition of user accounts, modification of group membership, resetting of passwords, backup of servers, and so on.

One advantage of the complete trust domain model compared to other multiple domain models is that the master copy of the user accounts database is on the same LAN as the machines storing the domain resources (files, printers, applications, and the like). Recall that, when you open User Manager for Domains or set access control lists (ACLs) on resources, the machine you are working on must pull the list of users and groups from the PDC. In the other two multiple domain models, the PDC containing user accounts is not located in the domain that stores the resources; such an arrangement leads to long delays when generating a list of users and groups for the purpose of changing ACLs or modifying a user's group membership.

Master Domain

A *master domain model* has the following characteristics:

- The accounts domain stores all user and group information, whereas the resource domains contain resources.

- The SAM in the account domain can be very large.

- The SAM databases for resource domains are small.

- One domain is designated to manage all user and group accounts.

- It supports centralized administration.

- It has a single point of failure for any of the domains (so if the PDC goes down, you cannot add users, modify group membership, or change ACLs).

- It lets you set permissions in resource domains for global users and global groups from the trusted master domain.

A master domain is probably the most popular and widely used NT domain model. It is a great choice for most small- to medium-sized corporations, and it scales reasonably well.

In a master domain model you have two types of domains: an account domain and a resource domain. Figure 5.3 illustrates a typical master domain model. The account domain, which is the master domain, stores all the user accounts and group membership information. Resource domains are used to organize and control access to resources. All resource domains trust the accounts domain.

Recall that users from a trusted domain can log on to workstations in the trusting domain—this is the fundamental concept behind the master domain model. Because all accounts are stored in a domain that is trusted by all resource domains, a user can log on from any workstation in any of the resource domains and be authenticated by the trusted accounts domain.

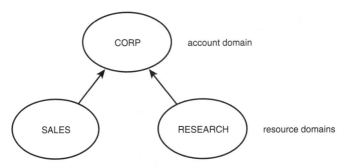

Figure 5.3 *A master domain model is formed by organizing resources into resource domains that trust a single account domain.*

Resource domains are typically organized in two ways:

- By geographic locations or regions (for example, New York and Los Angeles; or Northeast, Southwest, and so on)

- Departmental infrastructure (for example, sales, research, engineering)

Author's Note

When you establish domains based on geographic location, the design process is simplified because each trust relationship also represents a WAN network link. By associating the speed of the link with the trust relationship, you can easily plan the impact of replication traffic.

The SAM of a resource domain contains only computer accounts for the NT workstations and servers that are a part of the resource domain. In other words, there are no user accounts in the resource domains; all user and group accounts are stored in the account domain. Instead of having one SAM database with all user, group, and computer accounts, the master domain model uses smaller, separate SAMs that are logically organized for a specific purpose. The smaller SAMs result in more efficient authentication and faster synchronization if a full sync is needed.

You may wonder how the resource domains are administered if there are no user accounts there. This is where the model gets a little tricky. A typical approach is to create a global administration group in the accounts domain for the administrators of a resource domain, and then place that trusted global group into the local administrators group on each workstation and server in the resource domain. The possible variations of user and group strategies for multiple domain structures can get very complicated. Chapter 9, "Organizing Users," will offer detailed strategies for user and group organization in a master domain.

Multiple Master Domain

A *multiple master domain model* has the following characteristics:

- It is a good choice for companies with more than 15,000 users.

- Each corporate division can have its own administrative staff and implementation.

- It can scale to accommodate an organization of any size (currently there are BackOffice installations serving over 300,000 users).

- It requires very expensive implementation and administration.

The multiple master domain model is simply a master domain model with more than one master domain. An example of the model is illustrated in Figure 5.4; be sure to notice the two-way trusts between the master domains. The model shares many principles and fundamental concepts with the master domain model.

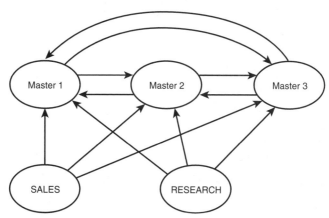

Figure 5.4   *A multiple master domain model has more than one master domain, with two-way trusts between all of them.*

The need for a multiple master domain model stems from the limitations of the SAM database. Recall from Chapter 3 that the SAM database has a limitation of 40MB. Although this offers a huge amount of user and group account storage space for most businesses, it is not accommodating for most true enterprise organizations. Consider the financial and telecommunications sectors, for example: Most of the larger financial corporations have over 100,000 users spanning worldwide networks. Of these large corporations, the ones running Windows NT have selected the multiple master domain model.

Because there are too many user accounts in these enterprise organizations to fit into a single SAM database (and work efficiently), they must logically group the user accounts into separate SAMs that are stored in each master domain.

Organizing Master Domains by Last Name

Figure 5.5 illustrates a multiple master domain organized by the user's last name. There are two master domains: The first contains only users whose last name starts with letters A through L, and the second contains users with the last initial M through Z. Each resource domain must trust all master domains (unless your company hires only sales people with last names beginning with A through L!).

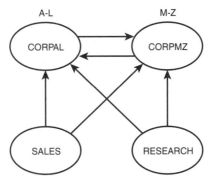

Figure 5.5   *In this multiple master domain, the user accounts databases are organized based on the first letter of the user's last name.*

Author's Note

A multiple master domain requires the creation of more global groups in the accounts domain. Suppose, for example, you needed to create a global Finance group. You would have to create a group in each domain: one for all Finance users whose last names begin with A through L, and another finance group for users whose last names begin with M through Z.

Organizing Master Domains by Company Divisions

Although you can organize the user accounts by last name, a better approach is to organize them based on company divisions (see Figure 5.6). This allows each division to have a separate administrative staff and generally works better politically (that is, each division can establish its own computing policy).

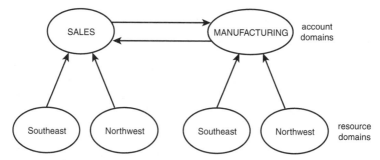

Figure 5.6   *In this multiple master domain, the user accounts databases are organized by company division, and resource domains are organized based on region.*

Drawbacks of the Multiple Master Domain Model

The multiple master domain model can be very expensive to implement due to the necessary load balancing. In some companies, the resource domains are organized based on geographic site location (see Figure 5.7). To alleviate performance bottlenecks, it is wise to place a BDC for each master domain at the site location of each resource domain. The need for the extra three BDCs per site makes this a very costly model.

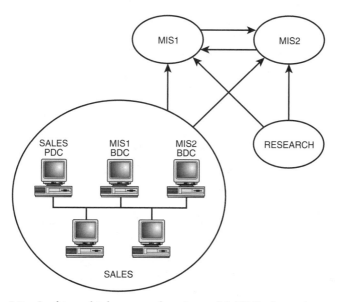

Figure 5.7   *In this multiple master domain model, BDCs for each master domain have been placed in each resource domain to decrease performance bottlenecks resulting from authentication traffic crossing the WAN.*

Author's Note

With Windows NT 4, you have only a single copy of the SAM that can be modified. When you set permissions or change ACLs, you must get your user and group information from the SAM on the PDC no matter how far you are from the PDC.

In a system such as Novell Directory Services (NDS), the database of user and group information is distributed among several servers, and you can modify the copy on any server. The database can be partitioned and replicated so that only parts of the database, rather than the entire database, are distributed. This is quite a programming feat because the system must carefully control modifications and the synchronization of the modifications. With NDS, the servers apply a timestamp to the modifications, making time synchronization among the servers crucial.

Microsoft's only attempt at a distributed read/write database with NT has been WINS, which uses version IDs to synchronize replication. Windows 2000 is scheduled to have a distributed, extensible SAM database and will use Update Sequence Numbers (USNs) instead of time to synchronize replication.

In addition to requiring more hardware, the multiple master domain model introduces extra administrative responsibilities. Suppose you need to create a global finance group, and your master domains are organized based on a user's last name. You would have to create the global group in each domain because each group can include only those global users from the domain in which it is created. In other words, the group in the first domain may include only users whose last initials are A through G , the second group would contain users whose last initials are H through N, and so forth.

Variations of Models

Each domain model has its own benefits and drawbacks, so it is likely that no one domain model completely satisfies the needs of your organization. Thus, most companies find they must introduce variations into the models.

The biggest reason for a variation is usually security. Perhaps your company is concerned about Internet hackers, or maybe you are worried about vendors who need access to information on your network. What if another company is responsible for modifications to your Web site, and you must grant them access to change and modify your Web servers? Without getting too specific about a rare corporate infrastructure, let's consider these and other examples.

The Internet is a fascinating technology, but it poses a security threat to most organizations. Unless you have a firewall configured by a security expert, there is no guarantee that an unauthorized person cannot read or modify your company's secret data. If a company must maintain an Internet presence and is concerned about data access, it is wise to establish a separate Internet domain containing Web and FTP servers. Recall that a domain is a security boundary and that, without trusts to other domains, a hacker cannot break into your Internet domain and access other untrusted domains.

Suppose that vendors need access to data in your manufacturing resource domain. You certainly do not want to give them an account in the master domain. If you were to do that, the vendors could not only access resources in the manufacturing domain but all other resource domains as well. This problem has a couple solutions:

- You could give the vendors user accounts in the manufacturing domain, allowing them to dial into it. The vendors could not access information in any other domains because no other domains trust the manufacturing domain.

- You could establish a separate resource domain specifically for vendors. However, instead of defining the vendor user accounts in the master domain, you would define them in the vendor resource domain (see Figure 5.8). Because the vendor domain would not be trusted (like the master domains), the accounts defined there could access only the resources in that domain.

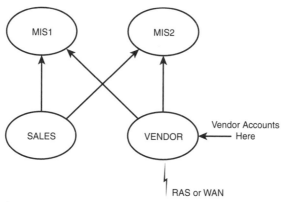

Figure 5.8   *Vendors can be granted controlled access to resources via a separate domain.*

Another popular variation is to implement a separate domain for the human resources department. The confidential nature of the data usually handled by the HR department suggests that a separate, untrusted HR domain should be implemented. In addition, many companies further protect the data by placing all HR-related equipment on a network that is wired and located separately from the other networks.

Drawbacks of Domains and Domain Models

Microsoft domains work well for most organizations when implemented properly. However, domains have some significant limitations and warrant the need for improvement in several areas. Most notably, domains should support a larger SAM and provide for granular delegation of administrative privileges. The following list offers some drawbacks of NT 4 domains:

- NT domains are flat with no hierarchy.

- The SAM database is not extensible. You need a user accounts database that can store additional properties such as a user's phone extension, home address, and so on.

- The SAM database is too limited. In large organizations, you have no choice other than multiple domains because the SAM database cannot hold all the user accounts.

- BDCs only have a read-only copy of the SAM. Although the failure of the PDC does not prevent user authentication, it does prevent the modification of user account properties and security on resources.

- There is no automatic failover of the PDC. The BDC can be promoted to a PDC if required, but you must do this manually after you discover the PDC has failed.

- The transition from a master domain model to a multiple master domain model can be tremendously expensive.

- Because of the default file system permissions, a trust relationship often permits the trusted users to gain more access than intended. Suppose your domain administrator establishes a trust relationship with another domain. If you do not change the default file system permissions (which are set to Everyone having Full Control), users from a trusted domain will be able to access your files—without your knowing about the existence of the newly created trust relationship.

- Logon scripts, policies, and other user properties should be automatically replicated along with the SAM to BDCs; however, you must explicitly replicate the scripts and policies. Otherwise, when the PDC fails and you promote a BDC, the BDC will not have a copy of the logon scripts and policies.

- It is nearly impossible to delegate administration to the level that is really needed in an enterprise environment. For example, how do you give lower-level administrators the level of access they need without making them a member of the Domain Admins group? The built-in groups Microsoft includes are not enough.

  Here is a common scenario: The help desk staff cannot properly troubleshoot situations because they cannot see the membership in the trusted global groups. The administrators of the trusted domain refuse to make help desk staff members of the Account Operators or Domain Admins group. The only good solution seems to require implementing emerging third-party add-ons that allow for a granular delegation of administrative rights for NT domains (see Chapter 9 for more details).

Author's Note

In September 1998, Sun announced Project Cascade. According to Sun, Windows NT requires too many servers that are dedicated to things like email, databases, file services, print services, authentication, and so on. Sun is introducing a technology that enables you to consolidate all native NT services onto a single multiprocessor server. The consolidation is intended to reduce complexity, lower total cost of ownership (TCO), and maximize uptime.

My experience tells me their claims have a great deal of truth. BackOffice products such as Microsoft Exchange and SQL Server require a dedi- cated, high-end server. As far as scalability is concerned, there is no doubt that a 64-processor Sun SPARC can outperform a 4-way or 8-way Windows NT machine. However, despite the euphoric information presented about the project, I am inclined to challenge many of the benefits of Project Cascade.

Consolidation translates to a single point of failure, and consolidating complex enterprise services does not reduce complexity and TCO. If all services are consolidated, you must interrupt all services whenever a hardware or software upgrade is performed. In addition, you cannot tune and optimize a server that runs multiple services. For example, giving SQL Server more memory reduces the amount available for Microsoft Exchange if both services run on the same machine.

continues

Continued

> *To make things even more complex, consider troubleshooting such a system. Unless you are an expert for all services running on the machine, it is very difficult to troubleshoot problems with the system. Hiring someone with such a broad skill set is unrealistic because there is no way any one person can reasonably manage multiple, complex enterprise services for a large company.*

The Impact of Windows 2000 on Domain Architecture

Microsoft supports the migration to Windows 2000 from Windows NT 4.0 centralized and decentralized domain models. To make the transition easier, Windows 2000 supports a mixed environment of NT 3.51, 4.0, and Windows 2000 domain controllers. By default, when you install a Windows 2000 domain controller, it operates in Mixed Mode. After you upgrade all NT servers to Windows 2000 and implement DNS, you can change your servers to Native Mode and take full advantage of Active Directory.

Windows 2000 introduces several new concepts and configurations related to domain architecture:

- *Tree.* A hierarchy of domains with transitive Kerberos trusts between the domains, sharing a contiguous namespace, common schema, and global catalog.

- *Forest.* One or more sets of trees having a disjointed namespace.

- *Site.* A well-connected set of TCP/IP subnets that does not contain any slow network links. Usually it is a single company location or multiple locations with fast network links (T1 or greater). An administrator defines a site by selecting one or more IP subnets.

- *Organizational Unit (OU).* An object container. For example, an OU can contain user and group objects.

Figure 5.9 illustrates a forest containing three trees. Notice that each tree maintains a separate namespace.

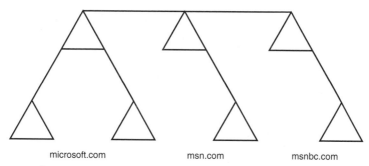

microsoft.com   msn.com   msnbc.com

Figure 5.9 *A forest is composed of two or more trees and exhibits a disjointed name-space.*

A domain in Windows 2000 is a partition in the namespace. Replication occurs on the domain level and is based on the individual properties of an object.

A site positively impacts the Windows 2000 domain architecture in two ways:

- Replication traffic of slow WAN links can be controlled and optimized.

- Clients can use site information to find a close domain controller.

In NT 4.0, the domain is the most granular unit of administration; in Windows 2000, you can use OUs for a finer distribution of administrative capabilities. For example, you can allow help desk staff to reset user passwords but not modify any other user account properties.

A fundamental problem with NT 4.0 has been its limitation on the size of the SAM (40MB is the recommended maximum size). Windows 2000's Active Directory solves the problem by increasing the limits to a 17TB database that can store up to 10 million objects.

Because Windows 2000 supports such a vast number of objects in the directory and OUs can be used to delegate administrative authority, there is no compelling technical need for a multiple domain structure. Thus, most vendors recommend flattening your domain structure in preparation for Windows 2000. The transition to Windows 2000 will be much easier if the NT 4.0 structure closely models the desired Windows 2000 structure.

Tip

Windows 2000 identifies all servers using a Globally Unique Identifier (GUID). The GUID allows you to move servers between domains.

Chapter 6

Domain Planning

This chapter will review:

- **Getting Started**
  Domain planning is a huge task and must start with the specification of your design goals.

- **Windows NT and Wide Area Networks**
  Wide area networks (WANs) significantly impact NT domain design and administration. In addition, the routers needed for WAN connectivity block broadcast traffic that is used for many domain functions.

- **Selecting a Domain Model**
  Choosing a domain model requires you to think on an enterprise scale and analyze issues from a different perspective.

- **Organizing Resource Domains**
  If you choose a master or multiple master domain model, you must decide on a strategy for organizing resource domains.

- **Preparing for a Transition to Windows 2000**
  Windows 2000's Active Directory solves many NT 4 domain problems and allows for the consolidation of users and resources into fewer domains. DNS is the name resolution protocol required by Windows 2000 to resolve names and locate services.

Getting Started

The goal of this chapter is to give you a methodical approach toward Windows NT domain design. Every network is different, and some portions of domain design are dependent on your particular infrastructure. During the design process, you must remember that there will be tradeoffs for almost every decision you make. When given more than one option, you should consider the nature of your business, your administrative staff, and the end users. For example, in some industries, such as banking and finance, the computing infrastructure is critical to the nature of the business; in other industries, such as manufacturing, a server being down for a short time may not be so critical.

Domain planning and design is no small chore. In fact, it is probably one of the largest projects a company can undertake. Creating a superb domain infrastructure is more work than just installing a BDC for every 2,000 users—it involves a great deal of careful, meticulous planning before you attempt to distribute servers.

There are two basic approaches you can take toward domain design:

- You can sit down for days, weeks, or even months calculating the estimated amount of network traffic generated by each workstation and each server for each application. Based on your calculations, you can design the best possible domain model.

- You can take an empirical approach of testing your current infrastructure and selecting a domain architecture based on your test results. After implementing the architecture, you can apply iterative measuring and tuning to the network to ensure an optimal configuration.

Every systems engineer and consultant would probably agree that the latter option yields the best model. Paper designs usually lead to implementation problems resulting from oversights. However, if you measure the average network throughput using a tool such as Performance Monitor, you get exact numbers without any assumptions or guesswork. You might not know from where the traffic is generated, but you will certainly be able to predict the impact of occurrences such as a BDC's full synchronization across the network.

Author's Note

It is likely that you already have Windows NT domains in place. Even if you have a domain architecture in operation, you must ask yourself if it is the best architecture. Perhaps one of the best tests of your design is to pretend you have no domains implemented; this chapter helps you understand how to approach a domain design for a new network.

If you decide that you need to modify a current design instead of creating one from scratch, see Chapter 7, "Domain Reconfiguration."

The following is an overview of the entire design process:

1. Define the goals of the design.

2. Conduct an enterprise analysis and a site-by-site analysis to resolve all design issues.

3. Select a domain model that best fits your company's network infrastructure, applications, and business processes.

4. Establish a strategy for user and group implementation.

5. Establish strategies for these enterprise services:

   DHCP

   WINS

   DNS

Common Domain Design Goals

Before getting into the issues of domain design and planning, you must ask yourself exactly what you want to achieve with your domain design. A major software implementation such as MS Exchange is often part of the design.

> **Tip**
>
> *Enterprise software packages, especially BackOffice applications, can be heavily dependent on your domain design. You should be careful not to overlook these products in your planning.*

The following are areas of domain design and planning that you should focus on:

- *Domain security.* A domain creates a security boundary that only a trust relationship can extend. You must decide where to establish security boundaries on your network.

- *Fault tolerance.* If a PDC fails, a BDC must be promoted to take over its role. You must be sure you can complete the promotion in a reasonably short time period, if necessary. You also should consider the impact of a severed network link between two sites.

- *Load balancing.* When data must be downloaded to the client machine, you should place the data as close to the client machine as possible. You also need to place a BDC on each subnet to load-balance authentication traffic.

- *Ease of administration.* You must set up the proper user and group strategy—otherwise, you will have an unmanageable monstrosity of a domain.

- *Fast, efficient logon and authentication.* In other words, the client should not download a 5MB roaming profile over a WAN link or authenticate against a BDC located across a WAN.

- *Fast access to resources.* Even if you have a resource server on a local segment, it must use pass-through authentication to validate your access to those resources. If the resource server has a secure channel set up with a BDC across a WAN link, your access to resources can be slowed significantly.

- *Future expansion.* You must account for future expansion and be able to extend your architecture to accommodate new sites. For this reason, you should pursue a modular approach that allows you to quickly and easily bring new sites online. You should also pursue a naming convention that uniquely describes every user, group, workstation, server, and network device. If you fail to implement a standard naming convention at each company location, you are bound to face many problems when converting to Windows 2000.

These are only basic goals, and I am sure that you have your own goals that are specific to your network and implementation. Take the time to extend this list by adding your own goals.

Why More Than One Domain?

A single domain is the easiest architecture to manage and maintain. However, there are several reasons why a single domain does not work for most businesses. From an engineering standpoint, the limitations of the SAM database can force the selection of a multiple domain model. The SAM database for many companies is simply too large and cannot be handled efficiently by a single Windows NT domain. Recall from Chapter 3 that the theoretical size limit of the SAM database is 40MB; rarely do companies pursue an implementation with a SAM this large.

Another common motivation for having multiple domains involves WAN-related performance issues. WAN links are slow and expensive. Windows NT's limitation of one PDC per domain becomes a serious issue when performing large amounts of administration from a remote site that is separated from the PDC by a WAN link. Setting access control lists (ACLs) and modifying user properties require you to download the PDC's SAM contents over the WAN—a frustrating process. (Group strategies to solve this problem are discussed in Chapter 9, "Organizing Users.") Establishing separate domains allows for a PDC at each location and provides much easier administration.

Organizational divisions within a company also provide a strong need for more than one domain. In most companies, each division is autonomous and self-sufficient. This leads to a separate administrative staff for each division and politically forces one domain per division at the very least.

Author's Note

An understanding of networking is essential to NT domain design. The next section discusses the impact of WANs on NT domain design. It would be impossible to explain local and wide area networking in this book; if you are unfamiliar with networking, I strongly suggest you consult additional reference material on the subject.

Windows NT and WANs

Many of the issues related to NT domain design and planning require a solid understanding of networking, especially TCP/IP networking. It is extremely rare to find a company that has no remote sites. Most companies have multiple locations and use routers to connect the locations over a WAN. The speed of the WAN line used to connect the sites can have a crucial impact on the domain design. In addition, the routers used to connect the WAN can block any broadcast packets used by Windows NT for some domain operations.

WAN Bandwidth and Pricing

Transporting data across WAN links is costly. The links are very expensive, and data transfer is often very slow. For example, ISDN service, which transfers data at up to 128Kbps, sells for $50 to $500 per month. A 256Kbps fractional T1 typically goes for about $1,200 per month, and a full T1 (1.544Mbps) sells for more than $2,000. When you compare the WAN bandwidth to the typical 10Mbps or 100Mbps on most LANs, you can easily see that the WAN can become a significant bottleneck for large amounts of data transfer.

Author's Note

Perhaps one of the most challenging problems of domain design is accommodating a remote network with no dedicated link and only a few machines. In most cases, the low number of machines makes it cost-prohibitive to purchase a dedicated link to the corporate network. As a result, a separate, untrusted domain is usually the best solution if the remote site has a server that can act as a PDC for the domain.

The driving idea behind a good WAN implementation is to keep your links free of consistent traffic flow and allow clients to use the full bandwidth to burst data. When considering your WAN architecture, you must consider more than just the link speeds from your network diagram—you must consider how much *available* bandwidth each link has. For example, a 56Kbps link is much faster than a saturated T1 link.

Even if you have fast links to some locations, those links are likely under heavy use for replication between database and email servers. See the "Enterprise Analysis" section later in this chapter for tips on measuring your usable bandwidth for an existing WAN architecture.

LAN Testing of a WAN Design

Perhaps the most common problem in domain design is the *"LAN mentality" syndrome*. This syndrome is characteristic of people who design and test a domain infrastructure on LANs operating at 10Mbps or greater. Such a design may work great in the test lab using real servers and applications; however, as soon as the domain controllers are distributed to remote locations, slow WAN links cause problems not encountered in the lab.

In addition to slow speeds, there are many other problems introduced by the routers used to connect the WANs. By design, routers block broadcast packets, which Windows NT uses for

- Setup of the NetLogon channel

- SAM synchronization

- Password changes

- Directory Replication

- Name resolution (if not using WINS or LMHOSTS)

- The browser (Network Neighborhood)

To overcome the problem of blocked broadcast packets, you must use WINS or LMHOSTS files to tell client machines how to route information directly to a domain controller rather than broadcast for a domain controller that may not be there.

> ### Tip
>
> *If you are using LMHOSTS for machines at remote sites, you must use the* #DOM *statement to differentiate the PDC from other machines listed in the LMHOSTS file. A* #PRE *statement is also used to preload the entry into the local NetBIOS name cache.*

To successfully test a WAN design, you must set up a detailed test lab using routers and links operating at the required WAN speeds. In most cases you can conduct the testing using a router with twin AUI ports. For such a setup, you would configure a router to allocate a specific amount of bandwidth between the two AUI ports simulating the WAN speed of the links.

Real-World Application

To further explain how an understanding of networking is helpful in solving NT problems, consider the following real world example. During a recent trip to Southeast Asia, I was called on by a large financial services company to assist with an NT authentication problem. The company had a remote site containing two TCP/IP subnets and only one BDC. After complaints of slow logons, it was determined the clients were being authenticated by a remote domain controller located in another city.

A representation of the network is illustrated in Figure 6.1. The entire problem resulted from the routed network architecture. During client logon, the machine issued a broadcast and a WINS query for all machines with a <1c> entry. Because there was no BDC on Subnet #2, the clients were receiving no reply to the broadcast and using the results of the WINS query to establish a NetLogon channel.

Although placing a BDC on Subnet #2 could have solved the problem, we decided that a switched ethernet solution would be better. A TCP/IP subnet is limited to about 60 to 80 clients using a hub, but a switch allows you to place nearly 400 clients on the same segment without severe network traffic implications. Because the switch passes broadcasts to all ports, the BDC is able to respond to the NetLogon requests from clients on Subnet #2.

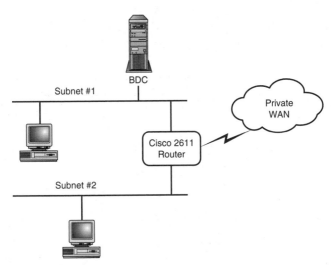

Figure 6.1   *Without a BDC on Subnet #2, user logon requests from workstations on Subnet #2 might be processed by domain controllers across the WAN.*

Selecting a Domain Model

The selection of the domain model is the most crucial part of the domain design. Although you can change the location of BDCs and reconfigure enterprise services such as WINS and DNS, you cannot easily change your domain model after you have completed its implementation. Thus, you must make sure you are considering all factors before making a decision.

Here are the three factors that most affect enterprise domain design:

- SAM database size
- Number of geographic sites
- Speed of network links connecting the sites

The size of the SAM database is directly related to the number of users, groups, and NT workstations in a domain. A small SAM database gives you the ultimate flexibility to select any domain model. For companies with a large number of users (greater than 20,000), it is typical to establish separate domains so the resulting SAM databases are smaller and replicate more efficiently. Consider the plight of an organization such as the U.S. Marine Corps. Its North Carolina base has been the administrative center for a Banyan VINES network for many years. The organization is now converting to a Windows NT network for nearly 300,000 users. A multiple master domain model is inevitable.

Having a small number of geographic sites gives you flexibility in selecting a domain model. However, a large number of sites almost always forces you into a master or multiple master domain model. Consider, for example, the U.S. Department of Agriculture, which has over 3,000 sites in the United States. Having a domain at each branch office would be ridiculous and unmanageable. Such an organization should probably pursue a regional domain model, establishing a domain for the northeastern U.S., the southwestern U.S., and so on.

WAN links play a big role in the domain architecture of your organization. Faster WAN links offer the greatest flexibility and will allow for optimal designs. If you have a location that has no dedicated WAN link or has a saturated WAN link, you will likely be forced to make the location a separate domain. Having a dedicated WAN link is a prerequisite for any geographic location if you wish to

- Establish a separate domain at the location and create a trust with another domain
- Integrate this location with others to form a domain

The following sections on enterprise analysis and site analysis will help you determine your requirements. Also, refer to Chapter 5 for a listing of the domain models and their characteristics.

Enterprise Analysis

An *enterprise analysis* covers the issues related to your overall design—in other words, it addresses the big picture that most people do not consider. Each characteristic of a domain design in the following list is accompanied by a series of questions you should answer for your situation. This is followed by general examples of acceptable implementations. (Please keep in mind these are generalizations; if your situation is rare, an alternative approach may be necessary.)

- *SAM size.* How many users will require a domain user account? How many global groups will you need? (To avoid going through detailed calculations for the size of each group, estimate your number of global groups and multiply it by 4K.) How many NT computers do you have? What size SAM would result with this many users?

<20MB	You can implement a single domain, complete trust, or master domain model.
>20MB	You are likely limited to multiple master domain model.

- *Number of sites.* How many facilities does your company have? (Of course, the fewer the locations the easier the implementation.)

<5 sites	You can choose a single domain, complete trust, or master domain model. A multiple master domain model is rarely used with so few sites and depends greatly on your number of users and whether you want a master domain for each company division.
>5 sites	It would be unwise to implement a complete trust model. Other choices depend on your number of users and design goals.
>100 sites	You will likely need to reduce the number of domains by combining several sites into one domain. You are most likely locked into a multiple master domain model with organizational or regional resource domains.

- *WAN links.* Create a list of all dedicated network links and corresponding sites. Are there any sites without a dedicated network connection? If so, they should be implemented as a separate domain. It is possible to establish a RAS-connected BDC, but that is highly inadvisable. Also, separate domains for sites with slow network links will prove to be a more manageable structure.

<512Kbps   You should consider the time it takes to do a full synchronization of the SAM database over this link.

Tip

If you currently have a network in place, you should measure the time it takes to copy a file from one site to another over your various WAN links. You can use CREATEFIL.EXE from the Windows NT Resource Kit to generate a file of any size, then copy the file from one location to the other, measuring the time it takes to copy the file. You can automate the time measurement using TIMETHIS.EXE, a utility also found in the Windows NT Resource Kit.

Be sure to try this several times throughout the day (your network may have heavy traffic patterns during specific portions of the day). Such a test is a true indicator of the performance you can expect from your WAN. In some cases you may be surprised to find that your fast links are saturated and your slower links yield faster throughput!

- *Centralized administration.* Do you require centralized administration? Only a single domain model and master domain model offer this. From a political perspective, most company locations want to control their own domain and will fight for decentralized administration. Furthermore, each location is often reluctant to trust any other locations. Complying with decentralization requests often results in chaos because each site ends up following different standards. For this reason, it is highly recommended that you pursue a model with centralized administration. The problem of delegating control of resources can be accomplished with the proper user and group strategy.

In many businesses it is often desirable to designate a pseudo-administrator for each department. Windows NT doesn't let you accomplish this very easily, but it does allow you to have separate administrator accounts that are responsible for different groups of users. Combine this limitation with the notion of giving a departmental "techie" a domain admin logon, and you have the dilemma most companies face. The solution might be to investigate third-party virtual administration tools. Chapter 9, "Organizing Users," features a listing of some of the third-party administration tools available.

- *Domain organization.* Do you want to establish separate domains based on geography or organizational divisions? Both methods provide a modular approach; however, the geographic approach makes it easier to add domains should your company be involved in a merger or acquisition. Also consider the need to create separate domains for vendors, Internet servers, extranet servers, the finance department, the human resources department, and so on.

- *Enterprise applications.* How is your domain model affected by the applications you run? Applications such as MS Exchange are very dependent on your domain model and influence your domain design greatly. Do you have centralized databases at a corporate site, or do you replicate your databases to remote sites?

- *Fault tolerance.* NT domains limit you to one PDC, which is a single point of failure. How many of your users and sites would be affected by a PDC failure? Models that support centralized administration would exhibit widespread effects if the PDC failed. Thus, you must be prepared for failure and establish a disaster recovery strategy that is accommodating to your line of business.

  If a PDC containing user and group accounts becomes unavailable, you cannot

  - Modify user or group properties

  - Set resource security (because you cannot access the users and groups on the PDC)

  - Change passwords

  - Add NT workstations or servers to the domain (because a computer account in the domain SAM is required)

- *Internet access.* Will any or all sites require Internet access? Will you grant Internet access to all users or only specific users or groups of users? On most networks, a single location has a network link to the Internet, and all other sites must travel through a private WAN to the corporate site to gain Internet access (see Chapter 8, "Domain Security," for information on Internet connectivity and related security issues).

Giving consideration to these criteria and your design goals should help you make an informed decision when selecting your domain model.

Site Analysis

If your company has numerous locations, you should perform a site-by-site analysis, determining how the sites should be connected and how they best fit into the proposed architecture. Companies with numerous sites should consider integrating two or more sites into regional resource domains.

Following are more criteria to consider at each site, along with questions you should answer for your situation:

- *Number of users.* How many domain users will the site have? If the number of users is fewer than 10, you may want to consider other technologies for connecting them to the corporate network. Such technologies include direct remote access to the corporate network via a modem, or Virtual Private Networking (VPN) devices that use the Internet to tunnel data back to the corporate network. You might also consider emerging technologies such as Terminal Server Edition.

- *Local servers.* How many local NT servers does this site have? If you are considering making the site a resource domain, you would need at least two servers—a resource domain PDC and an account domain BDC—for smooth operation. You should also have a third server for a resource domain BDC.

- *WAN connectivity.* Does this site have WAN connectivity? If so, to which locations? If no WAN links are present, the site would have to be an independent domain and access resources at other sites via modem. This gets messy—the only good solution is a dedicated link.

- *Administrative staff.* Does this site have qualified administrative staff that could support this site if it were a separate domain? If the site does not have qualified administrative staff, the users at this site would have to rely upon centralized administration controlled by another site.

- *Replication traffic.* Does this site have a local email or database server that replicates with other servers across the WAN? Does it have a local WINS server that replicates with other WINS servers? If so, how much replication traffic is generated? Does it occur during a particular portion of the day? Can the replication be scheduled for out-of-office hours? What is the tradeoff in doing so?

- *Resource Access.* Will users at this site need to access resources at other sites or in other domains?

- *User mobility.* Will users from other domains visit this site and log on to its workstations?

Organizing Resource Domains

If you have selected a master domain model or multiple master domain model, you must decide how to best organize your resource domains. In the following sections we describe several different methods, each with its advantages and disadvantages. The most popular choice for organizing resource domains is based on geography or geographical boundaries (such as regions).

Geographic Resource Domains

Organizing resource domains based on geography creates an infrastructure that is easier to troubleshoot and manage. Furthermore, it is modular and allows you to add new resource domains easily when your company establishes a presence in new cities. Figure 6.2 illustrates a master domain model with resource domains organized by city. Notice that the trust relationships also correspond to WAN links. This not only makes it easier to troubleshoot and isolate problems, but it also makes the diagram easier to understand.

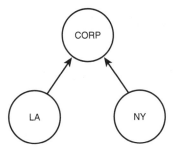

Figure 6.2   *The NY and LA domains trust the Corp domain. Organizing resource domains by location creates a design that is easier to troubleshoot and manage.*

To improve performance in the resource domains, it is a common practice to add a BDC for the master domain to the LAN at the remote site (see Figure 6.3). If you have more than one TCP/IP subnet at the remote site, you should consider a switched network or place a BDC on each subnet.

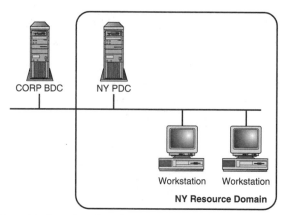

Figure 6.3   *A Corp BDC is placed at the New York location to handle trusted domain user authentication requests.*

Regional Resource Domains

Do you feel your organization has too many locations to make each one a resource domain? If so, you should divide the sites into regions, and then combine the sites within each region into a single resource domain. Figure 6.4 illustrates a simple example of a regional organization of resource domains. Each region is a single resource domain composed of offices in different cities (see Figure 6.5).

You can combine several locations into a regional resource domain.

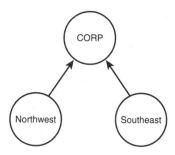

Figure 6.4   *The Southeast and Northwest domains trust the Corp domain.*

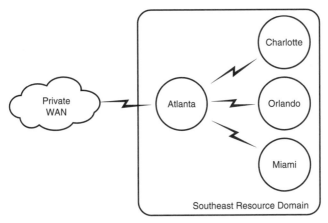

Figure 6.5   *The Southeast domain is broken into smaller offices.*

Divisional Resource Domains

Organizing resource domains based on divisional boundaries within your company is a less common approach that is rarely seen with master domain models but is more prevalent with multiple master domain models. Figure 6.6 illustrates a resource domain for a multiple master domain model organized by division. Each resource domain consists of a common department that spans multiple cities.

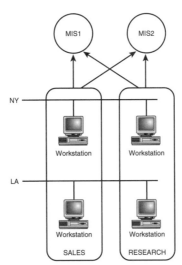

Figure 6.6   *Organizing resource domains by division usually results in fewer resource domains spanning numerous cities.*

A resource domain spanning multiple cities introduces the dilemma of where to locate the resource domain PDC. It also makes troubleshooting more difficult because there is no logical correspondence between trusts and WAN links.

> **Author's Note**
>
> *You should be wary of this resource domain implementation if you will be switching to Windows 2000. Windows 2000 is very dependent on TCP/IP, and the Active Directory uses service locator (SRV) records in DNS. Because each location is likely to have its own DNS server for the Active Directory, you would probably adopt a domain naming convention like this:*
>
>   <dept>.<city>.<company>.com
>
> *Thus, if you organize your resource domains based on city and not division, you will have an easier transition to Windows 2000.*

Preparing for a Transition to Windows 2000

The best preparation for Windows 2000 is a good NT 4.0 base. Because Active Directory supports numerous objects, you can likely fit all your domain resources into a single Windows 2000 domain.

Windows 2000 has everything you need to consolidate users and resources into a single domain infrastructure. *Organizational Units (OUs)* can be used to delegate administration and logically group resources. You can use sites to describe well-connected areas and control replication traffic across WANs. In fact, you can even control replication within a site using Windows 2000.

The Windows 2000 Active Directory implementation requires a solid understanding of TCP/IP and DNS. In Windows 2000 each domain is a DNS domain name, and DNS (not NetBIOS) is the required name resolution protocol. You have the option of running the Microsoft DNS or a third-party DNS on Windows NT or UNIX. Regardless of the DNS you choose, it must support SRV records as defined in RFC 2052. SRV records allow more than one server to advertise a similar service; in the case of Windows 2000, they are used to locate domain controllers.

To make your transition to Windows 2000 easier, you should limit your present NetBIOS names to the DNS character set (a–z, A–Z, 0–9, and -). Be aware that the hyphen character introduces problems for ODBC clients; it should be avoided in the naming of database servers.

A complete discussion of migrating to Windows 2000 is beyond the scope of this book. However, the following list of recommended design documents from Microsoft should give you a good start:

- Forest, domain, and global catalog architectures

- Site and replication architecture

- DNS design

- Schema extensions document

- DFS, file replication, and tree design

- CA trusts design

- Administrative/security roles document

- Namespace/naming standards design

- Risk assessment document

Author's Note

After a discussion of Windows 2000 and directory services, it is only fair to mention Novell Directory Services (NDS) for Windows NT. Released in the spring of 1998, NDS for Windows NT is intended for companies that are predominantly NetWare shops and have only a few Windows NT domains. The software offers true directory services with support for a tree of two million users. It eliminates the need for trusts among NT domains and allows you to manage NT domain objects with NDS tools such as NetWare Administrator.

The implementation of NDS for NT is quite interesting. You must install intraNetWare clients and NDS on all PDCs and BDCs. As a result, SAMSRV.DLL is replaced with a file from Novell that redirects all authentication requests to the NDS tree. Thus, there is no need for trusts or any accounts in the NT SAM; the NT SAM is ignored, and the NDS tree is used in its place. You must be extra careful when installing and testing NDS for NT. Because the SAMSRV.DLL is replaced, you must save the old one before installation in case you decide not to use NDS for Windows NT.

Netscape and Zoomit also offer metadirectories that are similar to NDS for NT and provide a single point of administration for heterogeneous networks.

Chapter 7

Domain Reconfiguration

This chapter will review:

- **Planning for the Transition**
  Domain reconfiguration projects are filled with many challenges. You must take the time to understand all the issues involved with a successful project.

- **Moving Accounts to a New Domain**
  Moving accounts is a difficult task. Although you can use utilities to automate the process, Windows NT's treatment of security identifiers forces you to reconfigure your access control lists (ACLs) and group memberships.

- **Moving NT Systems to a New Domain**
  Moving NT systems to a new domain involves more than just joining a new domain. In most cases, you must modify local group memberships to achieve the desired results.

- **Scaling from a Single Domain to a Master Domain**
  This architecture change is one of the most common. If you exercise caution, you can make the transition nearly transparent to your users.

- **Changing from a Complete Trust to a Master Domain**
  Because you must move user and group accounts, this domain reconfiguration can be the most demanding of all.

- **Integrating Two Resource Domains**
  In large enterprise networks, it is common to consolidate resources into fewer domains.

- **The Effects of a Company Merger**
  A company merger raises many issues with regard to network services and domain architecture.

Planning for the Transition

In Chapter 6 you were given the tools to select the best domain model for your company. However, it is likely that your company already has a domain structure in place. Following are three common changes you may need to make to your current domain structure:

- Scaling from a single domain to a master domain

- Changing from a complete trust to a master domain

- Integrating two resource domains

All three changes are discussed in separate sections at the end of this chapter.

A domain reconfiguration can be a huge project, so you can never spend too much time planning it. This is not impossible if you take the right approach. You must look at a complete overview of the project; in most cases you will have several options. When choosing a particular approach, you should weigh the amount of work involved in all possible choices.

The key to a successful domain reconfiguration project is standardization. Without standards, your staff will ultimately become confused by the complexity of the project, and chaos will ensue. If you have already been following standardized strategies for granting resource access, you will find your project much easier. On large networks, it is especially easy to stray from a standard practice for the sake of speed and convenience. However, nonstandard permission lists and group memberships can quickly change a large domain project from an overwhelming success to a failure.

The Dilemmas of Domain Reconfiguration

While there are two common dilemmas of domain reconfiguration, the dilemmas result from the same problem: security identifiers (SIDs). SIDS are used to identify everything in the domain: users, groups, computers and the domain itself. When you create a new user account or add a computer account to the domain Windows NT generates a new SID for the account.

User rights and resource permissions are controlled based on SIDs. For example, when you add a group to an ACL Windows NT associates the group SID, rather than the group name, with a particular permission level.

In a domain reconfiguration project, there are two common dilemmas you will face:

- *Moving users to a new domain.* One unfortunate shortcoming of Windows NT is the inability to move SIDs to a new domain. In other words, you cannot move a user (and their corresponding SID) to a new domain. You must create a new user account with the same name. Despite the fact the new user account has the same name, a new SID is assigned to the user account. If the new user is to have access to the same resources as the older user account, you must modify all ACLs to add the new user account.

> **Tip**
>
> *Creating users in a new domain can be automated using ADDUSERS.EXE from the NT Resource Kit.*

- *Moving NT systems to a new domain.* There is no tool that can automatically change a workstation from one domain to another. With a Windows 95 machine, you simply have to configure the machine to log on to a different domain. With an NT machine, however, you must disjoin it from the current domain and join it to the new domain. Upon doing so, a computer account for the workstation or server is created in the new domain SAM. The process does not require any modification of ACLs and is much easier than moving users to a new domain.

When you have a domain that contains both resources and user accounts, your first preference should be to use the existing domain as an accounts domain so that you do not have to move user accounts and modify ACLs—thereby making your transition much easier. However, when scaling away from a decentralized model to a centralized model, you must move accounts to the domain responsible for the centralized administration. This can be a cumbersome task that you should approach with caution.

> **Tip**
>
> *If you use a complete trust model because each of your company divisions want control of their own domain, you may want to consider a multiple master domain before trying to centralize accounts into a master domain. A multiple master domain gives each division its own master domain, and it solves the problem of delegating administration that a master domain model creates.*

Impact of a Domain Change on Enterprise Services

Enterprise services such as WINS, DNS, and DHCP are usually not impacted by your domain change. Only in the event that you change your IP addressing scheme or naming convention do you need to consider the impact on WINS and DNS. As a rule of thumb, you should try to minimize your number of WINS and DNS servers. In many cases, when people expand their domain architecture, they think it is wise to place a WINS and/or a DNS server at each company location. The result is usually an unmanageable configuration.

DHCP is a low-level service that automates the assignment of IP addresses to computers and network devices. Consequently, it is not impacted by your domain change unless you change your IP addressing scheme and assign it a different pool of addresses to delegate. For detailed information on how to perform this process smoothly, see Appendix C, "Changing IP Addressing Schemes."

Moving User Accounts to a New Domain

Moving user accounts to a new domain is a large undertaking; the amount of work required varies depending on your user/group structure and resource permissions strategy. To help you better understand the procedure, consider the illustration in Figure 7.1.

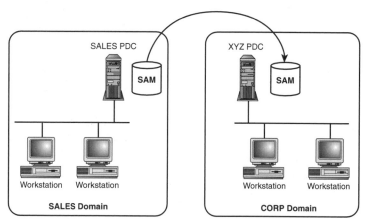

Figure 7.1   *Making the transition from independent domains to a master domain model requires a move of user accounts to the Corp domain.*

Suppose your job is to move the user accounts from the Sales domain to the Corp domain with minimal impact to the users. The following should be your strategy:

1. Establish a trust relationship between Sales and Corp such that Corp is trusted by Sales.

2. Use ADDUSERS.EXE (see the section on ADDUSERS.EXE in this chapter) to create new user and group accounts in the Corp domain based on the user and group accounts in the Sales domain.

> **Tip**
>
> *You must check the Corp domain for duplicate accounts. If this domain architecture has been in place for a period of time, it is likely you will find that user accounts have been created in the Corp domain for visiting Sales domain users. ADDUSERS.EXE does not overwrite existing user or group accounts.*

3. If you are not assigning resource permissions based on local groups (see the following note), you must modify all the ACLs for *all* resources in the Sales domain. You will add the new users and groups from the trusted Corp domain to the ACLs while leaving the existing ACL entries intact.

> **Author's Note**
>
> *According to Microsoft, you should add global users to global groups, add global groups to local groups, and set permissions based on local group membership. For a single domain, establishing a local group is an extra step; for simplicity, I advise people not to do it. However, if the Microsoft strategy were followed in this example, you would not be required to change each ACL—you would just have to change the local groups on all servers to include membership of the new trusted domain global groups.*
>
> *If all this seems confusing, see Chapter 9, "Organizing Users," which contains complete details on the various user and group strategies you can pursue with each domain model.*

If you are assigning resource permissions based on local groups, you will not have to modify any ACLs—you will simply need to add the new trusted global groups to your local groups.

4. You must create a global group in the Corp domain for Sales users, and you must add the trusted group to the local users group on all workstations and servers in the Sales domain. Likewise, you must create a global Administrators group in Corp for Sales administrators and add the trusted group to the local Administrators group on all workstations and servers in the Sales domain. Without these steps, users in the sales domain would not be permitted to log on because of a hitch with user rights. User rights will be discussed in Chapter 9.

5. Test the new arrangement by having users log on to their accounts in the trusted Corp domain. They should have their previous level of access to the resources in the Sales domain if you have set the ACLs properly.

6. If you are content with the modification, you must delete all user and group accounts from the Sales domain and clean up the ACLs on all resources. Specifically, you must delete references to the old user and group accounts from the Sales domain.

Upon completion, the finalized network configuration should resemble Figure 7.2.

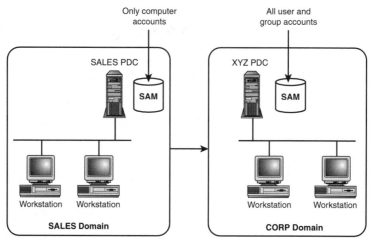

Figure 7.2 *The final configuration is a master domain model with centralized administration.*

Chapter 9 will have a complete explanation of user and group strategies for various domain models, and Chapter 11, "Controlling Access to Domain Resources," will cover permission strategies for controlling resource access.

Using ADDUSERS.EXE

The transition described in the previous section would be much easier if User Manager for Domains had an option to import and export an account list. Unfortunately, the option is not available. However, a utility included in the NT Resource Kit, ADDUSERS.EXE, gives you the capability to dump all user and group accounts to a text file. It extracts not only user account names but also user account properties such as the user profile path and home directory. When the list is extracted, it can be imported into a spreadsheet program (such as Microsoft Excel) and modified. The utility can also be used to create new accounts and groups in the SAM.

Tip

You must be a member of the Administrators group on the target computer to add accounts and a member of the Users group to dump accounts to a file.

ADDUSERS.EXE Syntax

```
addusers [ \\computername ] [{ /c ¦ /d ¦ /e } filename] [/s:x] [/?]
```

- \\computername is the computer on which you want to create user accounts or from which you want to write user accounts. If you do not specify a computer name, the local computer is used by default.

- /c creates user accounts, local groups, and global groups as specified by filename.

- /d dumps user accounts, local groups, and global groups to filename.

> ### Tip
>
> *Choosing to dump current user accounts does not save the account's passwords or any security information for the accounts. A tape should be used to back up security information for accounts.*
>
> *Also note that because password information is not saved in a user account dump, using the same file to create accounts causes all passwords of newly created accounts to be empty. All created users will then be required to change their password at logon by default.*

- /e deletes user accounts as specified by filename.

> ### Warning
>
> *Be careful when erasing user accounts—it is not possible to re-create the user account with the same SID. This option, however, cannot erase built-in default accounts.*

- filename is the comma-delimited input/output file that AddUsers will use for data.

- /s:x changes the character used for separating fields in the file. The x should be replaced with the new character to be used for separating fields. For example, /s:~ would make the tilde (~) the field-separation character. If this option is not specified, the default separator (a comma) is used.

- /? displays a usage screen.

To dump the contents of the Sales SAM to a text file, you would issue the following command:

```
addusers \\SalesPDC /d c:\samfile.txt
```

This command would create a text file called samfile.txt on the c: drive. samfile.txt would be a comma-delimited text file readable with any text editor. Because AddUsers does not extract any security information, it does not contain any passwords. The file contains three distinct sections—[Users], [Global], and [Local]—and is easily imported into a spreadsheet program (see Figure 7.3).

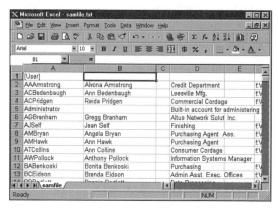

Figure 7.3   *You can easily import the comma-delimited file created by the ADDUSERS.EXE command into nearly any spreadsheet program.*

The last step in moving the user accounts from the Sales domain to the Corp domain is as follows:

```
addusers \\CORPPDC /c c:\samfile.txt
```

Note that you must have administrative privileges on the Corp PDC to complete the command.

Changing Resource Permissions

Changing resource permissions is an enormous task that requires a great deal of time. To make your transition easier, you need to classify all the resources on your network and each user's level of access to them. If you have followed a strategy of assigning resource permissions based on local or global groups, your domain change should be much easier. Otherwise, if you have resources with permissions assigned directly to individual user accounts, you should change your permissions before undertaking the project of changing domain architecture.

> **Warning**
>
> *Never place an individual user account on a permission list; you should always use a global or local group no matter how few users need access to the resource. If you do have individual user accounts on any ACLs, you must organize users into groups and assign resource permissions correctly before considering any domain change. Otherwise, your chances for a smooth transition are greatly diminished.*

There are four primary resources you should consider:

- *Shared Folders.* For shared folders, you must ensure that the share-level, folder-level, and file-level permissions do not inhibit your user's access when you change domain architecture. To get a full report on NTFS file system permissions, you can use a utility such as DumpACL (a shareware program covered in the next section).

If you permit users to share information from their NT workstations, you should avoid searching for network shares. You can use Net Watch from the Windows NT Resource Kit to list the shares of individual machines.

You can use SUBINACL.EXE to transfer file ownership and permissions from a user account in one domain to a new user account in a new domain. You can find SUBINACL.EXE in the NT Resource Kit Supplement Two.

- *Printers.* When moving users to another domain, you must be sure they can still access their printers. In some organizations it is common to restrict users to printers in their department or area. If you have changed any print permissions, you must consider how access to the printers would be affected by your domain change. You can treat the printer ACLs like the folder ACLs and follow the same guidelines. In some cases, when you split one domain into two or more domains, you need to move print queues. A clever way to automate the change for the users is to use a logon script utility such as KiXtart to install and configure printers as part of a user's logon script. See Chapter 10, "Logon Scripts, Profiles, and Policies," for information on using KiXtart.

- *Database.* Permission to the database software depends on the type of database product you are running. Some products can be run with integrated security—that is, the user authentication is integrated with Windows NT. If this is the case, you have to reconfigure your database server to create permissions based on trusted users and groups.

- *Email.* Once again, the impact of a domain reconfiguration depends on the email software you are using. However, if your email server assigns mailboxes to NT user accounts (like MS Exchange does), you can expect to change the assignment for each mailbox to the new accounts created in the trusted domain.

Depending on your network configuration, you will have more resources to consider.

Using DumpACL

DumpACL is a great utility for checking domain policies and NTFS permissions. You can download it from http://www.somarsoft.com. DumpACL gives you the option to report the following:

- Permissions for file systems
- Permissions for the Registry
- Permissions for printers
- Permissions for shares
- Users
- Groups
- Domain policies
- Domain rights
- Services

DumpACL (see Figure 7.4) is an indispensable tool for enterprise network administration and should be a requirement for a domain reconfiguration project.

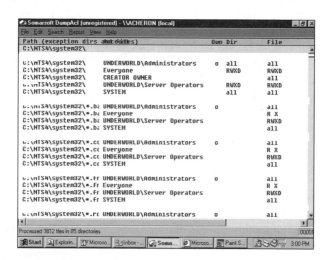

Figure 7.4 *DumpACL allows you to generate many useful reports related to users, groups, and NTFS permissions. Illustrated here is a permissions report for the nts4\system32 folder.*

Moving NT Systems to a New Domain

Changing an NT system's domain membership to a new domain is an easy task. The change only impacts the SID for the computer account and does not affect the user and group SIDs in the local SAM.

Users in the new domain are able to log on to the workstation immediately after the change. However, if you need to permit users from other domains to log on or administer the machine, some extra work is required. Consider Figure 7.2: To allow all members of the Corp domain to log on to a workstation in the Sales domain, you must add the Corp\Domain Users group to the local Users group on each workstation in the Sales domain. Furthermore, you likely need some of the administrators from the Corp domain to administer the workstations in the Sales domain. Your first step is to create a Sales Admins global group in the Corp domain. Then you add the Corp\Sales Admins global group to the local administrators group on each NT workstation in the Sales domain.

Automating Domain Changes with DM/Reconfigure

While you can use a combination of several NT Resource Kit utilities to help you automate your domain changes, you can save yourself a great deal of work by using an application like DM/Reconfigure™. DM/Reconfigure is a comprehensive domain reconfiguration application developed by FastLane Technologies, Inc.

The tool does not eliminate the need to thoroughly plan your reconfiguration. However, it offers several reports that are very useful in the project planning stage. Once you have a solid reconfiguration plan, you can use the tool to automate many tasks such as the moving of users, groups and computers to a new domain.

DM/Reconfigure divides the reconfiguration into a six stage process:

- Stage 1: Users
- Stage 2: Global Groups
- Stage 3: Local Groups
- Stage 4: ACLs
- Stage 5: Rights
- Stage 6: Computers

Each stage is thoroughly discussed in the documentation that accompanies the product (over 150 pages). You can download a 30-day evaluation copy from http://www.fastlanetech.com.

Scaling from a Single Domain to a Master Domain

The transition from a single domain model to a master domain model is probably one of the easiest domain changes you can pursue. Suppose XYZ Corp. has two primary divisions: Sales and Purchasing, and you are the project leader responsible for changing its single domain to a master domain (see Figure 7.5). Your goal is to establish two resource domains: a Sales domain and a Purchasing domain. Of course, you need to make the transition as smooth as possible. At present, the XYZ PDC and BDC pair are responsible for WINS, DNS, and DHCP. The XYZ BDC also has 10 print queues with Print permission for XYZ\Domain Users.

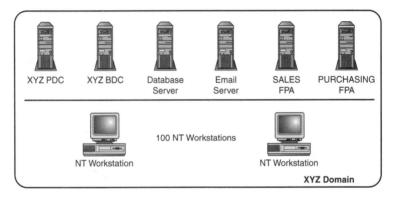

Figure 7.5　*The XYZ domain is a single domain configuration that must be changed to a master domain architecture.*

Author's Note

I realize the network architecture in Figure 7.5 is oversimplified compared to a real-world multiple-vendor network. However, the points and procedures are realistic and parallel the real-world approach to changing the domain architecture.

The first major decision is whether the current domain should become a resource domain or the accounts domain for the new master domain model. Establishing the current domain as the accounts domain creates the easiest transition because you are not required to move any user or group accounts. When you move the workstations to another domain, the SIDs on the ACLs attached to resources are preserved, which saves you the struggle of reconfiguring each ACL.

Transition Considerations

You need to consider the following issues when planning the transition from a single domain to a master domain:

- *Administration.* Who will be responsible for the administration of the workstations in the Sales and Purchasing domains? You can give the XYZ\Domain Admins responsibility for all workstations in both domains. A better and more modular approach is to create separate administrative groups for the administrators of workstations in each resource domain.

- *Naming conventions.* In most cases you should change the naming convention of your machines in the resource domains. For example, a workstation in the XYZ domain might be named XYZW001, whereas the new convention may call for something like SalesW001. The problem with changing the naming convention is how it relates to print queues and mapped drives. All workstations reference the servers based on name or IP address, depending on the client application. A changed server name leaves the workstations searching for resources on a nonexistent machine. Because of the complications involved, you should make the name changes after you change the domain model. See Appendix D, "Changing Naming Conventions," for more information.

- *IP addressing.* Much like the computer names, IP addresses are used by many applications to reference resources. Changing the IP address of a WINS or DHCP server can lead to chaos on a large network. See Appendix C, "Changing IP Addressing Schemes," for more information.

- *Print queues.* In this case, the print queues are unaffected if they remain on a machine in the XYZ domain. However, the printers belonging to each department should be moved to the proper domain. Moving print queues is not a critical issue and can be completed one-by-one after the domain reconfiguration is complete.

Steps for the Transition

The following steps outline the procedure for the transition from a single domain to a master domain:

1. Install a PDC for the Sales resource domain and a PDC for the Purchasing resource domain. For each domain, establish a one-way trust to XYZ in which XYZ is the trusted domain.

2. Create the following global groups in the XYZ domain for Sales and Purchasing administrators, respectively:

- XYZ\Sales Admins

- XYZ\Purchasing Admins

3. Join the file, print, and application (FPA) servers and workstations to the Sales or Purchasing domain. This operation removes the computers from the XYZ domain, and you are presented with a warning when you complete the operation.

4. Delegate user and administrative powers by modifying the local groups. You must add the global XYZ\Domain Users group to the local Domain Users group on all Sales and Purchasing computers (workstations, FPAs, PDCs and BDCs).For computers in the Sales domain, you must add the XYZ\Sales Admins group to the local Administrators group. For computers in the Purchasing domain, you must add the XYZ\Purchasing Admins group to the local Administrators group.

Congratulations! You have completed the transition. Your final configuration should resemble Figure 7.6.

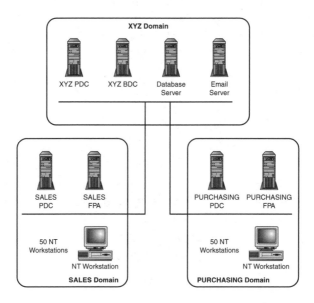

Figure 7.6   *The resulting XYZ domain is a modular architecture with centralized administration.*

Scaling from a Complete Trust to a Master Domain

Scaling from a complete trust to a master domain is challenging because you must move user and group accounts and modify resource permissions. Suppose your complete trust architecture consists of two domains—Atlanta and Orlando—with each domain corresponding to a corporate location (see Figure 7.7). Since the implementation of Windows NT, each domain has been independently administered.

Your first major difficulty in scaling to a master domain is deciding where you will locate the master domain—in Atlanta or Orlando? Where is more user and group administration performed? Because Atlanta has the largest user base (500 workstations versus 100 in Orlando), it would be wise to locate the master domain on the Atlanta network.

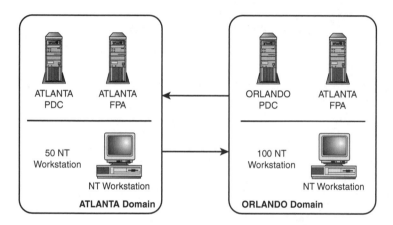

Figure 7.7   *The complete trust model offers independent administration but lacks the scalability of a master domain model.*

Transition Considerations

You would need to consider the following issues when planning the transition from a complete trust to a master domain:

* *Administration.* Who will be responsible for the administration of the workstations in the Atlanta and Orlando domains? You can still maintain the delegation of administration by creating two global administration groups—one for the Atlanta administrators and one for the Orlando administrators. The only problem is the overlap in administrative powers. By making an Orlando administrator a Domain Admin in the master domain, you also give that person the ability to administer accounts and groups for the Atlanta domain. From one point of view, this is nice because the Atlanta location can offload some support to the Orlando staff. On the other hand, the managers and staff at each location usually fear sharing control with another group and must work through the political issues before any progress is made.

- *BDC placement.* A BDC for the master domain should be placed on each LAN to improve logon and authentication performance.

- *Naming conventions.* See the previous section on scaling from a single domain to a master domain. For information on changing your naming convention, see Appendix D.

- *IP Addressing.* See the previous section on scaling from a single domain to a master domain. For information on changing your IP addressing scheme, see Appendix C.

- *Print Queues.* The change to a master domain allows all users to see the shared printers in each resource domain. By default, printers are installed with Print permission granted to the Everyone group. Unless the permissions have been modified to restrict printer access, you will not have to modify printer permissions after the transition.

Steps for the Transition

The following steps outline the procedure for the transition from a complete trust to a master domain:

1. Install and configure the Corp PDC and BDC.

2. Establish a one-way trust to the Corp domain from the Atlanta and Orlando domains, and leave the one-way trust between their domains in place.

3. Use ADDUSERS.EXE to export the Atlanta and Orlando SAMs to a text file, and then use it to create accounts in the Corp domain based on the exported text files. Be careful to avoid user and group name conflicts.

4. Classify all resources in the Atlanta and Orlando domains. If you are assigning resource access based on local groups, add the trusted global groups from the Corp domain to the local groups on each workstation and server in the resource domains. If you are assigning resource access based on global groups, you must inspect each ACL for resources in the resource domains. You must add the corresponding trusted global group to each ACL while leaving the existing ACL entries in place. In other words, if a file has access permissions assigned to the Atlanta\Accounting global group, you would add the Corp\Accounting group to the ACL.

5. You must create the following two global administrative groups in the Corp domain:

    - Corp\Atlanta Admins

    - Corp\Orlando Admins

6. You must add Corp\Domain Users to the local Users group on computers in the Orlando and Atlanta domains. Add the Corp\Atlanta Admins to the local Administrators group on every workstation and server in the Atlanta domain. Add the Corp/Orlando Admins to the local Administrators group on every workstation and server in the Orlando domain.

7. Test the new architecture by having users log on to the Corp domain with their new accounts.

8. After a sufficient testing period, you need to clean up the old unused trusts, accounts, and so on. Specifically, you must do the following:

    • Delete all user and group accounts from the Atlanta and Orlando domain controllers, leaving only the built-in accounts and groups.

    • Edit the ACL on each resource in the resource domains to remove reference to the deleted accounts.

    • Remove the trust relationships between the two resource domains, leaving a single one-way trust to the Corp domain.

Your final domain architecture should resemble Figure 7.8.

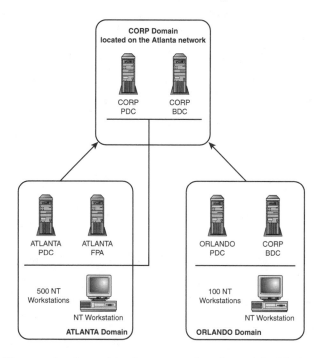

Figure 7.8   *The completed transition is a master domain model with the master domain Corp located on the Atlanta network.*

Integrating Two Resource Domains

Often an expanding company wants to consolidate resource domains into a regional configuration (see Figure 7.9). This change does not require moving any user accounts, so it is easily completed.

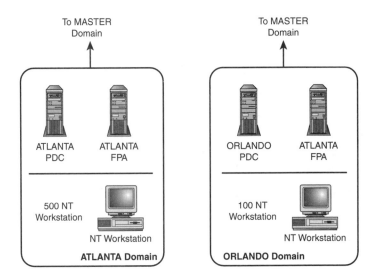

Figure 7.9   *The Atlanta and Orlando resource domains are part of a larger network. Both domains must be integrated into a single resource domain for the Southeast region.*

Integration Considerations

You need to consider the following issues when planning the integration of the two resource domains:

- *PDC placement.* You must decide which physical location will maintain the PDC. It makes sense to locate the PDC at the site with the largest number of end users.

- *WAN connectivity.* In most cases, you will want a direct WAN link between the two locations. The WAN link is used for replication of the SAM database.

- *BDC placement.* At the very least, you should have one BDC for the resource domain and locate it in the physical location opposite the PDC. Ideally, you should have a BDC at each location. If you were to experience a problem with the PDC, you could promote a LAN-attached BDC more quickly and efficiently than you could a BDC across a WAN link.

- *Naming conventions.* See the section on scaling from a single domain to a master domain. For information on changing your naming convention, see Appendix D.

- *IP addressing.* See the section on scaling from a single domain to a master domain. For information on changing your IP addressing scheme, see Appendix C.

- *Print queues.* In this case, the print queues are unaffected.

Steps for the Transition

The following steps outline the procedure for the integration of the two resource domains in Figure 7.9:

1. Establish a WAN link between the two locations if one is not in place.

2. Install and configure the Southeast PDC and BDCs.

3. Establish a one-way trust to the Master domain from the Southeast domain.

4. Move all workstations and servers from the Atlanta domain to the Southeast domain.

5. Move all workstations and servers from the Orlando domain to the Southeast domain.

6. Remove the Atlanta and Orlando domain controllers from the network.

The final domain architecture should resemble Figure 7.10.

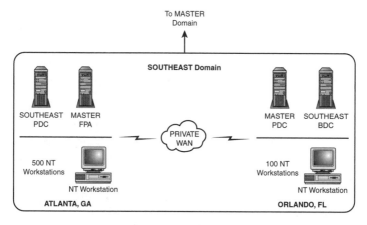

Figure 7.10   *The Atlanta and Orlando resource domains have been integrated into a Southeast domain.*

The Effect of a Company Merger

A company merger is often the impetus for a domain architecture change. The details related to the architecture change are greatly dependent on the network infrastructures of the merging companies, so it is nearly impossible to characterize them without specifics.

Contrary to popular belief, a company merger does not always result in a messy network integration. In some cases, each company has a master domain model that is easily changed into a multiple master domain model with master domains based on corporate divisions (that is, the two merged companies each maintain one of the master domains). In other cases, the situation is smoothed because one of the merging companies agrees to relinquish MIS control to the other.

Common Issues Related to a Company Merger

The typical merger raises many common issues that can seriously impact the domain architecture:

- *Who is in control?* This is usually more of a political war than anything else. However, security concerns are usually overemphasized, and a general lack of trust typically results. In the majority of cases, a misunderstanding of NT security leads to a fear of establishing any type of trust between the networks, particularly among the MIS people involved.

- *Centralized or decentralized administration?* If the companies involved are small enough, they may fight for a complete trust model for fear of centralizing (and possibly downsizing) MIS. A complete trust model is usually a bad idea, and you should steer the company toward a master or multiple master domain model.

- *No common TCP/IP addressing.* It is not impossible to connect TCP/IP networks with separate addressing schemes. However, a company-wide standard TCP/IP addressing scheme with address pools allocated to each office is ideal for expansion and flexibility.

- *No common naming conventions.* It is not mission-critical that the merging companies have a standard, companywide naming convention, but standards make it much easier to identify and troubleshoot problems.

- *Account conflicts.* You can expect to run into several user account, group account, and computer account conflicts. You should develop strategies for handling the conflicts before you encounter them. If you do not have a strategy, it is likely several variations will result, especially if many people are involved in the process of moving accounts.

Chapter 8

Domain Security

This chapter will review:

- **Introduction to Security**
  Security is often underemphasized. A logical approach leads you to the best security configuration for your network.

- **The Security Boundary of a Domain**
  One of the greatest benefits of a domain is the centralized security it provides. Understanding domain security and how it is affected by trusts greatly influences your network security policies.

- **Service Packs and Hotfixes**
  Service packs and hotfixes are used not only to patch bugs on NT systems but also to patch many security holes.

- **NT Security Measures Checklist**
  An exhaustive, detailed list would be beyond the scope of this book. However, a list of rudimentary security precautions is included in this chapter.

- **A Word on Firewalls**
  A firewall is a necessity when your business is connected to external networks you do not control. See this section of the chapter for tips on establishing an external security policy.

Introduction to Security

It would be impossible to cover all aspects of Windows NT security in this text. However, a domain is a security boundary, so we must consider the security issues associated with it.

Security can be divided into two categories: external security and internal security. *External security* is strengthened by firewall products. *Internal security*, however, depends greatly on your network architecture and configuration. If NT domain controllers or workstations are not configured properly, security becomes a serious issue.

To understand security, you must understand the type of people who break into networks and their motivation for doing so. Those attempting to penetrate a network from the outside may be trying to access the data on your network or use your network to get to another network and cover their tracks. On the other hand, those attempting to exploit a system from the inside are usually trying to obtain additional privileges. For example, a person with an ordinary domain user account may attempt to become a domain administrator. Of course, the more security you require, the more complex the network becomes, so additional configuration is required.

> **Author's Note**
>
> *Windows NT meets C2 security specifications. But what exactly does that mean?*
>
> *Most people do not fully understand C2 security, and they think that just because they have purchased Windows NT their network is more secure. Nothing could be further from the truth. Do you realize C2 security requires that you do not install any network components? How much business do you think a company can really do without having machines networked? Not very much.*
>
> *If you would like to learn more about C2 security and how the restrictions affect your system, run the C2 Configuration Manger from the Windows NT Resource Kit. C2 may be a requirement for military systems that store classified information, but it is certainly not a selling feature intended for the general marketplace.*

The Security Boundary of a Domain

A domain is not only a unit of administration but also a security boundary. Windows NT machines in a domain share common security policies (an account policy, audit policy, and so on) as well as a common list of users and groups.

Recall from Chapter 2 that NT machines configured to be a member of a workgroup do not run the NetLogon service. When an NT machine joins a domain, it starts its NetLogon service. The NetLogon service is responsible for establishing a secure channel with a domain controller and is used for authentication and pass-through authentication requests.

> **Tip**
>
> *You can use DOMMON.EXE from the Resource Kit to monitor the secure channel status of domain controllers and trusted domain controllers.*

To better understand the security issues involved in granting resource access to a user, consider the process of authenticating your request for a file located on a Windows NT server. Following are the four steps required to gain access to a file on a domain server:

1. Because the domain SAMs are the only locations where your account information is stored, the server containing the resource does not know who you are. It must verify your username and password with a domain controller using pass-through authentication. As soon as you are authenticated, the server generates a security access token containing security identifiers (SIDs) for your username and all your group memberships.

2. The SIDs on your security access token are compared to the share-level access control list (ACL) attached to the folder. In other words, the share-level permissions on the shared folder are checked to make sure you, or a group containing your account, are listed.

3. Assuming you pass the share-level permissions, your user and group SIDs are compared to the folder-level ACL.

4. Your user and group SIDs are compared to the file-level ACL.

> **Author's Note**
>
> *A file allocation table (FAT) file system has no security and would not require steps 3 or 4. With a FAT file system, the only method for controlling access to shared resources is with share-level permissions. Because NTFS provides folder- and file-level permissions, you should leave the share-level permissions set to Full Control for the Everyone group. The share-level permissions are not as granular as the NTFS folder level permissions and only present an unneeded layer of security.*

Notice that the first step in the entire process is to check your username and password with a domain controller. Consequently, no one can gain access to domain resources without a domain user account. Beyond step 1, your access depends on how your organization has set up users, group memberships, share-level permissions, folder-level permissions, and file-level permissions. Chapter 9, "Organizing Users," will present effective strategies for arranging your users and their group membership. Chapter 11, "Controlling Access to Domain Resources," will emphasize procedures for configuring optimal security permissions on domain servers.

Author's Note

The NetLogon shared directory has Read permission assigned to the Everyone group. You may have noticed this if you have ever tried to remotely edit a system policy file. If you use Directory Replication, you can connect to the REPL$ share and edit files because the share-level ACL lists Administrators with Full Control. If you do not use Directory Replication and you directly edit the items in the NetLogon share, you may want to add the Administrators group with Full Control to the share-level ACL.

The Impact of Your Client Choice

As you would expect, Windows NT Workstation provides security superior to Windows 95. The security of Windows NT is immediately noticeable by its requirement of a mandatory logon—you cannot simply click the Cancel button to access the local machine as you can with Windows 95. With Windows NT, you must have your credentials authenticated with the local SAM, the domain SAM, or a trusted domain SAM.

In general, Windows 95 lacks a robust and secure file system like NTFS and a mechanism for distinguishing users and groups. From a domain authentication perspective, Windows 95 also lacks the password encryption technology used by Windows NT. For backward compatibility with LAN Manager networks, Windows NT stores two encrypted versions of a user's password:

- An NT-encrypted version

- A LAN Manager–encrypted version

These encrypted passwords are commonly called the *NT hash* and the *lanman hash*, respectively. Windows 95 authenticates using the lanman hash, which is more easily exploited. The lanman hashing algorithm splits a user password by dividing it into two 16-byte encrypted sections corresponding to the first and last seven characters of a user's password. Knowing the hash representation of seven blank characters, a hacker can easily tell if a user's password is fewer than eight characters long by inspecting the last 16 bytes of the lanman hash. Password crackers can crack the lanman password more easily because of the two sections.

The lanman hash is converted to all uppercase characters when stored in the SAM. Likewise, when you submit a password from a LAN Manager or Windows 95 client, the password is converted to all uppercase, passed through the lanman hash, and sent to a domain controller for authentication. Because of the conversion to uppercase characters, Windows 95 machines that log on to the domain are not case-sensitive for user passwords. In other words, you can use uppercase, lowercase, or a mixed-case version of a password when logging on to a Windows 95 machine.

Author's Note

You can apply the latest service pack's hot fix to your Windows NT systems to force them to use only the NT hash for authentication, but only if all your clients are Windows NT clients. For more information on the hot fix and necessary Registry changes, see Microsoft Knowledge Base Article Q147706.

To compensate for the lack of security in Windows 95, you should familiarize yourself with the System Policies. You can use the System Policy Editor to create a policy for Windows 95 workstations that will accomplish such tasks as

- Disabling Registry-editing tools

- Forcing logon to an NT domain (mandatory logon)

- Limiting a user's access to the Control Panel

- Removing Network Neighborhood

Tip

If you use Windows 95 policies, you must add Group Policies to each individual Windows 95 machine so that it can properly interpret the domain group memberships when a user logs on. Windows 95 (versions A and B) must contact the PDC to get user and group information; thus, if the PDC is unavailable, Windows 95 is not able to process group information, and the user is given the default user policy. This is a confirmed problem you should keep in mind when creating policies that will be used by Windows 95 users.

Windows 2000 uses Kerberos version 5 as an authentication protocol. Kerberos not only provides better security and faster authentication, but it is also an industry standard that has been ported to other operating systems. For domains that contain both UNIX and Windows 2000, you can run Kerberos on the UNIX machines so that a user has to log on only once to access both Microsoft and UNIX resources. Kerberos operates based on time-stamped, encrypted tickets that grant users access to a particular server or application. The server responsible for the distribution of the tickets is the *key distribution center (KDC)*; placement of the KDC is important in Windows 2000 domain design.

To learn more about Kerberos, visit the Massachusetts Institute of Technology Web site:

`http://web.mit.edu/kerberos/www/`.

Author's Note

As of this writing, Microsoft's UNIX tools for Windows NT are in Beta 2. Included in the tools is a password synchronizer that updates user passwords on UNIX systems when domain users change them. A similar utility, Directory Service Manager for NetWare (DSMN), updates NetWare passwords for NT domain users. Using DSMN and UNIX tools for NT, you can keep user passwords synchronized among the three operating systems and eliminate the need for users to remember separate passwords.

Be Careful Whom You Trust

Trust relationships allow trusted domain users to access resources in a trusting domain. Suppose your system administrator establishes a trust with another domain, but you are unaware of the relationship. Perhaps you work in a research department with an understanding that the environment is safe and you can share your work with colleagues. Unless your workstation is protected with NTFS permissions that differ from the default permissions, you may be making your work available to the trusted domain users from another department. A trust relationship is transparent to the end users in the trusting domain; however, it gives trusted domain users the capability of accessing the end user's shared folders and printers.

If you have a department that deals with critical data, it may require a separate NT domain or may have to be on an entirely different physical network (the military C2 systems containing classified information are isolated with good reason). Once again, a domain is a security boundary, and creating a trust extends the boundary to include trusted domain users. A trust does not automatically mean trusted domain users can access your resources; you still control access permissions for your resources. However, if you do not take action to protect your resources, security is compromised.

Service Packs and Hotfixes

Periodically, Microsoft releases service packs for Windows NT. A *service pack* updates Windows NT system files that have been determined to have bugs or introduce problems. With all the hardware and various uses for computer systems, however, it is nearly impossible to design a system that is completely bug-free for everyone's situation.

Between the release of service packs for Windows NT, Microsoft releases small patches called hotfixes. *Hotfixes* address a specific NT problem and are not fully tested by Microsoft. They are intended for people who have an immediate need for a solution to a problem and cannot wait for the next service pack. Many of the hotfixes are related to security bugs; you should apply them to all your NT systems, especially your NT servers.

The latest service packs and hotfixes can be obtained from Microsoft's public FTP site at `ftp://ftp.microsoft.com/bussys/winnt/winnt-public/fixes/usa/nt40/` Service packs are inclusive. In other words, Service Pack 4 contains all of the fixes of Service Pack 3 and all post-Service Pack 4 hotfixes.

Author's Note

You can find another great resource for service pack and hotfix informa-tion at `http://www.ntbugtraq.com`. *On this site you can also find The International Windows NT Fixes Up-to-date Query Engine. The engine creates a Web page of all available fixes for your NT version and proces-sor type. You may also want to sign up for the email list that updates security holes and bugs in Windows NT.*

Tip

The hotfixes must be applied in a specific order. Consult the Microsoft FTP site to download a readme file containing all hotfixes and the spe-cific order in which you should apply them.

NT Security Measures Checklist

A detailed list of how to protect a machine from every available NT hack is beyond the scope of this book. However, the following list of security tools and methods should suffice for a moderate level of security:

- *Physical security.* All servers, especially domain controllers, should be locked away in a server room with controlled access.

- *Service packs and hotfixes.* You should apply the latest service packs and necessary security-related hotfixes to your servers.

- *BIOS protection.* Some available programs allow a person to boot a server from a floppy disk and change the administrator's passwords. You should disable the Boot from Floppy option and use a BIOS password on all machines. Most of the programs use a Linux kernel coupled with a limited NTFS driver to access the SAM. Because the hashing algorithms used by NT are publicly available, C programs have been written to encrypt a password of your choice and store it in the proper area of the SAM database. Physical security and BIOS passwords are your only protection against such attacks.

- *The built-in Administrator account.* The built-in Administrator account on a domain controller is one of the most powerful accounts in the domain, so it should be carefully guarded. This account is not subject to the account lockout policy you establish (unless you use SP3 enhancements). At the very least, you should rename the built-in Administrator account and assign a strong password to it. With networks on which security is a major concern, I use a C program to generate a 14-character, random, alphanumeric password. For even greater security, create a new account named "Administrator" and remove it from any group memberships. By the time a hacker breaks into the "Administrator" account and discovers its lack of privileges, he or she will move on to weaker prey.

Tip

A common dilemma associated with NT domain workstations is how you should set the local administrator password. You should not set all local administrator passwords to be the same; if someone discovers the password for one workstation, they know the password for all workstations.

A good approach is to establish your own encryption algorithm. A simple example would be to spell the workstation's name backwards. Obviously, a more complex algorithm is necessary, but the possibilities depend on the lettering and numbering used in your naming scheme.

- *Account Policy Settings.* Ideally, you should force users to change passwords on a periodic basis, and you should enable account lockout. See the "Enforcing Strong Passwords" section of this chapter for more details.
- *Audit Policy Settings.* The Audit Policy dialog box (see Figure 8.1) allows you to determine which type of events should be audited. The audited events are registered with the Security Log of the Event Viewer. At the very least you should enable some of the basic audit policies of the system. For example, you should audit failed logons to discover attempts to guess a user's password. You must enable File and Object Access auditing if you want to audit file, folder, and printer access through Windows NT Explorer. *Denial-of-service (DOS) attacks* do not exploit data on the system but rather make the system unavailable by forcing a blue screen or a reboot; you can enable the Restart, Shutdown, and System audit policy to capture DOS attacks that occur during the hours when you are out of the office.

Troubleshooting Tip

Do not audit process tracking; such auditing will fill your Event Logs very quickly.

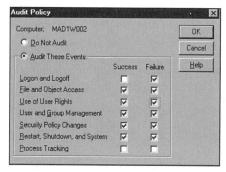

Figure 8.1   *The Audit Policy dialog box allows you to log users' actions on the system and hold users accountable for their actions.*

Tip

You should always increase the size of the Event Logs. By default, Windows NT assigns 512KB to each of the three Event Logs. You should increase the log size to 5MB or greater so that you do not overwrite important events.

Tip

A major problem with the Event Log is its difficulty of use. For example, you cannot monitor the Event Log of more than one machine at a time, and you do not have the capability to print from it. Furthermore, the log information can sometimes be cryptic and hard to understand.

*You can use third-party software to integrate the Event Logs of critical servers into a single Event Log database. One such product available is EventAdmin from Aelita Software Group (*http://www.aelita.com*).*

- *User Rights Policy Settings.* For all user rights, you may want to replace the Everyone group with the Domain Users group or the Authenticated Users group (added by Service Pack 3). You may want to remove the Administrators group from the Access This Computer from Network setting on servers storing critical data. Administrators could still log on locally to access the data, but anyone compromising the security of an administrative account would not be able to access the data without physically logging on to the local machine.

- *Protecting the Registry.* On all NT workstations, you should modify the permissions on the winreg key in the Registry to allow remote Registry access only to Administrators and System. You can find the winreg key in the following location:

  ```
  HKLM\CCS\Control\SecurePipeServers\winreg
  ```

- *Using password-protected screen savers and encouraging users to lock their NT workstations.* Locking workstations prevents internal users from gaining additional privileges. For those users who cannot get into the habit of locking their workstations, password-protected screen savers protect their machine if they abandon it for a lengthy period of time.

Tip

If you want to automatically log off users who leave their workstation for an extended period of time, you can use WINEXIT.SCR from the NT Resource Kit.

- *Do not use test accounts with blank passwords.* Accounts with blank passwords are quickly and easily exploited. Once such an account is compromised, it can be used to mask a hacker's identity as he attempts to use the account to gain additional system privileges.

- *Disable accounts for terminated employees on a timely basis.* It is easy for a terminated employee to use remote access from a home PC to perform malicious actions to the network. Avoid such actions by having your human resources department contact your MIS staff as soon as an employee is terminated or leaves voluntarily.

Tip

You can use USRSTAT.EXE from the NT Resource Kit to see the most recent logon time for each user. This can be helpful in determining if an account has been inactive for a long period of time.

- *Domain admins should never FTP to a server on your network.* FTP uses clear text passwords that are easily captured. If you are a domain admin and must FTP files, you should use a separate domain user account.

- *Do not use the same password for everything.* If you use a POP3 email client such as Eudora, your password is sent in clear text. If your email password matches your administrator password, someone can easily gain administrative access to your network.

- *Disable unnecessary services.* If the machine does not share resources, disable its Server service.

- *Remove unnecessary network bindings.* If a machine is not used to share files, folders, or printers, disable or remove its bindings for NetBIOS.

- *Use FLOPLOCK.EXE from the NT Resource Kit to disable floppy access for users.* FLOPLOCK.EXE allows only administrators (NTS) and power users (NTW only) access to the floppy drive. It runs as a service and can prevent viruses and unauthorized installation of software.

Enforcing Strong Passwords

Many security breaches and bugs are overemphasized by the media. The number one method for compromising a system is still the cracking of a user's password. Your top priority as the administrator of a secure NT network is to ensure the use of strong passwords, especially if you use technologies such as Microsoft's PPTP that allow users to access the corporate network via the Internet. Blank passwords and weak passwords leave the system open to attack, and as soon as an attacker gains access to a user's password, the auditing logs are useless because the attacker takes on the identity of the user.

Your first step in enforcing strong passwords is to configure a good Account Policy for your domain. Note that Account Policy settings are configured on a domain-by-domain basis; thus, if your company uses more than one domain with user accounts, you must configure the policy for each domain. Beyond a strong account policy, you can use Service Pack enhancements to further customize your requirements.

Figure 8.2 shows the Account Policy dialog box. Using the options in the dialog box, you can configure an account policy that forces users to periodically change their password.

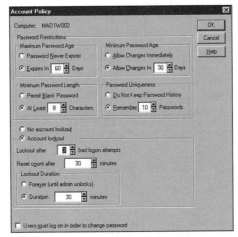

Figure 8.2   *You can use the Account Policy dialog box to force users to periodically change their passwords.*

You should apply the following settings for password security:

1. *Minimum Password Length*. Do not permit blank passwords. If you are unsure about password length, choose at least six characters.

2. *Maximum Password Age*. Windows NT systems keep track of how long a user has the same password. When the user's account password age is within 14 days of the maximum, Windows NT issues a password expiration warning to the user. Although this setting forces users to follow the procedure to change their password before the time limit expires, it does not force the user to use a different password unless you keep a password history.

> *Tip*
>
> *If you check the Users Must Log On in Order to Change Password check box (at the bottom of the dialog box), users will not be able to log on to the system after their password expires, and they must call the administrator to reset the password. Leaving the box unchecked causes the system to issue a Password Change dialog box during the logon process if a user's password has expired.*

3. *Password Uniqueness*. Stop. Re-read the last sentence of the previous step. Without a password history, a user can follow the password change procedure but keep the same password by entering the old password, new password, and new password confirmation.

4. *Minimum Password Age*. In some cases, users are very clever and really like to keep a favorite password. Suppose your favorite password is *abcdef*, and your system administrator keeps a password history of the previous five passwords you used. You could simply invoke the Password Change dialog box and rotate through five password changes very quickly (something like *abcdef1*, *abcdef2*, and so on). The five password changes would fill the history, and on the sixth password change you could reuse your favorite password. The only way to prevent such action is to enforce a minimum password age. This setting forces a user to keep the same password for a minimum period of time before issuing another password change.

Author's Note

If you enforce the minimum password age, users cannot change their password until the minimum password age expires, and they must change their password before the maximum password age is reached. Be careful to provide a password change time window that is sufficiently large and accounts for periods when users take company trips, vacation, and so on.

Author's Note

While we're on the subject of Account Policy settings, note that you should enforce an account lockout. By locking out an account after a number of failed logon attempts, you hamper password-guessing programs that issue consecutive logon attempts with a different password each time. Also note that, by default, the built-in Administrator account is not subject to the account lockout policy you configure for your domain. To enforce account lockout for the built-in Administrator account you can use PASSPROP.EXE (discussed in the next section).

After you have configured your domain Account Policy for password restrictions and account lockout, you can further improve the strength of user passwords using PASSPROP.EXE from the NT Resource Kit and PASSFILT.DLL with Service Pack 2 and later. These tools are described in the following sections.

PASSPROP.EXE

PASSPROP.EXE, included with the NT Resource Kit, goes beyond the Account Policy settings, allowing you to enforce a need for complex passwords and force lockout of the Administrator account.

If password complexity is enabled, the password must be mixed case or contain numbers or symbols. If Administrator account lockout is enabled, the administrator can log on interactively to any domain controller to unlock the account.

PASSFILT.DLL

PASSFILT.DLL, included with NT 4 Service Pack 2 and later, allows you to go beyond the limitations of the PASSPROP.EXE by creating your own custom DLL that describes the type of passwords you require. In case you do not program, Microsoft includes a PASSFILT.DLL. The Microsoft DLL requires the password to meet four criteria; see Microsoft Knowledge Base article Q151082 for more information.

Password Crackers

There are many security analysis tools available from third-party vendors. One of the most useful tools you can use to determine your users' password strength is a password cracking utility. Most of the password cracking utilities operate by dumping the SAM portion of the NT Registry and using dictionary-based techniques for discovering user's passwords. You must be an administrator to dump the NT SAM, so not just anyone can run such utilities. You will most likely be surprised by how simplistic most passwords are and how quickly they can be cracked.

> **Tip**
>
> *Perhaps one of the best password cracking utilities available right now is produced by L0pht. You can download LophtCrack from its Web site at* http://www.l0pht.com. *You may also want to check out the Kane Security Analyst for Windows NT by visiting* http://www.intrusion.com.

> **Author's Note**
>
> *By default, when you create an Emergency Repair Disk (ERD) with RDISK.EXE, the utility does not update the SAM and SECURITY Registry hive files. If you run* RDISK /S, *it updates the SAM and SECURITY hive files (assuming they are small enough to fit on a single disk). You must be extra careful with the ERD if you have created it using the* /S *option. If someone were to obtain the disk, he or she could run a password cracking utility directly against the SAM and easily obtain weak passwords. In addition to protecting the ERD, you should also protect the* %SYSTEMROOT%\SYSTEM32\CONFIG *and* %SYSTEMROOT%\REPAIR *directories.*

A Word on Firewalls

Firewalls, used to protect against external exploitation, fall into three categories:

- Circuit-level
- Packet-filtering
- Proxy-level

Circuit-level firewalls allow incoming connections only if the session is initiated from an inside machine. *Packet-filtering firewalls* allow you to block certain packet types and port numbers. *Proxy-level firewalls* allow one machine to initiate requests for other client machines on the network, protecting the requesting clients from harm. It is possible to get all three technologies in a single firewall product.

Firewall products vary and can be very misleading. You can purchase firewall software that runs on the NT operating system as well as hardware devices that have special cards to monitor network traffic. As stated earlier, security comes at the price of slower performance and additional configuration. In general, hardware firewalls offer greater throughput, and you may want to check with the manufacturer to ensure that your network would not be slowed tremendously by the presence of a firewall.

Figure 8.3 illustrates a typical Internet access configuration in which all sites funnel through the corporate site for Internet access. All sites access the Internet from a single point—a point that can be effectively controlled with a firewall.

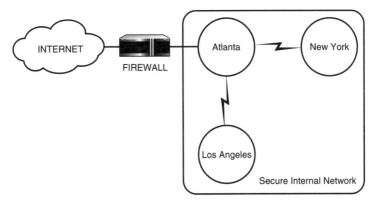

Figure 8.3   *A single Internet access point allows you to protect your entire internal network with a single firewall product.*

To further assist you with the setup of your firewall product, here is a list of ports you would typically open for inbound traffic from external networks:

Port Type	Port Number	Associated Service
TCP	21	FTP
TCP	25	SMTP mail
TCP, UDP	53	DNS
TCP	90	HTTP
TCP	443	SSL
TCP	1723	PPTP

This list is generalized and by no means complete—surely you will think of other ports necessary for your implementation. In most cases, you should be certain to disallow ports 137, 138, and 139. These ports are used for NetBIOS session and datagram services, and they should be considered extremely dangerous if left open to external networks. Many security breaches for Windows NT are formulated to attack using NetBIOS.

Tip

Many organizations refuse to use DHCP because their firewall products create logs that contain only IP addresses, not NT machine names or user names. Their argument stems from the possibility that a machine's IP address may be changed by the DHCP server before an administrator analyzes the log. Although the argument is valid, be aware that third-party auditing products exist that create logs based on NetBIOS machine names rather than IP addresses.

Tip

A common problem in many organizations is controlling Internet access. Most organizations funnel Internet access through one access point that is protected with a firewall product. The problem is how to limit Internet access to a specific group of individuals rather than allowing everyone access. Most firewall products give you the option of using TACAS or RADIUS authentication; however, with these you must create a separate list of users and passwords. A reasonable solution to the problem is to use Microsoft's Proxy Server product. This allows you to create an Internet Users group on Windows NT and control users' Internet access by adding or removing them from the Internet Users group.

Author's Note

My company strongly advocates the use of Cisco PIX firewalls, which you can configure to perform private link encryption. Such technology allows you to place PIX firewalls at multiple Internet access points and connect two or more remote networks over the Internet. This capability allows you to quickly and easily link networks involved in company mergers and acquisitions.

Chapter **9**

Organizing Users

This chapter will review:

- **User and Group Fundamentals**
  Seeing the big picture related to user and group administration is important to understanding enterprise strategies.

- **Understanding Rights and Abilities**
  Rights and abilities are granted to built-in local groups on Windows NT. They play a key role in the delegation of administration within NT domains.

- **The Impact of Trusts on Users and Groups**
  Trusts limit the flexibility of your user and group strategy by making only global users and global groups visible to the trusting domain.

- **Account Standards and Maintenance**
  Large networks demand standard practices for defining user and group accounts. Most networks also require ongoing account maintenance, including such tasks as disabling and deleting inactive accounts.

- **User and Group Infrastructure**
  Establishing a good user and group infrastructure for a large network is essential. The last section of this chapter presents the benefits of local groups and illustrates strategies for multiple-domain environments.

User and Group Fundamentals

Before delving into user and group strategies, it is important to understand user and group fundamentals. You should define a user account for every person who needs access to the system. By establishing separate user accounts, you gain the ability to control and audit each person's access to the system. Groups are used to organize users that require similar access to resources.

Groups are also used to grant administrative privileges such as the ability to create shared directories.

Groups simplify administration in the following ways:

- *Groups allow you to use fewer operations to control resource access.* Suppose you have 100 users in your engineering department who all need access to a shared folder containing design files. You can organize all 100 users into a single group, and then add the group to the folder and file access control lists (ACLs). This is easier than adding 100 individual accounts to the ACLs.

- *Groups make ACLs simpler.* By adding groups rather than users to ACLs, you create ACLs that are simpler and easier to understand. You also improve the system's efficiency because it has fewer ACL entries to compare.

- *Groups make it easier to manage users.* Suppose a new user enters the accounting department. If your system is set up properly, you should only have to copy a user account template for an accounting department user—after that, the new account has access to the proper accounting resources. In other words, if your resource access is set up properly based on group memberships, you can control it by adding or removing users from groups.

Windows NT supports two types of users and groups: local and global. Local users and groups are visible only on the machine on which they are defined; thus, the term *local* refers to a user's or group's limited scope. On the other hand, global users and groups must be defined in the domain SAM and are visible to all machines in the domain.

In addition to the local and global characterization, users and groups can be classified as *built-in* or *user-defined*. When you install Windows NT, the system creates built-in user and group accounts with specific privileges on the system. Although NT workstations and Member Servers have the same built-in users and groups, NT domain controllers include additional built-in groups. These built-in users and groups are outlined in the following section.

Built-in Users and Groups

On a Windows NT workstation and Member Server, Windows NT creates the following built-in users and groups:

Users:

Administrator

Guest (disabled)

Local Groups:

Administrators

Backup Operators

Guests

Power Users

Replicator

Users

Global Groups:

None

On a Windows NT domain controller, Windows NT creates the following built-in users and groups:

Users:

Administrator

Guest (disabled)

Local Groups:

Administrators

Account Operators

Backup Operators

Print Operators

Server Operators

Guests

Replicator

Users

Global Groups:

Domain Admins

Domain Guests

Domain Users

Tip

Windows NT keeps track of the built-in Administrator and Guest account, so you can rename them but not delete them. It is highly advisable for you to rename the built-in Administrator account because it is not subject to the account lockout policy you define for all domain accounts (see Chapter 8, "Domain Security," to review this topic).

Built-in local groups play an important role in the assignment of rights and abilities on NT systems. The additional built-in local groups on domain controllers exist for the purpose of domain administration. The global groups provide you with basic groups that are available to all machines in the domain for the purpose of assigning access to resources.

Special Groups

In addition to the built-in groups, Windows NT has the following special groups:

Authenticated Users (added by Service Pack 3)

Creator/Owner

Everyone

Interactive

Network

System

The special groups are not visible from User Manager or User Manager for Domains. However, they are available for assigning access to resources and can be added to any ACL.

User-Defined Users and Groups

Windows NT allows you to define local and global user accounts and local and global group accounts. Each of these accounts are described in the following sections. (The "User and Group Infrastructure" section later in this chapter provides detailed information and strategies for achieving the best arrangement for your circumstances.)

Local User Accounts

Local user accounts have a limited scope and are visible only on the machine on which they are defined. The account appears on all domain controllers because the SAM is replicated. A local user account does not support interactive logon. To create a local user account, you must explicitly set the account type to local on the user account property sheet (see Figure 9.1). Local user accounts are needed only in specific situations and are rarely used.

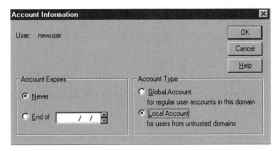

Figure 9.1   *By default, User Manager for Domains sets all account types to global unless otherwise specified.*

According to Microsoft, a local user account should be used for the purpose of granting untrusted users access to domain resources. A local user account provides extra protection through its limited visibility. An untrusted user has limited access to domain resources because the account is visible only on the machine in which it is defined. In other words, because the account is not visible to other machines, it cannot be added to the ACLs of resources on the other machines.

Tip

> *If an untrusted user requires access to resources on more than one server, you must define more than one local user account and set the same password for each one.*

Global User Accounts

The new accounts you create on Windows NT are automatically set to a global account type. *Global accounts* are visible on all machines in the domain for the purpose of assigning resource access.

Local Group Accounts

Local group accounts are limited in scope and visible only on the machine in which they are defined. Depending on your user and group strategy, you may or may not need to use local groups. In certain cases, local groups can simplify administration and eliminate certain speed problems associated with assigning resource permissions over a WAN.

Local groups can contain

- Local users
- Global users
- Global groups

Global Group Accounts

Global groups are visible on all machines in the domain. Thus, you can assign global groups to any resource in the domain.

Global groups can contain

- Local Users
- Global Users

Understanding Rights and Abilities

You must understand rights and abilities to understand how administrative capabilities are delegated to Windows NT users. The NT operating system assigns rights and abilities to the built-in local groups on NT servers and workstations. *Abilities* are inherent powers that cannot be modified. They are granted by virtue of membership in built-in local groups. The only way to change a user's ability is to change the user's group membership. For example, suppose you must give a user the ability to back up the system. You can do so by adding the user's account to the Backup Operators group, giving them the ability to back up and restore files and directories.

Tables 9.1 and 9.2 show the abilities assigned on NT workstations, Member Servers, and domain controllers. Users and Guests have no defined abilities on domain controllers.

Table 9.1   Abilities on Workstations and Member Servers

Abilities on Workstations and Member Servers	Administrators	Power Users	Users	Everyone	Guests	Backup Operators
Assign user rights	X					
Create and manage global groups	X					
Create and manage local groups	X	X	X			
Create and manage user accounts	X	X				
Create common groups	X	X				
Format server's hard disk	X					
Keep a local profile	X	X	X			X
Lock the server	X	X		X		
Manage auditing of system events	X					
Override lock of the server	X					
Share and stop sharing folders	X	X				
Share and stop sharing printers	X	X				

Table 9.2   Abilities on Domain Controllers

Abilities on Domain Controllers	Administrators	Server Operators	Account Operators	Print Operators	Backup Operators	Everyone
Create and manage user accounts	X		X			
Create and manage global groups	X		X			
Create and manage local groups	X		X			
Assign user rights	X					
Manage auditing of system events	X					
Lock the server	X	X				X
Override lock of the server	X	X				
Format server's hard disk	X	X				
Create common program groups	X	X				
Keep a local profile	X	X	X	X	X	
Share and stop sharing folders	X	X				
Share and stop sharing printers	X	X		X		

Rights are similar to abilities, but they can be controlled by administrators. Specifically, a *right* is an authorization for a user to perform an administrative task on the system, such as managing the security log or changing the system time. Tables 9.3 and 9.4 show the rights assigned on NT workstations, Member Servers, and domain controllers. No rights are defined for Users or Guests on domain controllers.

Tip

You can use NTRIGHTS.EXE from the Windows NT Resource Kit to automate the modification of user rights on multiple machines.

Table 9.3   Rights on Workstations and Member Servers

Rights on Workstations and Member Servers	Administrators	Power Users	Users	Everyone	Guests	Backup Operators
Access this computer from network	X	X		X		
Back up files and directories	X					X
Change the system time	X	X				
Force shutdown from a remote system	X	X				
Load and unload device drivers	X					
Log on locally	X	X	X	X	X	X
Manage auditing and security log	X					
Restore files and directories	X					X
Shut down the system	X	X	X	X		X
Take ownership of files and other objects	X					

Table 9.4   Rights on Domain Controllers

Rights on Domain Controllers	Administrators	Server Operators	Account Operators	Print Operators	Backup Operators	Everyone
Access this computer from network	X					X
Back up files and directories	X	X			X	
Change the system time	X	X				
Force shutdown from a remote system	X	X				
Load and unload device drivers	X					
Log on locally	X	X	X	X	X	
Manage auditing and security log	X					
Restore files and directories	X	X			X	
Shut down the system	X	X	X	X	X	
Take ownership of files and other objects	X					

Without membership in a built-in local group (either directly or indirectly), an account has no rights or abilities and is unusable. Recall that a workstation's local groups are modified when it joins the domain. The specific modifications are as follows:

- The Domain Admins global group is added to the local Administrators group on the workstation.

- The Domain Users global group is added to the local Users group on the workstation.

- The Domain Guests global group is added to the local Guests group on the workstation.

These modifications give the Domain Admins group the necessary rights and abilities to administer all domain workstations. The modifications also give the Domain Users group the needed rights and abilities to log on and use any workstation in the domain. These modifications are important because enterprise domain models require you to manually apply similar modifications to workstations in trusting domains.

Author's Note

To see the effect of an account with no rights or abilities, try the following example:

1. *Create a new group called "Test."*

2. *Create a new account and add it to the Test group only. You must set the account's primary group to Test to remove the Domain Users group from the Member Of list box.*

3. *Try to log on to the account. You should receive an error message saying the local policy of the system does not permit you to log on interactively. Because the account does not have the needed right to log on locally (refer to Table 9.3), the user is not permitted to log on.*

Author's Note

If you are new to NT rights and abilities, do not fret. When adding a new user account, you should not think, "What rights do I grant to this user?" or "Will the user have the needed abilities?" Unlike the NT file system permissions, NT rights and abilities are set up very well out-of-the-box and warrant little change. In general, you do not have to make any modifications to user rights; if you do, you should modify them by adding or removing groups and not individual user accounts.

continues

Continued

The most common user right I modify is the right to change the system time. It is often desirable to synchronize a workstation's time with a server. You can use the net time *command in a login script, but a user must have the right to change the system time to successfully complete the command.*

Another user right that is sometimes modified is the right to access a computer from the network. On some networks, the security policy dictates that administrators must work from the console of the server. Consequently, the Administrators group is removed from the right to access the computer from the network on all servers. Because administrators cannot access the server remotely, potential hackers are forced to gain physical access to the system or compromise security using an ordinary user account.

The Impact of Trusts on Users and Groups

Trust relationships introduce limitations on group membership in the trusting domain. Local users and groups from a trusted domain are not visible in the trusting domain and cannot be included in any trusting domain groups or added to ACLs in the trusting domain. Thus, users from the trusted domain must be organized at the global level.

As a domain admin of a trusting resource domain, you depend on the domain admin of the trusted domain (usually the accounts domain) to properly organize global users into global groups. Otherwise, your resource administration is complicated, and extra steps are introduced.

Author's Note

You cannot specify whether a user is trusted in User Manager for Domains. A user is considered trusted based on a trust relationship established between two domains, not based on an account definition. As soon as a trust is in place, all users and groups in the trusted domain are considered trusted by the trusting domain.

Figure 9.2 illustrates the group membership possibilities for users and groups within a single domain.

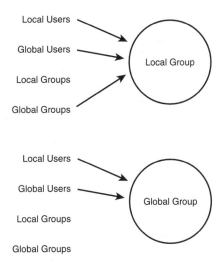

Figure 9.2 *You have many group membership options within a single domain.*

In a single domain, you have a large degree of freedom for organizing your users and groups. However, when your network consists of multiple domains the flexibility is limited. Figure 9.3 shows the group membership possibilities for users and groups from a trusted domain.

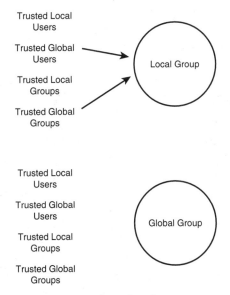

Figure 9.3 *If your domain is trusting of another domain, you are limited to adding trusted global users and trusted global groups from the other domain to your local groups.*

Notice that you cannot add a trusted global user to a global group in the trusting domain. Consider the illustration in Figure 9.4. Suppose you manage the 20 workstations in the ATL domain and want to grant domain administrator privileges to Tom in the Corp domain. You cannot add Tom (a trusted global user) to the Domain Admins group. Your only choice is to add Tom to the local Administrators group on your domain controllers. This gives Tom the ability to administer the domain controllers, but what about the domain workstations? To give Tom administrative control over the workstations, you must explicitly add the Tom account to the local Administrators group on each workstation. The next section presents precautionary steps you can take to avoid this situation.

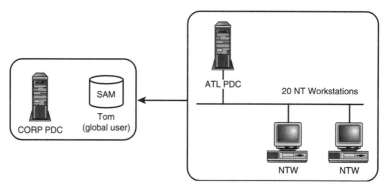

Figure 9.4   *Granting administrative control of all ATL workstations to Tom can be a difficult task.*

Account Standards and Maintenance

Conventions are important when administering an enterprise NT network. You should establish standard naming conventions for all user and group accounts. You may notice the convention of starting all global groups with the letter G and all local groups with the letter L later in this chapter. Such conventions save time and clarify the user and group structure. You should also note that NT does not allow you to rename a group account. Your only solution is to re-create the group with a new name and add all the necessary members.

> ### Tip
>
> *There are a couple of conventions I would recommend for enterprise networks with a large SAM. First, you should use an underscore at the beginning of all template account names. This moves the template accounts to the top of the list in User Manager for Domains and allows you to quickly copy them for new users. You can extend this idea further by using two underscores (__) at the beginning of service accounts to separate them from the ordinary user accounts.*
>
> *Secondly, when you disable an account, you should rename it with a Z at the front of the account name. This moves all disabled (and unused) accounts to the bottom of the list in User Manager.*

A typical problem on most large networks is unused accounts. Unused accounts can result from several actions. Sometimes accounts are created with the wrong username and are never deleted. In other cases, you may have test accounts with simplistic passwords lying dormant in the Security Accounts Manager. If you work with several other administrators or if you are a new administrator, it is likely there are unused accounts on the system that you do not know about. Thus, you should periodically inspect the system for unused accounts and delete them.

A great utility to help you determine whether an account is active is USRSTAT.EXE from the NT Resource Kit. USRSTAT.EXE generates a list of all accounts and their most recent logon time. You can easily import the USRSTAT.EXE output into a spreadsheet, sort by last logon time, and —voilá—you quickly know which accounts are experiencing a period of inactivity.

Another problem associated with large networks occurs when no one sets up a communication system to let administrators know when a user leaves or changes a position within the company. To solve the problem, you should establish a good line of communication with the human resources department. It is important that you are notified immediately when users leave the company or change positions within the company—otherwise, you are left with dormant accounts and unneeded group memberships. When a user leaves the company, you should disable their account immediately. If you do not take action to disable the user's account, they may be able to dial in and destroy network resources, enter fictitious product orders, and so on.

Author's Note

You should always disable—not delete—accounts of former users because of the SIDs used by NT. If you disable the account, you can rename it when someone else takes the previous user's place, and the new user will have access to all the resources needed by the old user.

On the other hand, if you delete the old account, the SID associated with the account is gone forever. For a deleted account, your only choice is to take ownership of all resources belonging to the deleted account and delegate them to a new user or other users on the network. Such an operation is meticulous and time-consuming. Disabling and later renaming the account is a much better solution.

User and Group Infrastructure

Your organizational strategy depends on the domain model your company selects. It also depends greatly on the number of domains and number of global groups required by your organization. The remainder of this section provides information to help you develop a successful user and group strategy for your network.

There are two key issues concerning your user and group strategy that you must address:

- You must organize users and groups in a way that simplifies the administration of network resources.

- For centralized-administration domain models, you must create groups for the purpose of delegating control of servers and workstations in the trusting domains.

Figure 9.5 presents the two primary approaches to user and group organization. Each triangle in the figure represents a layered pyramid that describes a particular organizational approach. Each pyramid starts with a large number of global users at the base, which are then organized into a small number of global groups. For an organization with 10,000 users, you may only have 200 global groups, which are created on the domain controller.

Notice the pyramid on the left side in Figure 9.5 contains a local group layer. The local groups are defined on the servers that store resources, and the ACLs illustrated in the pyramids are attached to those resources. Thus, an ACL contains permission assignments to local groups, the local groups contain global groups, and the global groups contain global users.

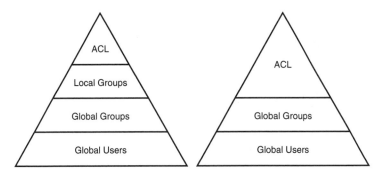

Figure 9.5   *There are two major approaches to user and group organization.*

Microsoft recommends the strategy on the left side of Figure 9.5: organizing global groups into local groups. Although the approach makes sense for most enterprise organizations with hundreds of global groups, it is not the best design for most networks. In most cases, local groups offer no significant benefit and only complicate the user and group structure. To better understand when and if to use local groups, you must consider the advantages they offer and whether your infrastructure can benefit from the advantages. The following section explains these topics in greater detail.

The Role of Local Groups

Local groups have two benefits:

- In organizations with a large number of global groups, they help you simplify administration and improve system efficiency through the addition of local groups.

- They can be used to alleviate speed problems introduced by slow WAN links.

To illustrate the simplified administration created by local groups, suppose your company has a master domain model with 12 resource domains located at 12 different company locations (see Figure 9.6). Now suppose you have a shared research directory on a NY marketing server, and you must grant read access to the marketing users of 10 resource domains. Although you can add the 10 trusted global groups directly to the ACL of the research directory, you would benefit more by creating a local group on the marketing server (see Figure 9.7).

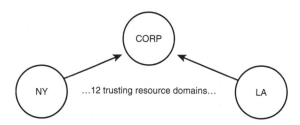

Figure 9.6 *This company has one master domain and 12 resource domains that are geographically separated.*

Figure 9.7 *Administration is simplified by combining the trusted global groups into a local group.*

The second benefit of local groups is that they help you overcome the administrative problems associated with slow WANs. When setting the ACLs on resources, the list of users and groups is pulled from a PDC. If the PDC is located across a WAN link, a serious delay in retrieving the users and groups is introduced. The length of the delay depends on the size of the SAM database containing the users and groups you must enumerate. Although you cannot shorten the delay, you can arrange an alternate group structure that allows you to quickly modify resource permissions on networks that communicate with the PDC over a WAN. The trick is to mirror each global group located across the WAN with a local group that contains the global group. With local groups defined in the machine's local SAM, you can quickly modify ACLs by assigning permissions to local groups.

Consider the network in Figure 9.8. The Corp domain is located in Chicago across a 64K WAN link, and the resource domain is located in New York. When you set up the NY file server, you can create a local group for each global group in Corp and add the Corp global group. There is no doubt that this increases your setup time; however, you only have to pull the global groups from Corp once. After all Corp global groups are mirrored to local groups in the local SAM, you can assign permissions quickly based on the local groups. For instance, suppose you have a shared Sales folder and need to give access to the global sales group GSales. Instead of waiting to pull all the global groups across the WAN, you can add the LSales group to the ACL more quickly (see Figure 9.9).

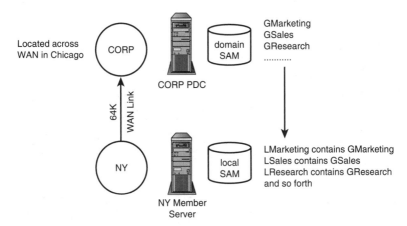

Figure 9.8   *The administration problems introduced by the 64K WAN link are alleviated through the mirroring of global groups to local groups on each server in the NY domain.*

Figure 9.9   *Administration is simplified by combining the trusted global groups into a local group.*

Author's Note

I know it is impractical to mirror hundreds of global groups to local groups, and I do not advocate mirroring every single group. However, servers usually have a specific purpose, and if you mirror the groups related to the server, the advantage can be realized. For instance, if you have a research file server, you would likely benefit from mirroring 10 to 12 global research-related groups.

Ideally, you should avoid the use of local groups. However, if you have a large number of global groups, or if your resource administration is significantly degraded by a slow WAN link, you should consider using them.

Delegating Administrator and User Privileges

In multiple domain structures that use centralized administration (master and multiple master domain models), you must create groups in the accounts domain specifically for users and administrators of the resource domains.

Let's go through an example to illustrate the user and group interaction in a centralized administration model. Consider the network in Figure 9.10. (The figure shows only one resource domain, but the network likely contains many more.) Following is an outline of the user and group interaction:

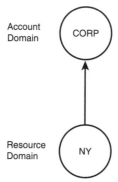

Figure 9.10   *Corp and NY are part of a master domain model.*

1. *Grant logon privileges for NY users.* Even though NY trusts Corp, Corp users cannot log on to workstations in the NY domain. Consider a single workstation in the NY domain: To be able to log on, the account or group must possess the right to log on locally (see Table 9.3). On a workstation, the right is assigned to the local Users group. Because the workstation has been joined to the NY domain, the local Users group contains the global NY Domain Users group. However, all accounts are

defined centrally in the Corp domain, not the NY domain. So your challenge is to allow users from the Corp domain log on to workstations in the NY domain.

The problem is solved by organizing all the accounts for New York users into a global group in the Corp domain. Then add the global group (we'll call it NYDomain Users) to the local Users group on each workstation in the NY domain (see Figure 9.11).

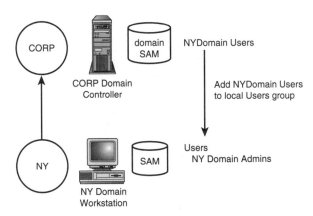

Figure 9.11 *NYDomain Users are added to the local Users group on each NY domain workstation to permit New York users to log on.*

Notice that only members of the NYDomain Users group can log on to the NY workstations. What if you want to allow users from other domains to visit the NY domain and use the workstations there? If you want to grant total mobility, you can add the Corp\Domain Users global group to the local Users group on each workstation. Otherwise, you must add only the groups from other selected domains.

2. *Grant administration privileges for NY domain controllers.* The second challenge is deciding how the NY domain should be administered. Should the Corp\Domain Admins be responsible for NY domain controllers, or should you create a separate group for the administration of the NY domain controllers? This can be a tough question, and the answer really depends on your infrastructure.

   For example, it is not plausible to give two help desk users from the NY domain membership in the Corp\Domain Admins group so that they may reset passwords for NY users. Let's assume two people at the New York office, Tom and Sally, will be responsible for the administration of all domain controllers, servers, and workstations in the NY domain. Now the challenge is clearly defined: You must give Tom and Sally control over the NY domain controllers. You can solve the problem by creating a NYDomain Admins global group in the Corp domain and adding the NYDomain Admins group to the local administrators group on the NY PDC (see Figure 9.12). Because the SAM is replicated, you only need to add the trusted global group to the local group on the PDC.

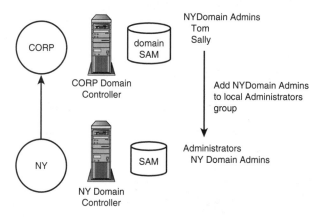

Figure 9.12 *NYDomain Admins is added to the local Administrators group on each NY domain controller to grant administrative control of the NY domain to Tom and Sally.*

3. *Grant administration privileges for NY workstations.* Although Tom and Sally can administer the NY domain controllers, they cannot administer the NY workstations without one more group modification: You must add the NYDomain Admins to the local Administrators group on all NY domain workstations (see Figure 9.13).

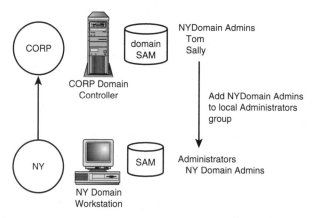

Figure 9.13 *To grant control over all NY domain workstations, the trusted global NYDomain Admins must be added to the Administrators group of each NY domain workstation.*

This example covered the basics of delegating user and admin privileges for resource domains. If necessary, you should go beyond the example and create global print operators, backup operators, or whatever is needed for the resource domain.

NT's Lack of Granular Administration

Windows NT 4.0 does not provide the granular level of administration demanded by enterprise networks. For example, suppose you are a help desk administrator and someone calls because they cannot access a file. How do you check their access and permissions? You can likely view the permissions on the file and display the groups on the ACL, but how do you ensure the user is a member of one of the listed groups? Unless you are a domain administrator, you cannot.

There are many administrative powers that need to be delegated for enterprise networks. Such powers include resetting user passwords, unlocking accounts, granting dial-in access, and so on. Fortunately, several third-party tools exist for the purpose of subdividing administration on a granular level. Following is a list of third-party administration tools for NT 4 and contact information for the manufacturer:

Enterprise Administrator
Mission Critical Software
http://www.missioncritical.com

Trusted Enterprise Manager
Master Design & Development
http://www.mddinc.com

Virtual Administration Tool
FastLane Technologies
http://www.fastlanetech.com

Windows 2000 will offer a greater ability to delegate administrative powers. However, Windows 2000 and Active Directory will not natively provide the advanced administrative functions needed to deploy NT on an enterprise scale. The Active Directory falls short of providing the multiple lines of administration needed by most companies. You should be able to organize administrative units based on geographic sites as well as functional divisions. You should also be able to have an administrator who is responsible for all user and group accounts in Chicago and an administrator who is responsible for all user and group accounts in the Sales division, which may span several geographic networks. For such functionality, you will be pressed to seek third-party administration add-ons for Windows NT.

Chapter **10**

Logon Scripts, Profiles, and Policies

This chapter will review:

- **The Role of the NetLogon Share**
  Every domain controller has a NetLogon share that is used to store logon scripts, policies, and a network default user profile.

- **Logon Scripts**
  Logon scripts provide a way to initialize a user environment with mapped drives.

- **Profiles**
  Roaming profiles give users the ability to change workstations while maintaining their preferences and environment. Mandatory profiles lower support cost by imposing a standard Desktop environment for one or more users.

- **Policies**
  Policies not only give you granular control over the user environment but also allow you to distribute Registry changes to users, groups, and computers.

- **Directory Replication**
  Directory Replication, used to synchronize the contents of the NetLogon share on domain controllers, is essential for large networks with numerous domain controllers.

The Role of the NetLogon Share

When discussing policies, profiles, and logon scripts, it is important to have a good understanding of the NetLogon share. All domain controllers have a NetLogon share and use it during the authentication process. The share is used to store three types of items:

- Logon scripts

- Policies (for Windows 95 and Windows NT clients)

- The Network Default User Profile

The items in the NetLogon share are completely optional and not required by a Windows NT network or domain. However, most businesses use logon scripts, and many use policies for Windows 95 clients. Because a user can authenticate with any domain controller, the contents of the NetLogon share must be exactly the same on all domain controllers. You can use the Directory Replication service to automatically synchronize the contents of the NetLogon shares based on an export directory. The Directory Replication service and its implementation are discussed at the end of this chapter.

> **Tip**
>
> *If users complain about intermittent problems with logon scripts, it is likely the scripts are not synchronized on the domain controllers. To help troubleshoot the problem, you can have the user run Windows NT Diagnostics and tell you the name of the logon server. Then you can check the server to make sure it contains the correct logon script for the user.*

The contents of the NetLogon share are used during the authentication process. When the domain controller authenticates a user, it checks the account properties. If the user has been assigned a logon script, the domain controller checks the contents of its NetLogon share for a logon script to execute on the client machine. If it is the user's first logon to the domain and a network default user profile exists, the profile is downloaded to the client machine and used to create the initial Desktop environment for the user. Additionally, if there is a policy file for the user's client platform (Windows 95 or Windows NT), the file is downloaded and the Registry of the client machine is changed.

Permissions for the NetLogon Share

The NetLogon share corresponds to the following path (in which %SYSTEMROOT% is the environment variable for the installation folder):

%SYSTEMROOT%\System32\Repl\Import\Scripts

The Scripts folder of the preceding path has the following folder-level permissions:

Administrators	Full Control
Creator/Owner	Full Control

System	Full Control
Replicator	Change
Server Operators	Change
Everyone	Read

The NetLogon share has the following share-level permissions:

Everyone	Read

You can see that only Administrators and Server Operators can modify or update the contents of the NetLogon share. The Replicator group appears with Change permission, but users should not have membership in that group—it is intended for use by the Directory Replication service.

Notice that the share-level permissions are set to Read for the Everyone group. This prevents ordinary users from modifying the contents of the share. The permissions also prevent administrators from remotely updating the contents of the share.

Updating the Contents Remotely

If you do not use Directory Replication, you must assume the responsibility of synchronizing the NetLogon shares of all domain controllers. Thus, if you modify a logon script, you must copy the modified script to the NetLogon share on all domain controllers.

The share-level permissions of the NetLogon share allow you to connect to the share but not copy files. As a result, you may want to change the share-level permissions on the NetLogon share to include Administrators with Full Control (see Figure 10.1). Otherwise, you can connect to the ADMIN$ share and drill down into System32\Repl\Import\Scripts folder.

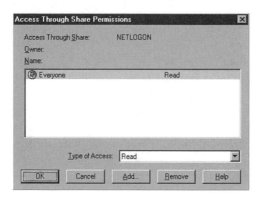

Figure 10.1 *You may want to modify the share-level permissions of the NetLogon share so that you may connect to it and modify its contents directly.*

If you have Directory Replication in place, you can use the Repl$ share on the export server to modify the NetLogon share contents. Administrators have Full Control share-level permission on the Repl$ share, allowing them to directly connect and modify files and folders in a single location. The files and folders contained in the Repl$ share are automatically copied to the NetLogon share of all domain controllers.

Logon Scripts

Logon scripts are used to initialize user settings during the logon process. Logon scripts can be .bat files, .cmd files, or custom executables. In most cases, administrators use batch files; only Windows NT and OS/2 understand how to process .cmd files, and custom executables are simply too much work to create. Logon scripts are stored in the NetLogon share on all domain controllers.

When a user logs on to an NT domain, the domain controller that authenticates the user account looks in its NetLogon share for the logon script assigned to the user account. Because a user can authenticate with any domain controller, all domain controllers must have copies of each logon script used by accounts in that domain. You can control the logon script for each user by setting the Logon Script Name field of the User Environment Profile dialog box (see Figure 10.2).

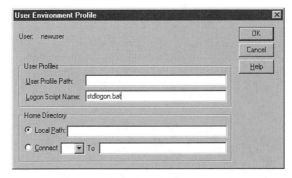

Figure 10.2   *A logon script is specified as part of a user's account properties. More than one user can share the same logon script.*

Notice that only the logon script name is listed in the Logon Script Name field in Figure 10.2. No path information for the logon script is given because domain controllers always look in their NetLogon share for the script. If the script is not present, the user does not receive it and no error messages are given.

Because a logon script is assigned by the machine that authenticates the user, you do not have to distribute logon scripts to domain controllers of other domains. In a master domain model, the domain controllers in the master domain authenticate user logons, even if the user is logging on to a workstation in a resource domain. Thus, you need to distribute logon scripts only to the domain controllers of the master domain—you need not place any logon scripts on domain controllers in resource domains. Likewise, in a complete trust model, the domain controllers of each domain should contain the logon scripts only for users who have accounts in that domain.

A typical logon script maps drives and synchronizes the workstation's time with a server. To avoid having a logon script for each user, you can specify environment variables such as %USERNAME% to make the script generic to a group of users. Listing 10.1 presents an example logon script that maps three drives and synchronizes the workstation's time:

Listing 10.1 *A Sample Logon Script*

```
echo off
rem filename: stdlogon.bat
echo Removing any persistent connections
net use * /delete /y
echo Mapping home directory
net use h: \\ATLS01\%USERNAME%
echo Mapping drive P to Public share on ATLS002
net use p: \\ATLS002\Public
echo Mapping drive S to Sales share on ATLS003
net use s: \\ATLS003\Sales
echo Synchronizing time with ATL domain
net time /domain:ATL /set /y
```

Tip

The %USERNAME% *variable does not work in logon scripts for Windows 95 clients. If you use batch file logon scripts to map home directories for Windows 95 end users, you must have a logon script for each user account. See the "KiXtart Logon Scripts" section later in this chapter to learn how to create a single logon script for all your Windows 95 users.*

Author's Note

If you want to synchronize a workstation's time in a logon script, you must grant the right to change system time to the Users group on each NT workstation. This can be a tedious and time-consuming task.

Maintaining Numerous Logon Scripts

A common problem in a multiple domain structure is the need to maintain and distribute numerous logon scripts. Although you do not always have a logon script for every user account, you typically have a script for each company location or department (see Figure 10.3). It is not uncommon for a company with multiple locations to have 20 or more logon scripts.

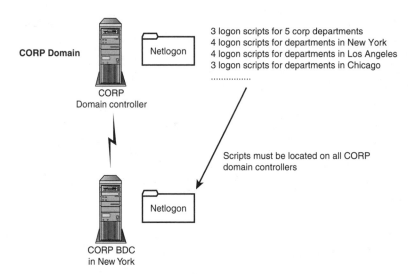

Figure 10.3   *The logon scripts for each location and department must be distributed to all Corp domain controllers.*

The need for multiple logon scripts results from the archaic command set used in batch files. Because you cannot include sophisticated logic in a batch file, you must have multiple single-purpose files instead of a single multipurpose logon script that is used by everyone in the company. For instance, you usually need to map drives to a particular file server based on a user's group membership. The users in the Sales department may need a mapping to one server, whereas the users in the Engineering department need mappings to a different server. When you use a batch file, you cannot test for group membership and map drives to the appropriate file server based on the user's group membership. Thus, you are forced to create a batch file for each group and assign it to all group members.

Fortunately, there is a better way to implement logon scripts. Later in the chapter, you will find information on KiXtart scripts and learn to create a single logon script for everyone.

User Home Directories

You may have noticed the mapping of a home directory in Listing 10.1. *Home directories* are important because they encourage users to save their work to a file server. By locating all user work on a file server, you gain the ability to back up all files to tape and restore them if a user accidentally deletes an important file or directory.

There are two methods for assigning a server-based home directory:

- You can map the directory in a logon script to a drive letter and assign the drive letter in the Local Path field in the User Environment Profile dialog box (see Figure 10.4). The drive listed in the Local Path field (H:\ in the figure) must be mapped with a logon script. This method is more work intensive because you must create a home directory for each account, set permissions for it, share it, and map it to a drive letter in a logon script.

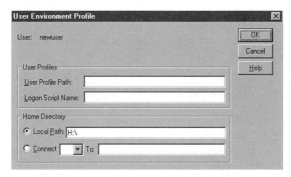

Figure 10.4   *You can map a drive in a logon script, specifying the drive letter in the Local Path field as if it is a local drive.*

- You can assign a home directory in the User Environment Profile dialog box by filling in the Connect and To information. For the example in Figure 10.5, it is assumed that you have created and shared a Users directory. Windows NT takes care of creating the home directory and setting the directory permissions on a per-user basis when you use the %USERNAME% variable. Windows NT's automation makes this method much easier; however, this drive mapping works only for Windows NT clients.

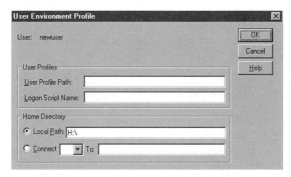

Figure 10.5   *This method maps home drives only for Windows NT clients.*

> *Tip*
>
> *Some administrators are reluctant to give users a home directory on a server because they cannot control the amount of information a user stores in it. In some cases, users copy entire CD-ROMs to their home directory and use too much space on the file server. To stop such problems, you can install third-party software such as Quota Advisor, Quota Manager, or Quota Server. Such utilities allow you to establish quotas for each user and report the amount of space used by each one. Windows 2000 has quota capabilities built-in.*

If you map a user's home directory in a logon script, you must share each home directory separately because you cannot map a drive to a subdirectory of a shared directory; otherwise, you could share the parent folder and map drives to all home directories below it. For example, in Figure 10.6 you cannot map a drive to \\ATLS001\Users\Tom (assuming Users is shared). You must share the Tom directory and specify the home directory as \\ATLS001\Tom.

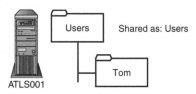

Figure 10.6   *You must share the Tom folder and map a drive to \\ATLS001\Tom because mapping a drive to \\ATLS001\Users\Tom does not work.*

Hiding Shares and Servers

Having a large number of shared home directories on file servers with other shares creates a browsing mess in Network Neighborhood. Suppose you have a server with 10 shared printers, 15 shared directories for various departments, and 120 shared home directories. Browsing for one of the department shares would be difficult because of the numerous home folders that appear in the browser.

One solution to the problem is to hide the shared home directories for user accounts by appending a dollar sign to the share name. This eliminates the appearance of the 120 home directories in the browser and makes the other resources more apparent to end users.

> **Author's Note**
>
> *You can also prevent servers from appearing in Network Neighborhood by issuing the following command:*
>
> ```
> net server config /hidden:yes
> ```
>
> *This is a great way to deploy and beta test new servers without having to worry about curious users exploiting your test machines.*

Problems with Template Accounts

Although hiding shared home directories solves one problem, it creates another problem if you use template accounts. When you copy a template account to create a new user account, Windows NT checks the template to see if the home directory matches the account name for the template. If so, Windows NT checks whether the home directory of the new user matches the account name. However, if you introduce a $ to the end of the home directory for the template, the match is eliminated, and the new account is assigned the home directory of the template account instead of a new home directory.

Table 10.1 shows a Tom account created based on two sales templates. The account copied from Template #1 correctly sets Tom's home directory, whereas the account copied from Template #2 creates a new account with the wrong home directory.

Table 10.1   Sales Template Accounts

	Username	Home directory
Sales Template #1	_salesuser	\\ATLS001_salsuser
Sales Template #2	_salesuser2	\\ATLS001_salesuser2$
	Tom	\\ATLS001\Tom
	Tom	\\ATLS001_salesuser2$

For Windows 95 clients, you may consider the idea of establishing two home directories. Windows 95 has a nasty habit of using a home directory as a storage location for a user's profile (profiles are discussed later in the chapter). This makes for a messy home directory and confuses end users.

To alleviate this problem, you may consider creating two "home directories" for each user: one to store the user's profile, and another to store the user's work. To do this, you must map two drives and tell Windows NT—in the User Environment Profile dialog box (refer to Figure 10.4)—to use one of the mapped drives as a home directory. Then assign the home directory to the mapped drive intended to hold the user's profile.

KiXtart Logon Scripts

KiXtart is a freeware scripting language available for Windows NT. KiXtart goes beyond the power of batch files by giving you a superb set of scripting commands that allow you to do such things as modify a user's Registry settings or install a printer during a user's logon. An older version of KiXtart is included with the Windows NT Resource Kit; however, you download the latest version from the KiXtart Archive (`http://netnet.net/~swilson/kix.html`). KiXart includes 94 pages of documentation. However, if you want sample scripts or additional assistance you can point your browser to the KiXtart discussion group in the General discussion board (`http://www.extracheez.com/boards`) or the Win32 Scripting page (`http://cwashington.netreach.net`).

KiXtart offers the following advantages:

- It is free.

- It is easy to use.

- You can use KiXtart to establish a single logon script for everyone in your company. The script language contains commands that allow you to map user drives and process information based on a user's group memberships. With KiXtart, there is no more distribution of numerous batch files on BDCs or variation in logon scripts among users.

- KiXtart saves you time by allowing you to automate certain client workstation changes using a logon script.

To use KiXtart, perform the following steps:

1. Copy kix32.exe, kix32.dll, and kix16.dll to the NetLogon share of your domain controllers.

2. Define a logon script and name it with a .scr extension. If the script will be used with Windows 95 clients, you must name the logon script kixtart.scr.

3. Assign the script to a user account (see Figure 10.7). You can specify `kix32` as the logon script if you are using a script named kixtart.scr; otherwise, you must also specify the name of the logon script (see Figure 10.7).

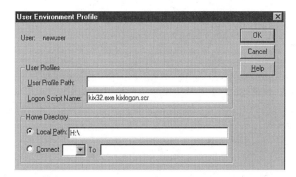

Figure 10.7 *You can assign a KiXtart script by specifying* `kix32 <script name>` *in the Logon Script Name field. For Windows 95 clients, you must name the logon script kixtart.scr, and you need not specify the* `<script name>`.

Listing 10.2 gives an example of a KiXtart script that accomplishes the same tasks as the batch file version in Listing 10.1.

Listing 10.2 *A Sample KiXtart Script*

```
; filename: kixtart.scr
;
; Remove Persistent Connections
USE * /del
; Map Drives
USE H: "\\ATLS001\@userid$"
USE P: "\\ATLS002\Public"
USE S: "\\ATLS003\Sales"
; synchronize workstation time with ATLS001 server
SETTIME "\\ATLS001"
```

Suppose you have users in two groups, Sales and Marketing, who need drives mapped to two separate servers. If you were to use batch files, you would need a separate logon script for each group. However, you can use the ingroup command in KiXtart to easily solve this problem and combine the needs of both groups into a single logon script. Listing 10.3 gives an example of how to use the ingroup command.

Listing 10.3 *An Example of the* ingroup *Command*

```
; filename: kixtart.scr
;
; Remove Persistent Connections
USE * /del
if ingroup("sales")
; Map Drives
USE H: "\\SALES01\@userid$"
USE S: "\\ SALES01\Sales"
endif
if ingroup("marketing")
    USE H: "\\MRKGT01\@userid$"
    USE S: "\\ MRKGT01\Marketing"
endif
```

Now suppose you want to give the Marketing department Internet access through Microsoft's Proxy Server product, but you do not want to go to each computer in the Marketing department and tell Internet Explorer (IE) to use the proxy server. You can use KiXtart to distribute the Registry change needed for IE to use a proxy server. Your only limitation on distributing Registry changes with KiXtart is that the user must have access to the portion of the Registry you need to modify. If the Registry modification requires administrative access, you may still be forced to visit each client Desktop (or remotely edit the Registries). Listing 10.4 illustrates a KiXtart script used to propagate IE proxy settings to the users in the Marketing department.

Listing 10.4   *Using KiXtart to Push Out Registry Changes for a Proxy Server*

```
; filename: kixtart.scr
;
; Remove Persistent Connections
USE * /del
if ingroup("sales")
; Map Drives
USE H: "\\SALES01\@userid$"
USE S: "\\ SALES01\Sales"
endif
if ingroup("marketing")
    USE H: "\\MRKGT01\@userid$"
    USE S: "\\ MRKGT01\Marketing"
    ;Set Up Internet Explorer to Use Proxy Server and Default to www-int
    ; Check Enable Proxy Server Box

$Enable=ReadValue("HKEY_CURRENT_USER\Software\Microsoft\Windows\CurrentVersion\
Internet Settings", "ProxyEnable")
    If $Enable="01000000"
        ;Proxy Already Enabled - Do Nothing
    Else
$Hidden=WriteValue("HKEY_CURRENT_USER\Software\Microsoft\Windows\CurrentVersion\
Internet Settings", "ProxyEnable", "01000000", "REG_BINARY")
    Endif
;
; Configure Browser with Proxy Server Address
;
$Server=ReadValue("HKEY_CURRENT_USER\Software\Microsoft\Windows\CurrentVersion\
Internet Settings", "ProxyServer")
    If $Server="proxy.yourcompany.com:80"
        ;Proxy Server Address is Configured - Do Nothing
    Else
$Hidden=WriteValue("HKEY_CURRENT_USER\Software\Microsoft\Windows\CurrentVersion\
Internet Settings", "ProxyServer", "proxy.yourcompany.com:80", "REG_SZ")
    Endif
;
; Enable HTTP1.1 Through Proxy
;
$Http11=ReadValue("HKEY_CURRENT_USER\Software\Microsoft\Windows\CurrentVersion\
Internet Settings", "ProxyHttp1.1")
    If $Http11="1"
        ;Proxy Already Enabled for HTTP 1.1 - Do Nothing
    Else
$Hidden=WriteValue("HKEY_CURRENT_USER\Software\Microsoft\Windows\CurrentVersion\
Internet Settings", "ProxyHttp1.1", "1", "REG_DWORD")
    Endif
;
; Bypass Proxy for all Local LAN Sites
;
```

```
$Bypass=ReadValue("HKEY_CURRENT_USER\Software\Microsoft\Windows\CurrentVersion\
Internet Settings", "ProxyOverride")
   If $Bypass="*.yourcompany.com;<local>"
      ;Proxy Already Bypassed for Local Sites - Do Nothing
   Else
$Hidden=WriteValue("HKEY_CURRENT_USER\Software\Microsoft\Windows\CurrentVersion\
Internet Settings", "ProxyOverride", "*.yourcompany.com;<local>", "REG_SZ")
   Endif
;
endif
```

KiXtart's ability to make Registry changes during client logon is similar to a system policy. However, KiXtart scripts run under the context of the user account, whereas system policies run under the context of the system. In other words, a KiXtart logon script has the same level of access to the system as the user account; a system policy has a system level of access.

Profiles

A *profile* is a series of folders and files that describe a user's environment and preferences. By default, Windows NT creates a profile for each user who logs on to the system. When a user modifies his or her settings and environment, the changes are saved back to the user's profile. Profiles allow more than one user to use the same machine but keep each user's environment separate.

A profile consists of a series of folders and a ntuser.dat file. A description of each folder is presented in Table 10.2:

Table 10.2   Profile Contents

Folder/file	Contents
Application Data	Application-specific data, such as your Outlook signature.
Desktop	All files and shortcuts on the Desktop.
Favorites	Favorites list from Internet Explorer.
NetHood	Shortcuts to Network Neighborhood items.
Personal	Shortcuts to Program items.
PrintHood	Shortcuts to Printer folder items.
Recent	Shortcuts to recently used files.
SendTo	Shortcuts that appear on the context menu in Explorer. For example, you can right-click in Explorer to send the selected file or folder to a floppy drive.
Start Menu	Shortcuts in the Start menu.
Templates	Shortcuts to Template items.
ntuser.dat	Settings for the Control Panel, Windows NT Explorer, Taskbar, Accessories, and network printer connections.

A profile is always stored on the local machine, but it may be located on a server too. Windows NT machines create a folder with the same name as the user account beneath the %SYSTEMROOT%\Profiles folder in which to store each user's profile.

> **Tip**
>
> *In a complete trust domain model, you might experience problems if users of different domains have the same account name. Suppose Tom from the LA domain logs on to a workstation used by Tom in the NY domain. The workstation would already have a Tom folder beneath the %SYSTEMROOT%\Profiles folder, so it would consider the Tom profile folder for NY\Tom to be corrupt and create a new profile folder labeled Tom.000 for LA\Tom.*

Windows NT has four types of profiles:

- *Local profile.* This profile is always created for each user who logs on to the system. The profile is stored on the local machine in the %SYSTEMROOT%\Profiles folder. Each time you log on and modify your settings, your changes are saved to your profile.

  Storage location: local machine

- *Network default user profile.* This profile is stored in the NetLogon share on all domain controllers. When the user logs on for the first time (and only the first time), the network default user profile is downloaded to the user's local machine and used to establish the user's initial environment. Such a profile is great for new NT rollouts because it allows you to establish an enhanced initial environment for all new logons. For example, you can prime the IE Favorites list with helpful links for new users.

  Storage location: NetLogon share on all domain controllers

- *Roaming profile.* This profile moves the concept of a local profile to a server. Roaming profiles are easy to create, and they enhance user mobility by allowing users' environments to follow them when they log on to different workstations. When the users change their preferences or environment, the changes are saved to the local profile and the roaming profile. A roaming profile is specified in the User Profile Path field of the User Environment Profile dialog box (see Figure 10.8).

  Storage location: network server

- *Mandatory profile.* Stored on a server, this profile imposes a mandatory environment on the user. Such profiles are great for groups of users that should have a standard Desktop with common icons and menu items. A mandatory profile makes troubleshooting easier because each person has the same icons and menus, and it tends to lower support costs. A mandatory profile is specified in the Profile Path field of the User Environment Profile dialog box (see Figure 10.8).

Storage location: network server

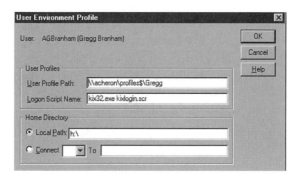

Figure 10.8   *The server storage location of a roaming or mandatory profile is indicated in the User Profile Path field in the User Environment Profile dialog box.*

Server-based profiles are downloaded during client logon and uploaded during client logoff. When a user logs on, Windows NT stores a local copy of the user's profile beneath the %SYSTEMROOT%\Profiles directory. If a workstation you have previously logged on to cannot retrieve your server-based profile, you are given the option of using your local profile. Later, when the server is available, you are informed that your local profile is newer than your server-based copy, and you are given the option of logging on with your local profile. Upon logoff, your changes are saved to the server-based copy, and the two profiles are once again in synch.

The size of a user profile depends on the user's settings and configuration; it generally ranges from 300 to 500K. For the purpose of estimating server storage space, you should assume 500K per user. If you use a server-based profile, it should be located on a LAN server; it should not be located on a server across a WAN due to its size.

Troubleshooting Tip

Be sure to warn users not to save files directly to their Desktop. If users save large files to their Desktop, their profile increases by several megabytes. The Desktop and Start menu should contain shortcuts only. Such a policy is hard to enforce, and user education is the key to avoiding problems in this area.

> *Tip*
>
> *If you have a workstation that is shared among several users or perhaps temporary users, you should consider automatically deleting each user's local profile during logoff. If not, the number of profiles builds over time, and no one ever deletes them. You can use a System Policy file to automatically delete cached copies of roaming profiles.*

Modifying a User's Roaming Profile

If a user has a roaming profile, Windows NT saves the user's profile changes to the server during logoff. Because a profile is composed of several files and folders, Windows NT must use one of the files to keep track of the profile's timestamp. The ntuser.dat file (user.dat for Windows 95 profiles) is used for this purpose. During a logon, Windows NT checks the timestamp of the ntuser.dat file. If the ntuser.dat located on the server is newer, Windows NT downloads the profile from the server; otherwise, the local profile is used.

Suppose Sally has a roaming profile, and you need to add a shortcut to her Start menu. First, you must make sure Sally is not logged on; if she were, your changes to the server-based profile would be overwritten when she logged off. When you are sure Sally is not logged on, you can connect to the server that stores her profile and make the addition to the Start menu. Then you must complete a very important step: Use TOUCH.EXE from the Windows NT Resource Kit to update the timestamp on Sally's ntuser.dat. You would use the touch utility by executing the following command:

```
F:\Profiles\Sally> touch ntuser.dat
```

This forces Sally's workstation to download the updated server-based profile during her next logon.

Windows 95 Profiles

To establish a profile for a Windows 95 user, you must enable User Profiles on the Windows 95 machine. To do this, click the Passwords icon found in the Control Panel to invoke a tabbed dialog box. Click the User Profiles tab and select the option labeled Users Can Customize Their Preferences and Desktop Settings.

Your next step is to assign a home directory to the Windows NT user account. Fill in the Connect and To sections of the User Environment Profile dialog box; this causes Windows 95 to use the specified path to download and upload profiles. However, it is important to note that Windows 95 never shows the path as a mapped drive, and it uses the path to save profile information only. To give the users a directory to save their work, you must establish another shared directory for them and map it using a logon script.

Policies

A *policy* is a series of Registry settings for a particular user, group, or computer. The Registry settings are described in a file called a *policy file*, which is placed in the NetLogon share on all domain controllers. When a user logs on to a workstation, the policy file is downloaded from the server that authenticates the user and is applied to the user's Registry (ntuser.dat) and the workstation's Registry.

Policy files offer two distinct advantages:

- A policy can strengthen Windows 95 and make it more secure.

- A policy file can lower network support costs by disallowing client access to certain parts of the operating system.

For example, you can simplify the operating system for novice users in a data entry department by removing many of the Desktop icons and Start menu shortcuts. The simplified system is easier to use and demands less support because the user cannot access certain portions of it.

Policies are created using the *System Policy Editor (SPE)* (see Figure 10.9). The SPE does not come with Windows NT Workstation, but you can install it there by installing the server-based Network Administration Tools. It also comes with Windows 95 and can be found on the Windows 95 CD in the Admin\Apptools directory.

By default, the Windows NT SPE comes with two templates:

- The common.adm template contains Registry settings common to both the Windows 95 and Windows NT platforms.

- The winnt.adm template contains Registry settings specific to Windows NT.

The Windows 95 SPE has two templates: common.adm and windows.adm. As you might guess, windows.adm contains Registry settings specific to Windows 95.

It is important to note the chronology when considering the interaction between policies and profiles. First, the user's profile is loaded either from the local machine or from a network server, and then the policy file applies Registry changes to the Registry of the local workstation and to the ntuser.dat portion of the user's profile.

You can have only one Windows NT policy file and one Windows 95 policy file per domain. The policy for Windows NT clients must be named NTCONFIG.POL, and the policy file for Windows 95 clients must be named CONFIG.POL. Both files must be saved to the NetLogon share on all domain controllers.

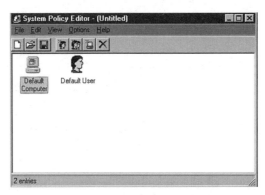

Figure 10.9   *You can use the System Policy Editor (SPE) to create policy files for Windows NT and Windows 95 clients.*

Policy files are nothing more than a combination of Registry settings that are applied to the system during client logon. In fact, if you need to modify certain Registry keys during client logon, you can write your own system policy templates to include the Registry changes in your policy file. A policy file is somewhat special in the sense that it can access portions of the Registry that are disallowed to the user logging on to the system. Because it runs under the context of the system, a system policy is much more powerful than a logon script.

Tips for Defining a Policy File

Defining a good policy file can be tricky and dangerous. It has the potential to affect numerous users and computers with changes that are difficult to remove. You should always thoroughly test a policy file before deploying it. Here are some tips to help you get started on the right track:

- Browse the user and computer policies supplied with the SPE and make a list of the policies that can benefit your network.

- Decide which users, groups, and computers will receive each policy.

- Decide on the restrictions for the default user. Users or groups not directly specified in the policy file receive the Default User policy. You can make the Default User very limited and add groups to the policy file to remove the restrictions, or you can make the Default User very unlimited and impose restrictions on the groups you add. Your approach depends entirely on the number of restrictions you must impose and the number of groups affected by the restrictions.

- When defining the policy file, you must be sure to reverse each policy for those not intended to be affected by the policy. For example, if you remove Network Neighborhood from the Sales group and a salesman logs on to a computer in the Marketing department, the computer will download the policy and remove Network Neighborhood from the computer. Unless you specifically add the Network Neighborhood icon for the marketing group, the marketing user will lose access to Network Neighborhood. The best way to handle this problem is to keep track of each policy you implement and reverse the policy for the users and groups that should not be affected by it.

While performing these steps, you should create a table like the one illustrated in Table 10.3.

Table 10.3   Sample Policy File

Policy	Default User	DataEntry	Sales	Domain Admins
Hide Network Neighborhood	☒	☒	☐	☐
Remove Run command from Start Menu	☐	☒	☐	☐
Disable Registry Editing Tools	☒	☒	☒	☐
All other policies	■	■	■	■

☐ = *No*
☒ = *Yes*
■ = *Ignore*

Table 10.3 shows three policies. For each policy that is implemented for one user or group, you must be sure to reverse the policy for the other groups. For example, suppose a DataEntry user logs on to a computer in the Sales department; the Network Neighborhood shortcut would be removed from the Desktop, as commanded in the policy file. However, when a Sales user logs on to the same machine, the Network Neighborhood shortcut is not restored unless the policy for the Sales group specifically clears the policy restriction.

Author's Note

One weakness of policy files is the inability to group machines and propagate Registry changes to a group of machines. Windows 2000 solves the problem, allowing you to group machines for the purpose of policy distribution.

Windows 95 Policies

Windows 95 machines do not understand how to interpret Windows NT groups until you load Group Policies from the Windows 95 CD. To add Group Policies, go to the Control Panel and choose Add\Remove Programs, Windows

Setup, Have Disk. Enter `Admin\Apptools\Poledit` for the path, and choose OK. When prompted, install the Group Policies. You must do this for each Windows 95 client machine that will use the policy file.

When interpreting Windows NT groups, Windows 95 queries the primary domain controller (PDC) directly. This can introduce significant delays for Windows 95 machines located across a WAN. In addition, if the PDC is unavailable, the Windows 95 user gets the Default User policy from the cached policy on the local machine. For more information, see Microsoft Knowledge Base Article Q150687.

Directory Replication

The *Directory Replicator* is an optional service you can run on Windows NT to export files and folders to import servers. The most common use of the Directory Replicator service is to synchronize the contents of the NetLogon share among domain controllers. The NetLogon share plays a major role in the operation of the domain if you are using policies, profiles, or logon scripts. Figure 10.10 illustrates many of the items that require placement in the NetLogon share. The Directory Replicator service is not intended for large amounts of information, but it is well-suited to the contents of the NetLogon share.

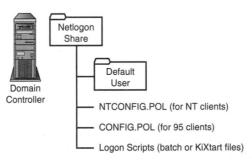

Figure 10.10   *The NetLogon share of domain controllers is used to store many items.*

Directory Replication Operation

The operation of Directory Replication is illustrated in Figure 10.11. In this example, you would modify the contents of only the Export directory with new or updated files. The Directory Replicator service periodically checks for new or updated files in the Export directory. The new or changed files are then replicated to the Import directory on all import servers. In most cases, the export server is a domain controller and must be configured for both export and import operations, as depicted in Figure 10.11.

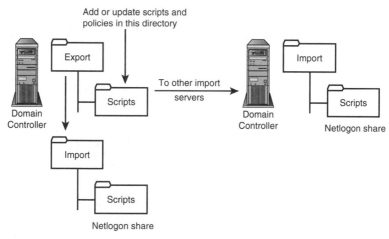

Figure 10.11   *An export server contains a master copy of all items that must be auto-matically copied to all import servers.*

The import server must read the following Registry key of the export server to know which files to replicate:

HKLM\System\CCS\Services\Replicator

By default, Windows NT 4.0 does not allow the Replicator account on the import server access to read this key in the Registry of the export server. There are three solutions to the problem:

- Add the Replicator account on the import server to the local Administrators group on the export server.

- Publish the Registry location by adding it to the following Registry key:

  HKLM\System\CCS\Control\SecurePipeServers\Winreg\ AllowedPaths

- Install the latest service pack (Service Pack 3 and beyond perform the solution mentioned in the previous paragraph).

Installing Service Pack 3 is the best solution to the problem. After Service Pack 3 is installed, there are three steps required to implement Directory Replication. These steps are described in the following sections.

Step 1: Create an Account for the Directory Replication Service

You must create an account for the Directory Replicator service (see Figure 10.12), naming it something like "_Replicator." Clear the boxes for User Must Change Password at Next Logon and check the boxes for User Cannot Change Password and Password Never Expires. You don't need to modify the account's group membership; thus, the account is a member of the Domain Users group by default.

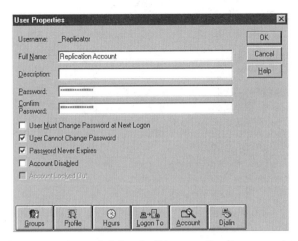

Figure 10.12   *An account is needed for the Directory Replicator service.*

Step 2: Configure and Start the Directory Replication Service

Open the Control Panel and click on the Services applet. Select the Directory Replicator service and click the Startup button (see Figure 10.13). In the Service dialog box, set the Startup Type to Automatic and make the service log on using the account created in Step 1. When you click OK, you receive a message stating that the account is granted the right to log on as a service and that the account has been added to the Replicator local group. Although you are not informed, the account is also added to the local Backup Operators group.

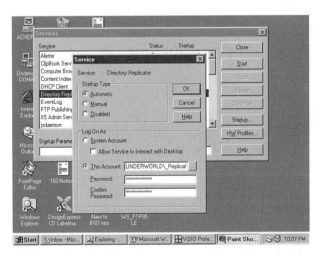

Figure 10.13   *The Directory Replicator service must be configured to log on to a Windows NT account.*

Step 3: Configure Export and Import Servers

You can use Server Manager to configure both the import and export servers. Select the machine you want to use as the export server and choose Properties from the Computer menu. Click the Replication button to invoke the Directory Replication configuration dialog box (see Figure 10.14).

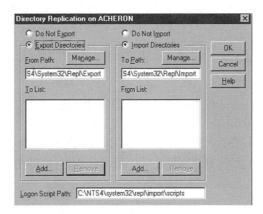

Figure 10.14 *You must configure the Directory Replication properties on each import and export server.*

Click the Export Directories or Import Directories option as required for the machine you are configuring. By default, machines are configured to import and export to the domain, and broadcast packets are used to communicate with import and export servers. This works fine on LANs but causes problems when routers are introduced. If the import and export servers are located across routers, you must configure the To List area in the Replication dialog box (see Figure 10.12) with the machine names of the computers.

Replication Registry Parameters

You can find the Registry parameters related to Directory Replication in the following Registry location:

HKLM\System\CurrentControlSet\Services\Replicator\Parameters

There you will find two parameters that control replication:

Value:	*GuardTime*
Date Type:	REG_DWORD
Default Data:	2
Description:	GuardTime is the amount of time the directory must be stable before replication can occur.

Value: *Interval*

Date Type: REG_DWORD

Default Data: *5*

Description: *Interval* describes how often the export server
                        checks for changes in the Export directory.

Troubleshooting Directory Replication

If the Directory Replicator service fails to start, check the Application Log in
Event Viewer. Refer to Table 10.4 to associate the event IDs with problems and
solutions.

Table 10.4   Events Related to Directory Replication

Event ID	Problem	Resolution
3208, 3216	The import server cannot read a needed Registry key on the export server, and it does not know what to replicate.	Install Service Pack 3 or modify the AllowedPaths key of the Registry on the export server (described earlier in this chapter).
7000	The permissions on the system32 or system32\ repl directory do not allow access to the Replicator account.	Change the permissions to give the Replicator account access.
7023, 7024	The Import and Export paths for Directory Replication in the Server Manager properties setup screen are set to nonexistent paths.	Check your spelling of the Import and Export paths and make sure they are accessible by the Replicator account.
1057, 1069	These errors can result from incorrect configuration of the Directory Replicator service or incorrect configuration information in the Registry, or because domain user account information has not been synchronized.	Check the password for the Replicator account. Check the Logon as a Service User right.

Chapter **11**

Controlling Access to Domain Resources

This chapter will review:

- **Windows NT Resources**
  Windows NT treats files, folders, and printers as objects and attaches access control lists (ACLs) to the objects to protect them.

- **Understanding NT Permissions**
  Windows NT has permissions at the share level, folder level, and file level. The permissions for every user are cumulative.

- **Building a Strategy**
  Although every company has a different security policy, there are some common guidelines every company should follow.

- **Useful Utilities**
  There are many useful utilities for verifying and modifying permissions. Some of the more helpful utilities are covered in this chapter.

Windows NT Resources

When discussing NT security, it is common to refer to files and printers in a generic sense as *resources*. Windows NT protects resources by attaching an *access control list (ACL)* to each resource. The ACL describes the users and/or groups who can access the resource along with their level of permission.

Folders are container objects used to organize files and other folders. Just like you organize similar users into groups, you organize similar files by placing them into folders. By classifying files into more categories (folders), you gain a better ability to control access to them.

The example in Figure 11.1 illustrates an important point. The figure shows two directory structures: one with a single directory for all files and another with multiple directories for files. As you can see, if XYZ were to use a single directory, security would be more difficult to control. From this example, you can conclude that the better you create and organize the directory structure on your file server, the easier you are able to control resource access. If your files are poorly organized, your permission settings may be unnecessarily complicated.

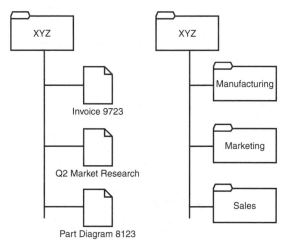

Figure 11.1 *The more specific the directory structure, the more easily you can control file access.*

Your first step toward securing access to files and folders is to locate data on NTFS drives. The file allocation table (FAT) file system offers no security at the file and folder level and is a poor choice for locating data. By locating files and folders on an NTFS system, you force the user to go through a minimum of four security checks (see Figure 11.2).

Using Figure 11.2, suppose Dan is a member of the Sales group and wants to access the Q2 Research document located in the shared Marketing folder. When Dan double-clicks on ATLS001, ATLS001 performs pass-through authentication to authenticate Dan's username and password with the domain SAM. The shared Marketing folder is then displayed, and Dan is allowed to map a drive to it because the share-level permissions are set to Full Control for Everyone. Because Dan is a member of the Sales group, he can list the contents of the Marketing folder; however, he cannot open the Q2 Research file because his account is assigned the No Access permission to the file.

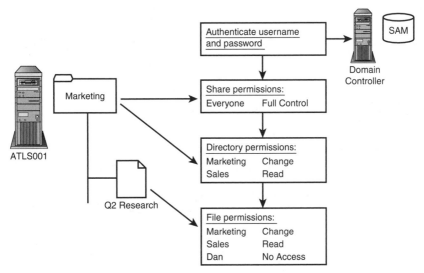

Figure 11.2 *Access to files on a network server requires a series of security checks.*

The share-level permissions on an NTFS system are unnecessary and only complicate security settings. Microsoft advocates the use of share-level permissions only on FAT drives and suggests leaving the default share-level permissions (Everyone, Full Control) for NTFS drives. By accepting the default share-level permissions, you can rely on the underlying NTFS folder and file-level permissions to control user and group access.

> **Tip**
>
> *You can convert a FAT file system to NTFS using CONVERT.EXE. However, be aware that this conversion is a one-way process—you cannot change back to a FAT file system later.*

Understanding NT Permissions

You can assign the following individual permissions (called *special permissions*) to a file or folder on an NT system:

- Read (R)
- Write (W)
- Execute (E)
- Delete (D)
- Change Permission (P)
- Take Ownership (O)

To make things easier, the designers of Windows NT grouped common combinations of these special permissions into what are known as *standard permissions*. Standard permissions are available in the Type of Access drop-down list box (see Figure 11.3) near the bottom of the Directory Permissions dialog box. If you prefer to set the permissions individually, you can select Special Directory Access or Special File Access (see Figure 11.4). In most cases, the standard permissions offer sufficient flexibility; rarely do you need to apply a nonstandard combination.

Figure 11.3   *The Type of Access drop-down list box contains standard permissions.*

Recall the four security checks mentioned earlier in this chapter. The first check verifies the user's credentials in the domain SAM, whereas the last three checks relate to permissions you can set. There is a standard list of available permissions at the share level, folder level, and file level. Table 11.1 summarizes the available standard permissions for each level.

Table 11.1   Available Standard Permissions

Share Level	Folder Level	File Level
No Access	List (RX) (Not Specified)	Read (RX)
Read	Read (RX) (RX)	Change (RWXD)
Change	Add (WX) (Not Specified)	Full Control (All)
Full Control	Add & Read (RWX) (RX)	No Access (None)
	Change (RWXD) (RWXD)	
	Full Control (All) (All)	
	No Access (None) (None)	

> **Author's Note**
>
> *Notice the two sets of parentheses for folder level permissions in Figure 11.3. The first set of parentheses describes the folder permissions, and the second set describes the permissions inherited by new files created in the folder. For more information, see the "Permission Inheritance" section later in the chapter.*

Windows NT permissions are *cumulative* (rather than being calculated). In other words, a user's level of access is the cumulative result of their user and group permissions defined on the resource. For example, referring to Figure 11.2, assume you are a member of both the Marketing and the Sales group. Your total level of access to the Marketing folder would be as follows:

Read (RX) + Change (RWXD) = Change (RWXD)

If you were only a member of the Sales group, you would have only Read and Execute access to the Marketing directory on ATLS001. However, with additional membership in the Marketing group, you would gain Write and Delete permissions to the directory.

The one exception to the cumulative permissions used by NT is the No Access permission. If a user is assigned No Access to a resource (or if the user is a member of any groups assigned No Access to the resource), the user is denied access to the resource regardless of other group memberships that grant resource access. For example, consider the Dan account in Figure 11.2; although Dan is a member of the Sales group, which has Read access to the Q2 Research document, Dan's account has explicitly been assigned No Access. As a result, Dan cannot access the document.

A user can be given access to a resource directly or indirectly. A user has direct access to a resource if his or her username is explicitly listed on the ACL; a user has indirect access if he or she is a member of a group that is listed on the ACL. Users not listed on the ACL directly or indirectly do not have access to the resource. Thus, if a user is not listed on an ACL and is not a member of any groups on the ACL, there is no reason to grant the user the No Access permission. The action would be redundant because the user already cannot access the resource.

Permission Inheritance

In Windows NT, a directory has two sets of permissions. In Figure 11.4, notice the two sets of parentheses that follow each standard security setting. The left set defines the permissions related to the directory, and the right set describes the permissions given to any new files created in the directory. The concept of establishing an initial set of permissions for a new file is called *file inheritance*. You can set the file inheritance on any directory.

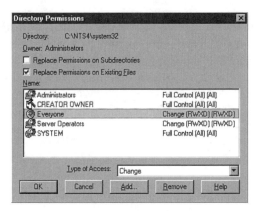

Figure 11.4   *The two sets of parentheses following each standard permission describe the directory permissions and the file inheritance.*

Moving and Copying Files

When you move a file, it retains its original owner and ACL. When you copy a file, it inherits its ACL from the target directory, and the user performing the copy operation becomes the owner. When moving a file across partitions, the operation is treated as a copy and a new ACL is inherited.

When users want to share information with others, they usually copy files from their home directory to a shared directory on a server. If the directory permissions are set up correctly on the target directory, the copied file inherits the permissions of the parent directory and is accessible to the other accounts on the ACL. However, if the user mistakenly moves the file to the server, the original ACL is retained. Because the home directory permissions typically grant Full Control to the user only, the moved file is inaccessible to others.

Author's Note

Because copied files inherit ACLs, you should rarely have to modify the ACLs of individual files. If you have set up the correct directory permissions on all shared directories, the new files placed in them will all receive the correct permissions without any user intervention. The task of planning and setting up a file server may be time-consuming, but it usually demands very little follow-up attention.

Hidden FDC Permission

The Full Control permission in Windows NT includes a hidden permission called the *File Delete Child (FDC) permission*. This permission is related to POSIX compliance, which is based on the UNIX file system. UNIX users with Write permission to a directory can delete its files. Under the FDC implementation in Windows NT, users with full control over a directory can delete any of its files even if they do not have access to the files.

The FDC permission is a serious concern when you must control access to a directory shared by many people. Suppose a shared Sales directory has an ACL containing Sales with Full Control, and the manager of the Sales department creates a confidential document in the Sales directory and assigns No Access to a user named Bob. Suppose the document is related to Bob's job performance and Bob is a member of the Sales group. Although Bob cannot read the contents of the document (because of the No Access permission), he can delete the document because he has the FDC permission by virtue of the Full Control permission assigned to the Sales group for the Sales directory.

> **Tip**
>
> *Because of the FDC permission, you should never give a user or group Full Control of a top-level folder that contains data belonging to two or more users. Granting Full Control of the top-level folder allows one or more users the ability to delete underlying files regardless of the permissions on the files. Consider Change permission rather than Full Control.*

Automating Permission Assignments

You can use CACLS.EXE and XCACLS.EXE to automate the setting of security permissions for files and folders. For most organizations, it is quite common to make at least a few security changes before delivering new NT client workstations to end users. Rather than changing each ACL manually, you can write a batch file that uses CACLS and XCACLS to automatically set permissions on the workstation. The batch file can then be used as part of an unattended installation script to automatically configure permission settings during the installation procedure.

Listing 11.1 gives an example of such a script. CACLS.EXE and XCACLS.EXE are described in detail in the "Useful Utilities" section later in this chapter.

Listing 11.1   *A Sample Script to Lock Down the File System Permissions*

```
cacls c:\ /g administrators:f system:f users:r
cacls c:\*.* /t /c /g administrators:f system:f users:r
cacls c:\temp /e /p users:c
xcacls c:\winnt /e /t /g users:ex;ewx "creator owner":c
xcacls c:\winnt\repair /e /r users "creator owner"
xcacls c:\winnt\system32 /e /g users:ex;ewx "creator owner":c
xcacls c:\winnt\system32\spool /e /g "creator owner":f
xcacls c:\winnt\cookies /e /g users:c
xcacls c:\winnt\forms /e /g users:c
xcacls c:\winnt\history /e /g users:c
xcacls c:\winnt\occache /e /g users:c
xcacls "c:\winnt\temporary internet files" /e /g users:c
xcacls "c:\powercerv applications" /e /t /g users:c
xcacls "c:\program files\microsoft office\office" /e /g users:ewxd;ewx
xcacls "c:\program files\microsoft office\templates" /e /g users:ewxd;ewx
```

The Impact of Trusts on Resource Access

Trusts have a great impact on controlling domain resources because they allow you to make resources available to users from trusted domains. In essence, a *trust* extends the security boundary of a domain. It has the effect of allowing the administrator of the trusting domain to set permissions based on the global users and groups in the trusted domain. So even if a trust exists, it does not automatically allow trusted users to access resources in the trusting domain.

> **Warning**
>
> *The default file system permissions for most directories on Windows NT Server are Everyone, Full Control. If the permissions are not changed, a trust relationship appears to grant automatic access to trusting domain resources for trusted domain users. To protect your domain resources, you should always be careful when giving the Everyone group access to any resource.*

In Figure 11.5, the Corp domain is trusted by the Atlanta domain. Corp users can open Network Neighborhood and see the shared directories in the Atlanta domain. However, Atlanta users cannot list the shares on any server in the Corp domain. Because the ACL of the Sales directory on ATLS001 is set to Everyone with Full Control, all users from the Corp domain can access resources in the Sales directory. Security on the directory is strengthened by removing the Everyone group and replacing it with the specific groups that need access to the directory (see Figure 11.6).

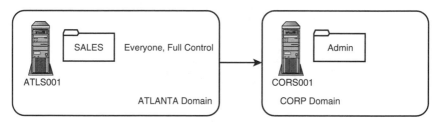

Figure 11.5   *All users from the Corp domain can access the Sales folder in the Atlanta domain.*

> **Author's Note**
>
> *One of the first tasks I perform on a file server after installing Windows NT is to change the ACLs in most of the file system. In fact, I typically automate the process with a script. My primary concern is the Everyone group with Full Control sprinkled throughout the file system. Everyone is replaced with Authenticated Users (or Domain Users) in most cases.*

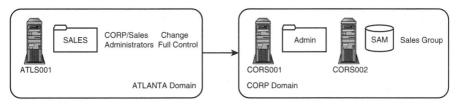

Figure 11.6 *Security on the Sales folder is increased by explicitly giving access to those groups who need to use the Sales directory resources.*

Building a Strategy

Permissions are closely tied to the user and group structure of your organization. In fact, the security needs of the organization should dictate the number of groups needed by the organization.

Suppose a company has no need for security and wants all users to be able to view, modify, and delete the work of other users. In such a case, the company has no need for groups—groups are only needed to delegate resource access or grant administrative powers. All users are a member of the Everyone group and, as long as the Everyone group has access to all resources, the company can function as desired.

On the other hand, if the company is security-conscious and wants to control resource access on a more granular level, it should have numerous groups, each containing a small number of users.

Take Time to Plan

Resource security involves a huge amount of planning. To properly set up a file server, you must classify all of its data. To whom does the data belong? Who are the primary users of the data? Who decides which users get access to the data and at what level of access? Extracting this information can be difficult and time-consuming, but it is necessary if you want to plan effectively.

> *Tip*
>
> *Email is a great way to gain information about the data in a file server. For example, if you don't know who needs access to an Accounting directory, a broadcast email to the Accounting department is a quick, nearly effortless way to discover who is responsible for the data and who grants others access to it.*
>
> *To go a step further, you may want to create email forms that the resource owners can use to quickly request the addition or deletion of accounts to files and folders on the server.*

Exploring a Common Approach

A file server is typically set up with top-level folders for each department (see Figure 11.7). From there, the content and organization within each department's folder is dictated by the individual department. Some departments have very few types of data. For example, a Manufacturing group may only need to store a shared Access database on the server. On the other hand, a group of research scientists may require several directories to contain project information, research data, analysis reports, and so on. Furthermore, a research environment likely demands many varying levels of security to protect the research data and discoveries.

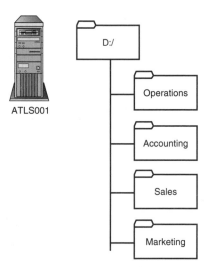

Figure 11.7   *Creating a top-level directory for each department is a common approach to setting up a file server.*

Use Only Groups on ACLs

ACLs should never contain individual user accounts. Consider the example in Figure 11.8. The ACL on the left grants access to three users, and so does the ACL on the right. However, the right ACL grants access indirectly via a group. In this case, some people may argue that there is not a significant difference between the two approaches. Both involve a nearly equal amount of work because a group has to be created for the right ACL. But suppose you are working with 300 users instead of 3, and you must assign access to multiple folders and files. It is far easier to organize the 300 users into several groups that you can add to the ACLs than to assign 300 individual accounts to ACLs.

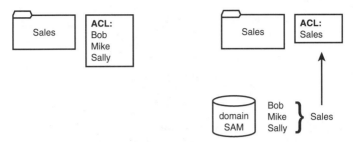

Figure 11.8   *Both ACLs accomplish the same result, but the ACL on the right is a better approach.*

When you are convinced groups are a much better approach, you must decide whether to use local or global groups. This decision is influenced by your domain architecture, and you should refer to Chapter 10 for helpful information to determine which arrangement is best for your company. In any case, if there is not a suitable group for the resource you want to control, create one (or have your administrator create it if you do not have an account with the proper privileges).

If you follow the standard practice of granting permissions on ACLs based on global or local groups, you create a modular system that is easy to verify and change. Otherwise, a mixture of individual accounts and local and global groups on the ACLs eventually leads to chaos when you must make changes.

Use the No Access Permission Properly

Recall that the No Access permission is the exception to NT's treatment of cumulative permissions. The only use of the No Access permission is to block a user or group that is already listed on the ACL. For example, suppose you want to give all Accounting users except Jim access to a folder. To accomplish the task, you add the following entries to the ACL:

```
Accounting    Full Control
Jim           No Access
```

The Accounting entry gives all Accounting users access to the resource; the Jim entry blocks Jim's access, successfully completing the assigned task.

But what if you need to give all Accounting users Full Control and give Jim read-only access? Because NT permissions are cumulative, you cannot solve the problem by assigning Full Control to the Accounting group and Read access to Jim; the cumulative NT permissions would result in Jim getting Read and Full Control access to the resource.

This is a common dilemma, and the next section provides details on the solutions you can pursue.

Use Separate Groups for Each Access Level

A common question is "Do you need a separate group for every level of access you want to define for a resource?" The unfortunate answer is yes, you must assign separate groups for every level of access to a resource.

> **Tip**
>
> *If you get confused when creating groups, always refer to this guideline: A user should gain additional privileges (that is, resource access) for membership in an additional group to be worthwhile. For example, it is pointless to add a domain administrator to the Domain Users group because no additional privileges are gained.*

The following sections illustrate how to create the necessary groups in several example situations.

Example 1: Assigning Users Read and Change Access

Problem: Group A contains 10 users: Five users need Read access to a file, and 5 users need Change access to the file.

Solution: Create a new group, Group B, for the users who require Change access. Assign the following permissions:

```
Group A    Read
Group B    Change
```

Example 2: Limiting Jim's Permissions

Problem: Jim, a data entry worker, is a member of the Accounting group. The Accounting group needs Change access to a directory. For protection, the Accounting manager wants to restrict Jim's access to read-only.

Solution: Because NT permissions are cumulative and Jim is a member of the Accounting group, adding the Accounting group with Change access would give Change access to Jim. The simplest solution is to create a separate group (called Power Accountants) containing all Accounting users except Jim. The resulting ACL would look like this:

```
Jim                 Read
Power Accountants   Change
```

Following the advice given earlier, you should never place individual accounts on ACLs. Thus, you should go one step further in this example. You should create a global group called Data Entry and place Jim in it. You should then remove Jim from the ACL and add the Data Entry group with Read permission. The ACL now looks like this:

```
Data Entry          Read
Power Accountants   Change
```

Creating the group seems like extra work in this example. However, you achieve a modular system in which you can simply alter the membership in the Data Entry group to control resource access.

Example 3: Extending Steve's Permissions

Problem: Steve, the manager of the Sales department, creates weekly sales reports and places them in a folder on the server. Steve wants sales users to have Read access to the reports, but he does not want them to be able to modify them.

Solution: Create a group called Sales Managers and place Steve in it. Modify the permissions on the folder as follows:

```
Sales     Read
Sales Managers    Change
```

Avoid Redundant Permissions

Consider the following ACL found on a domain workstation:

Administrators	Full Control
Domain Admins	Full Control
Sales	Full Control
System	Full Control

There is no need to include the global Domain Admins group because the local Administrators group already contains it. Recall that the Domain Admins group is added to the local Administrators group on all domain workstations (refer to Chapter 5).

The Impact of Email

With many of today's email servers, you have the ability to email files as attachments. As a result, there is less of a need to set up directories on a file server specifically for the exchange of files among users. With most email programs, users can simply attach the files in an email message and send it to the appropriate person to complete the file exchange. In fact, this method is encouraged because the communication is documented by the email server.

Useful Utilities

There are numerous useful utilities you can use to examine and modify file system security. Many utilities are included in the Windows NT Resource Kit, and others are available from third-party vendors. The following sections describe several of these utilities.

PERMS.EXE

PERMS.EXE is a Windows NT Resource Kit utility that lists a user's access to files and/or directories. You must be an administrator to run PERMS.EXE.

PERMS.EXE has the following syntax:

```
PERMS [domain\¦computer\]username path [/i] [/s]
```

The elements of the PERMS.EXE syntax are described in the following list:

`[domain\¦computer\]username`	Name of user whose permissions are to be checked.
`path`	A file or directory, with wildcards (*,?) accepted.
`/i`	Assumes the specified user is logged on interactively to the computer where the file/directory resides. With this switch, PERMS assumes the user is a member of the Interactive group. Without this switch, PERMS assumes the user is a member of the Network group.
`/s`	Checks permissions on files in subdirectories.

The output access mask contains the following letters:

R	Read.
W	Write.
X	Execute.
D	Delete.
P	Change Permissions.
O	Take Ownership.
A	General All.

-       No Access.

*   The specified user is the owner of the file or directory.

A group the user is a member of owns the file or directory.

?   The user's access permissions cannot be determined.

CACLS.EXE

CACLS.EXE, which comes with Windows NT 4, gives you the ability to modify ACLs. You can usually create a batch file of many CACLS.EXE commands. The syntax of CACLS.EXE is as follows:

```
CACLS filename [/T] [/E] [/C] [/G user:perm] [/R user [...]]
              [/P user:perm [...]] [/D user [...]]
```

The elements of the CACLS.EXE syntax are described in the following list:

filename	Displays ACLs.
/T	Changes ACLs of specified files in the current directory and all subdirectories.
/E	Edits the ACL instead of replacing it.
/C	Continue on access denied errors.

Author's Note

The /c switch is needed if you plan to use the command in an automated script. For example, Windows NT locks the pagefile and denies access when CACLS.EXE tries to modify the access permissions on pagefile.sys. If you do not use the /c switch, the command stops execution on such an access problem. However, the /c switch will result in CACLS skipping those files it cannot access.

/G user:perm	Grants specified user access rights. The perm can be R Read, C Change (write), or F Full Control.
/R user	Revokes specified user's access rights (valid only with /E).

/P user:perm	Replaces specified user's access rights. The `perm` can be N None, R Read, C Change (write), or F Full Control.
/D user	Denies the specified user access.

Wildcards can be used to specify more than one file in a command. You can also specify more than one user in a command.

XCACLS.EXE

XCACLS.EXE is a Windows NT Resource Kit utility that extends the capability of the CACLS.EXE command included with Windows NT. Using XACLS.EXE, you can automatically set any special permissions you want to control.

XCACLS.EXE has the following syntax:

```
XCACLS filename [/T] [/E] [/C] [/G user:perm;spec] [/R user [...]]
               [/P user:perm;spec [...]] [/D user [...]] [/Y]
```

The elements of the XCACLS.EXE syntax are described in the following list:

filename	Displays ACLs.
/T	Changes ACLs of specified files in the current directory and all subdirectories.
/E	Edits the ACL instead of replacing it.
/C	Continues on access-denied errors.
/G user:perm;spec	Grants the specified user access rights. The `perm` can be: R Read, C Change (write), F Full Control, P Change Permissions (Special access), O Take Ownership (Special access), X Execute (Special access), E Read (Special access), W Write (Special access), or D Delete (Special access). The `spec` can be the same as `perm` and is applied only to a directory. In this case, `perm` is used for file inheritance in this directory. If not omitted, `Spec=Perm`. Special values for `spec` only: T Not Specified. At least one access right has to follow. Entries between ; and T are ignored.
/R user	Revokes the specified user's access rights.

/P user:perm;spec	Replaces the specified user's access rights. For access right specification, see the /G option.
/D user	Denies the specified user access.
/Y	Replaces the user's rights without verification.

Wildcards can be used to specify more than one file in a command. You can specify more than one user in a command, and you can combine access rights.

DumpACL

DumpACL is a freeware utility that offers several administrative features not found in Windows NT. (You can download it from http://www.somarsoft.com.) One of the most notable features of DumpACL is its ability to generate a report of NTFS permissions for a directory and its subdirectories (see Figure 11.9).

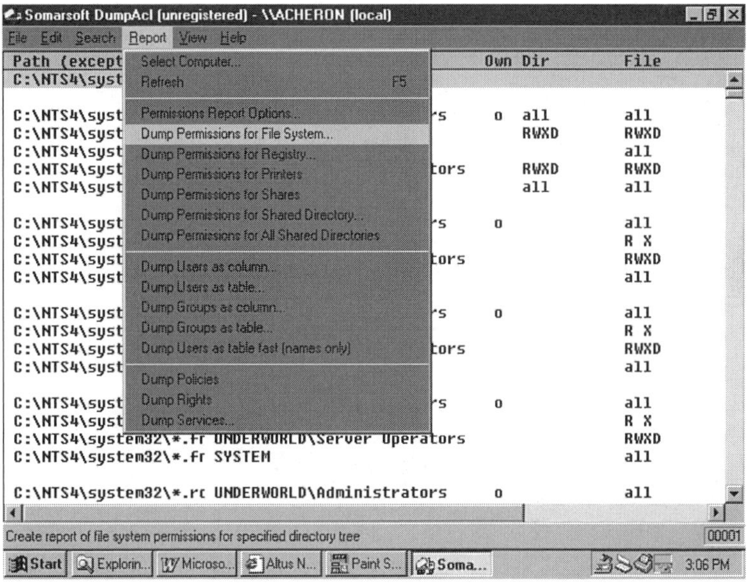

Figure 11.9 *DumpACL allows you to generate a report of all permissions for a directory and its subdirectories.*

Chapter **12**

The Browser

This chapter will review:

- **Browser Concepts**
  Understanding the fundamentals of the browser is the first step toward becoming a browsing expert.

- **Browser Client Operation**
  Browser clients announce their presence to a master browser and retrieve browse lists using API calls to master or backup browsers.

- **Browsing and NetBIOS Names**
  The browser uses NetBIOS names for communication and identification of browser servers.

- **Browser Communication**
  Browser communication takes place by sending broadcast datagrams to mailslots.

- **Understanding Browser Elections**
  Browser servers are elected based on several criteria.

- **Browsing Across Subnets**
  Domain membership and a WINS server are necessary for smooth browsing over enterprise WANs.

- **Tuning the Browser**
  Tuning the browser for better performance and consistency is essential in an enterprise environment.

- **Browser Troubleshooting**
  Browser troubleshooting is made easier by two NT Resource Kit utilities.

Browser Concepts

The browser is the gateway to resources on a Microsoft network. More specifically, the *browser* is a software component responsible for discovering all NetBIOS servers on the network. Browser servers maintain a list of all available servers, workgroups, and domains. Other machines query a browser server and display the list via Network Neighborhood and Windows Explorer.

With regard to the browser, the term *server* is loosely interpreted to identify any machine capable of sharing NetBIOS resources. Both Windows NT Server and Windows NT Workstation run a Server service that allows the sharing of folders and printers. Consequently, both operating systems are considered to be servers by the browser. In addition, Windows 95 machines configured for file and print sharing are also considered servers and appear in the browse list. Note that machines deemed as servers by the browser appear in the browse list even though they may have no shares to offer.

The browser is not limited to machines running Microsoft operating systems. Even machines running UNIX can participate in browsing and publish resources in the browse list. By loading SAMBA onto a UNIX workstation, it can participate in browsing and share resources like a Microsoft operating system.

On all networks, browser servers are responsible for maintaining the browse list. There are many types of browser servers, and each network must maintain at least one master browser. A browser server can assume one of the following roles:

- Domain Master Browser
- Master Browser
- Backup Browser
- Preferred Master Browser

On a network of two machines, one machine becomes the Master Browser and the other becomes the Backup Browser. On larger networks, the Microsoft algorithms result in one Backup Browser per 32 machines. An *election*, as discussed in the next section, is used to determine which machines become browser servers.

Figure 12.1 illustrates a small network with two browser servers: a master browser and a backup browser. The master browser, XYZDC01, maintains the server list—a list of available servers, workgroups, and domains. The backup browser, XYZW001, periodically contacts the master browser to update its server list. Clients can retrieve the server list from a master browser or a backup browser.

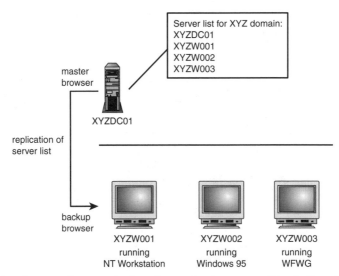

Figure 12.1 *A master browser is elected to maintain a server list of all available servers on the network.*

> **Tip**
>
> *You can use the Browse Monitor from the NT Resource Kit to see the status of master and backup browsers. Browse Monitor not only lists the computers responsible for maintaining the server list, but it also gives you statistics on each one. For example, you can see the number of server announcements, server enumerations, and so on.*

> **Tip**
>
> *You can use the* net view *command to help troubleshoot browser problems. Although the client's browse list may be retrieved from a backup browser,* net view *retrieves it directly from the master browser. Because there is a timing delay associated with the update of the backup browser server list, a server list received from a backup browser may not be as consistent or accurate as the server list received from the master browser.*

Browse lists are maintained on a per-protocol and per-workgroup/domain basis. Thus, if your LAN has three workgroups, a master browser is elected for each workgroup. Assuming each workgroup has at least two machines, a backup browser is also elected for each workgroup. A network with multiple workgroups usually results in client machines within the workgroup assuming the role of a browser server. End users often reboot their machines many times per day, which causes many elections to take place and results in an unstable browsing environment. One remedy is to consolidate client machines into fewer workgroups and run fewer protocols on client machines.

The "Tuning the Browser" section later in this chapter provides information on reducing browser-related network traffic and a sample KiXtart script that can be used to eliminate workgroups.

Browser Client Operation

When a machine boots, it sends out a host announcement to the broadcast address of the network (see Figure 12.2). The announcement is heard by the master browser, and the machine is added to the server list. The machine then requests a list of backup browsers for the network so that it can contact a backup browser if a master browser becomes unavailable. The list of backup browser servers is sent to the client from the master browser. At this point, the client is ready to use the browser to list servers and attach to shared resources. In addition, the client machine continues to send host announcements to the master browser every 12 minutes.

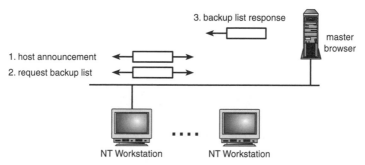

Figure 12.2   *A client machine issues a host announcement and backup list request during the boot process.*

Figure 12.3 illustrates a Network Monitor capture of the startup of a Windows 95 machine named Pokey. Looking at the first three packets, you can see the host announcement, backup list request, and backup list response. Note that the first two packets are sent to the broadcast address, whereas the response to the backup list request is a directed datagram sent to the requesting client's specific address.

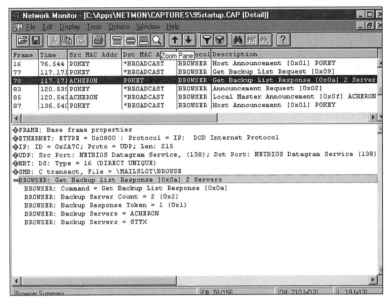

Figure 12.3 *This Network Monitor capture illustrates the traffic associated with the startup of a Windows 95 client.*

When a user opens Network Neighborhood, the client machine sends a NetServerEnum2 API call to the master browser to retrieve the server list, which is presented in Network Neighborhood. When you click on a computer listed in Network Neighborhood, the client machine sends a packet to the selected server requesting a list of available resources.

If a client machine cannot contact the master browser, an election is forced and a new master browser is elected. The new master browser takes the responsibility of maintaining the server list. To expedite the filling of the server list, the master browser can issue a RequestAnnouncement datagram. All computers that receive the datagram issue a host announcement at a random time within the following 30 seconds. The randomized delay ensures that the network and the master browser are not overwhelmed by the responses.

Browsing and NetBIOS Names

Microsoft networking uses *NetBIOS records* to describe various network services. The browser uses NetBIOS records to identify servers and describe the various browser servers on the network. For example, all servers that appear in the browse list have a NetBIOS <20> record, and all domain controllers have a NetBIOS <1C> record indicating they are part of an Internet group. An *Internet group* is a list of up to 25 domain controllers and machines on the list that are used for pass-through authentication.

You can see the NetBIOS records a machine has registered by issuing an
nbtstat -n command to show the local NetBIOS names. Here is the output of
an nbtstat command on a primary domain controller (PDC):

```
H:\>nbtstat -n
Node IpAddress: [10.1.1.1] Scope Id: []
ACHERON      <00>    UNIQUE    Registered
ACHERON      <20>    UNIQUE    Registered
UNDERWORLD   <00>    GROUP     Registered
UNDERWORLD   <1C>    GROUP     Registered
UNDERWORLD   <1B>    UNIQUE    Registered
UNDERWORLD   <1E>    GROUP     Registered
ACHERON      <03>    UNIQUE    Registered
AGBRANHAM    <03>    UNIQUE    Registered
UNDERWORLD   <1D>    UNIQUE    Registered
_MSBROWSE_   <01>    GROUP     Registered
```

NetBIOS names can be either unique or group names. *Unique names* are
unique on the network, whereas *group names* can exist on more than one
machine in the domain or workgroup.

Tables 12.1 and 12.2 list the NetBIOS unique and group names related to the
browser.

Table 12.1   Unique NetBIOS Names

Name	Description
<00>	This record indicates the computer name. It must be registered to receive mailslot requests.
<20>	This record indicates the machine is a server. For Windows NT machines, it means the server service is running. For Windows 95 machines, it means the computer is configured for File and Print Sharing.

Table 12.2   Group NetBIOS Names

Name	Description
__MSBROWSE__.<01>	Used by master browsers to announce their domain on a local subnet.
<00>	Used by workstations and servers to process server announcements to support LAN Manager. Servers running WFWG, Windows 95, and Windows NT do not broadcast this name unless the LMAnnounce option is enabled in the server's properties.
<1B>	Identifies the domain master browser (the PDC).
<1C>	Identifies an Internet group name. All domain controllers register this record.
<1D>	Identifies a master browser. Workstations announce their presence (via host announcements) to this name.
<1E>	Used for all workgroup or domainwide announcements by browser servers in a Windows network. All browser election packets are sent to this name.

Browser Communication

Browser communication uses two APIs:

- `NetServerEnum` (for compatibility with LAN Manager networks)

- `NetServerEnum2`

The API calls are sent using mailslots as the communication mechanism. Browser datagrams destined for LAN Manager, WFWG, Windows 95, or Windows NT machines are sent to the mailslot name \MAILSLOT\LANMAN. Browser datagrams destined for only Windows NT computers are sent to the mailslot name \MAILSLOT\BROWSE.

On TCP/IP networks, the mailslot datagrams are sent to UDP port 138 (NetBIOS datagram services). In addition, the packets are sent to the IP broadcast address of the local subnet.

The browser system on Windows NT is composed of two components:

- The browser service

- The datagram receiver

The *browser service*, which runs in user mode, maintains the browse list and issues API calls. The SERVICES.EXE and BROWSER.DLL files provide support for the browser service. The *datagram receiver* runs in kernel mode and is responsible for receiving datagrams and mailslot messages; it is implemented by the BROWSER.SYS file.

Browser communication results in a significant performance degradation on most networks because of the frequency and broadcast nature of the packets. Table 12.3 illustrates some of the packets and the frequency of each.

Table 12.3   Browser Traffic Summary

Packet	Frequency
Host announcement	Every 12 minutes
Workgroup announcement	Every 15 minutes
Local master announcement	Every 12 minutes
Backup browser server list request	Every 15 minutes

In addition to the packets listed in Table 12.3, there are many other packets associated with elections. If the elections are not biased, or if there are many peer workgroups on the LAN, many elections can result.

When a machine is not powered down gracefully, it never informs the master browser it is going offline. In such a case, the master browser waits for the client to miss three consecutive host announcements before removing it from the server list. When you consider the 15-minute delay between updates of the backup browser server list, you can see that a machine can incorrectly appear in the browse list for up to 51 minutes if it is not powered down properly.

Understanding Browser Elections

A *browser election* determines which machines become browser servers and the role of each one. Computers running WFW, Windows 95, and Windows NT can all become browser servers.

An election is always triggered by any of the following events:

- A computer cannot locate a master browser.

- A backup browser cannot contact the master browser to update itself.

- A computer designated as a preferred master browser comes online.

- A PDC comes online.

- A master browser shuts down correctly.

When a server needs to force an election, it broadcasts an election datagram that contains the election version and election criteria. When an election is initiated, all machines that are potential browsers compete for the opportunity to become a browser server. Figure 12.4 illustrates a Network Monitor capture of an election packet.

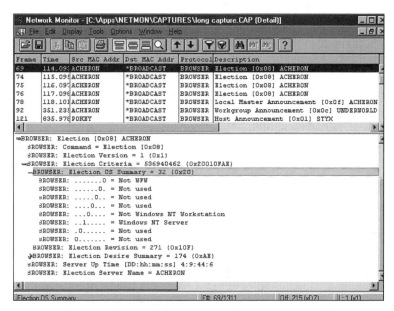

Figure 12.4   *A sample election packet from a Windows NT Server machine.*

Election Criteria

The election process is weighted to give certain machines an advantage over others. The browser election criterion consists of three components:

- Operating system type

- Election version

- Per-version criteria

The election criterion is a 4-byte hexadecimal value. Figure 12.5 illustrates the structure of an election packet.

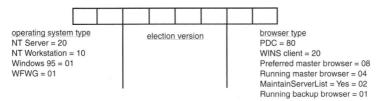

operating system type
NT Server = 20
NT Workstation = 10
Windows 95 = 01
WFWG = 01

election version

browser type
PDC = 80
WINS client = 20
Preferred master browser = 08
Running master browser = 04
MaintainServerList = Yes = 02
Running backup browser = 01

Figure 12.5 *An election packet.*

If the election criteria are identical among a group of machines, the master browser is determined based on the machine that has been running the longest. If two machines have been running for an equal amount of time, the machine with the name that comes first alphabetically is selected to be a master browser.

When a browser receives an election datagram indicating that it wins the election, the browser enters the *running election state*. In this state, the browser sends an election request after a delay based on the browser's current role, as follows:

- 200ms delay for master browsers

- 400ms delay for backup browsers

- 800ms delay for all other browsers

Although machines compete to become master browsers and backup browsers, the role of domain master browser is always given to the PDC of the domain. If you promote a backup domain controller (BDC) to a PDC, a browser election is forced and the new PDC takes over the role of domain master browser. The domain master browser is very special because it allows you to browse across TCP/IP subnets.

Browsing Across Subnets

TCP/IP subnets are separated by routers and routers block broadcast messages. Unfortunately, most of the browser functionality relies on broadcast datagrams. Thus, on a TCP/IP network, each subnet is a separate browsing entity. As a result, a master browser is elected for each subnet. If the master browser happens to be part of a domain, it can communicate with the domain master browser (Figure 12.6). When a domain spans multiple subnets, the master browsers for each subnet announce themselves to the domain master browser using MasterBrowserAnnouncement directed datagrams. The domain master browser then sends a NetServerEnum call to the master browser that announced itself to collect that subnet's list of servers.

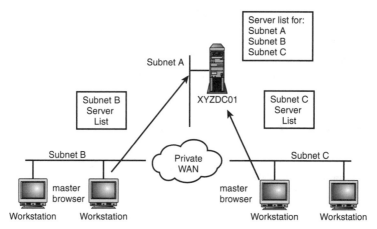

Figure 12.6   *The master browser on each subnet communicates with the domain master browser.*

There are two requirements for a machine to browse across subnets:

- The machine must be a member of a domain.

- The machine must use WINS or LMHOSTS to communicate with machines on other subnets.

The first requirement is easy: Simply install a PDC and join all machines to the domain. The second requirement is a bit more difficult: If you use LMHOSTS, you must use the #DOM directive to identify the PDC to the client. Otherwise, the client is able to contact the PDC by IP address, but it doesn't realize it must use that IP address for domain functions such as authentication and browsing.

Author's Note

WINS is a solution superior to LMHOSTS and is less problematic. Furthermore, WINS allows you to dynamically assign IP addresses on remote subnets, whereas LMHOSTS requires static IP address assignments.

Following are the characteristics of browsing across subnets:

- Workgroups cannot span subnets. If a workgroup includes machines on separate subnets, each functions as a separate workgroup.

- The ability to expand a workgroup or domain depends on the ability to resolve the master browser's computer name.

- The ability to connect to a resource in a workgroup depends on the ability to resolve the computer name.

- The <1B> records registered with WINS are used to build domain lists.

Tuning the Browser

Tuning the browser for performance and consistency is an essential task in an enterprise environment. You can control the browser by controlling the machines that can become master browser servers. A client workstation should never become a browser server because it is usually rebooted more frequently than network servers. The reboot of a browser server forces elections and creates inconsistent browse lists. Only select servers should be master browsers.

There are many steps you can take to improve browser performance on large networks. Here is a list of tasks you should consider:

- Prevent client workstations from becoming master browsers or backup browsers.

- Weigh selected servers to win browser elections.

- Reduce the number of network protocols.

- Reduce the number of servers in the server list.

- Reduce the number of workgroups.

The method for preventing client workstations from becoming browser servers differs depending on the operating system:

For WFW:

1. Open the SYSTEM.INI file.

2. Go to the [Network] section.

3. Set `MaintainServerList` to `No`.

For Windows 95:

1. Open the Control Panel.

2. Click on the Networking icon.

3. Select File and Printer Sharing for Microsoft Networks.

4. Click on Properties.

5. Set `BrowseMaster` to `No`.

For Windows NT:

1. Open the Registry using REGEDT32.EXE.

2. Go to HKEY_LOCAL_MACHINE\System\CurrentControlSet Services\ Browser\Parameters\.

3. Set the `MaintainServerList` value to `No`.

In addition to restricting a computer's capability of becoming a browser server, you can also weigh the criteria for a Windows NT system so that it is favored in an election. Follow these steps to weigh an NT machine's participation in an election:

1. Open the Registry using REGEDT32.EXE.

2. Go to HKEY_LOCAL_MACHINE\System\CurrentControlSet Services\Browser\Parameters\.

3. Set the `IsDomainMaster` value to `True`.

Only machines that share resources should appear in the browse list. Consequently, you should disable File and Printer Sharing for Microsoft Networks on all Windows 95 and WFW machines that do not have resources to share on the network.

Eliminating Workgroups

One of the biggest problems on larger networks is that of numerous Windows 95 workgroups. Because the browser traffic uses broadcast messaging, a large number of workgroups introduces a major performance degradation on most networks. The only solution to the problem is to consolidate workgroups or eliminate them altogether.

Windows NT Workstation forces the computer to be a member of a domain or a workgroup, but not both. However, Windows 95 allows you to log on to a domain, yet establish a separate workgroup (see Figure 12.7). This often results in a single domain LAN with numerous workgroups used to classify the machines.

Although the workgroups help organize the machines, they do so with an increase of broadcast traffic on the network; this reduces network performance and should be eliminated. A great way to consolidate all workgroups into a single domain is to modify the Windows 95 Registry with a KiXtart script during user logon. The script in Listing 12.1 consolidates all Windows 95 workgroups into a single XYZ domain.

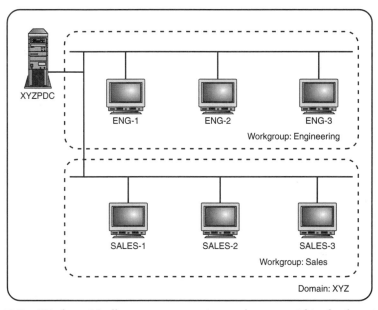

Figure 12.7   *Windows 95 allows you to organize workgroups within the domain.*

Listing 12.1   *A KiXtart Script to Eliminate Workgroups*

```
; Force 95 Machines into Workgroup XYZ and Disable their Browser Service
;
If @InWin=2 ;We're running 95
$Browser=ReadValue("HKEY_LOCAL_MACHINE\System\CurrentcontrolSet\Services\VxD\
VNETSUP", "MaintainServerList")
    If $Browser=0
        ;Browser Already Disabled - Do Nothing
    Else
$Hidden=WriteValue("HKEY_LOCAL_MACHINE\System\CurrentcontrolSet\Services\VxD\
VNETSUP", "MaintainServerList", "0", "REG_SZ")
```

continues

Continued

```
    Endif
;
;
$Workgroup=ReadValue("HKEY_LOCAL_MACHINE\System\CurrentcontrolSet\Services\VxD\
VNETSUP", "Workgroup")
    If $Workgroup=XYZ
        ;Workgroup Already XYZ - Do Nothing
    Else
$Hidden=WriteValue("HKEY_LOCAL_MACHINE\System\CurrentcontrolSet\Services\VxD\
VNETSUP", "Workgroup", "XYZ", #REG_SZ")
    Endif
;
;
    If $Browser=0 and $Workgroup=XYZ
        ; Everything is Already Set - Do Nothing
    Else
        $Confirm=MessageBox("The MIS Department has just updated your machine.
Please Shutdown and Restart your machine to initialize the new settings. Thanks
for your cooperation.", "MIS Staff", 64)
    Endif
Endif
;
```

Browser Troubleshooting

Browsing is difficult to control and even more difficult to troubleshoot. However, most browsing problems are usually related to timing issues, and they end up correcting themselves. For example, when a master browser shuts down, the clients must retrieve a potentially incomplete server list from a backup browser, at which time an election is forced and the new master browser quickly fills its server list by forcing all servers on the network to announce themselves.

Here are some guidelines to help you troubleshoot browser problems:

- Check the client's network configuration. You must ensure the computer has the Microsoft or Novell client loaded, the correct protocols installed, and the correct configuration for each protocol.

- If a domain is missing from the browse list, check WINS to ensure that the PDC of the appropriate domain has registered a <1B> record.

- If you suspect a problem with a browser server, you can use BROWMON.EXE or BROWSTAT.EXE from the Windows NT Server Resource Kit to help you determine which computers are acting as master and backup browsers.

There are two utilities in the Windows NT Server Resource Kit that are useful for troubleshooting enterprise browser problems: BROWMON.EXE and BROWSTAT.EXE. These are discussed in the following sections.

BROWMON.EXE

BROWMON.EXE is a graphical utility that is useful for determining the browser servers on the network (see Figure 12.8).

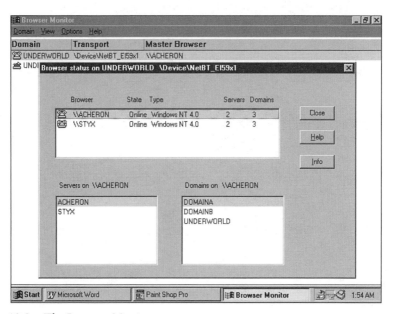

Figure 12.8 *The Browser Monitor.*

BROWMON.EXE provides the following statistics for each browser server:

    Number of Server Announcements

    Number of Domain Announcements

    Number of Election Packets

    Number of Mailslot Writes

    Number of GetBrowserServerList Requests

    Number of Server Enumerations

    Number of Domain Enumerations

    Number of Other Enumerations

    Number of Duplicate Master Announcements

    Number of Illegal Datagrams

BROWSTAT.EXE

BROWSTAT.EXE is a command-line utility that is generally more useful than
BROWMON.EXE. You can use BROWSTAT.EXE not only to gather statistical
information but also to force browser events such as a master browser stop or
an election.

The syntax of the browstat command is

```
BROWSTAT Command [Options ¦ /HELP]
```

where <Command> is one of the following:

ELECT	(EL)	Forces election on remote domain.
GETBLIST	(GB)	Gets backup list for domain.
GETMASTER	(GM)	Gets remote master browser name (using NetBIOS).
GETPDC	(GP)	Gets PDC name (using NetBIOS).
LISTWFW	(WFW)	Lists WFW servers that are actually running browsers.
STATS	(STS)	Dumps browser statistics.
STATUS	(STA)	Displays status about a domain.
TICKLE	(TIC)	Forces remote master to stop.
VIEW	(VW)	Remotes NetServerEnum to a server or domain on transport.

In server (or domain) list displays, the following flags are used:

```
W=Workstation

S=Server

SQL=SQLServer

PDC=PrimaryDomainController

BDC=BackupDomainController

TS=TimeSource

AFP=AFPServer

NV=Novell

MBC=MemberServer

PQ=PrintServer

DL=DialinServer

XN=Xenix

NT=Windows NT

WFW=WindowsForWorkgroups

MFPN=MS Netware
```

```
SS=StandardServer

PBR=PotentialBrowser

BBR=BackupBrowser

MBR=MasterBrowser

DMB=DomainMasterBrowser

OSF=OSFServer

VMS=VMSServer

W95=Windows95

DFS=DistributedFileSystem
```

Many of the BROWSTAT.EXE functions require you to provide the transport used by your machine. You can get the transport information by issuing a net config rdr command. For example, the following net config rdr reveals a transport of NetBT_El59x1:

```
H:\>net config rdr
Computer name                   \\ACHERON
User name                       AGBranham

Workstation active on           NetBT_E159x1 (00A02475D133) NetBT_NdisWan5
(000000000000)
Software version                Windows NT 4.0

Workstation domain              UNDERWORLD
Logon domain                    UNDERWORLD

COM Open Timeout (sec)          3600
COM Send Count (byte)           16
COM Send Timeout (msec)         250
```

Chapter 13

Enterprise Services: DHCP, WINS, and DNS

This chapter will review:

- **DHCP Implementation**
  DHCP is a Windows NT service that you can use to automatically assign
  TCP/IP properties to client workstations. If used properly, DHCP can
  save you a tremendous amount of time when you must make network
  changes. This section explores DHCP operation and implementation
  strategies.

- **NetBIOS and Domain Names**
  NetBIOS names are used by all Microsoft operating systems for file and
  print sharing. Domain names are used to identify and distinguish TCP/IP
  clients.

- **WINS Overview**
  WINS is the premier solution for NetBIOS name resolution. It offers
  dynamic registration of computer names and allows browsing across
  TCP/IP subnets.

- **DNS Overview**
  DNS is not a requirement for Microsoft networks. However, it is a key
  service in Windows 2000 and will surely be a necessary skill for any
  network administrator in the near future.

DHCP Implementation

A typical TCP/IP client machine requires the following TCP/IP parameters:

- IP address
- Subnet mask
- Default gateway

- Primary and secondary WINS servers

- Primary and secondary DNS servers

Setting these parameters for each workstation on a large network is time-consuming and error-prone. To automate the process, Windows NT Server provides a Dynamic Host Configuration Protocol (DHCP) service. Only Windows NT server can act as a DHCP server, but you can configure Windows NT workstations and servers as DHCP clients.

The DHCP server is configured with a pool of available IP addresses called a *scope* and optional parameters to assign to DHCP clients (see Figure 13.1). Typical DHCP clients include Windows for Workgroups, Windows 95, and Windows NT Workstation.

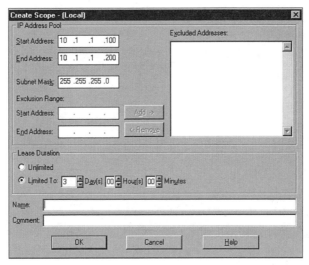

Figure 13.1   *The DHCP server is configured with a pool of IP addresses to fulfill incoming requests from DHCP clients.*

Warning

If you install Routing and Remote Access Server (RRAS) and use virtual private networking (VPN), be careful when using DHCP to assign addresses to VPN clients. According to the number of VPN clients you specify, the RRAS server will remove that number of addresses from the DHCP server. For example, if you have a DHCP pool of 200 addresses and configure 100 VPN clients, the RRAS server immediately leases 100 DHCP address on behalf of the VPN clients. Such action can result in using the entire DHCP pool unexpectedly.

A DHCP client obtains its IP address by contacting a DHCP server. The conversation between the client and the server consists of four packets, all of which have a fixed length of 342 bytes and are sent to the limited broadcast address of 255.255.255.255. The entire process takes about 300ms on a LAN. Table 13.1 outlines each of the four packets.

Table 13.1   DHCP Client-Server Packets

Packet	Description
DHCP Discover	This is the first packet. Its purpose is to locate any DHCP server with available addresses. Because the client is not configured with an address of a DHCP server, this is a broadcast packet that is accepted by any DHCP server. The source IP address in the packet is set to 0.0.0.0.
DHCP Offer	The DHCP server hears the DHCP Discover packet and selects the next available IP address from its pool of addresses. The address is encapsulated in a DHCP Offer packet that is sent to the requesting client. Every DHCP server that hears the packet makes a DHCP Offer.
DHCP Request	Although the DHCP client may hear more than one DHCP Offer, it responds to the first DHCP Offer with a DHCP Request packet. Because the DHCP Request is a broadcast packet, it is heard by all DHCP servers that have made an offer to the client. The servers whose offers were not accepted return the offered IP address to their pool of available addresses.
DHCP Acknowledge	To finalize the client settings, the DHCP server whose offer is requested issues a DHCP Acknowledge packet. Depending on the lease duration for the IP address, the client may have to periodically contact the server to continue using its assigned IP address.

Figure 13.2 illustrates the traffic used by a DHCP client to obtain an IP address from a DHCP server.

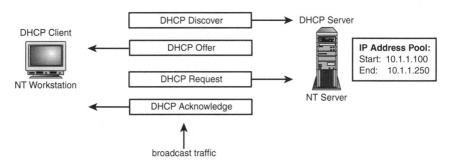

Figure 13.2 *Discover, Offer, Request, and Acknowledge are the four steps to acquiring an IP address from a DHCP server.*

You can configure the DHCP server to make three types of IP address assignments:

- *Random leased addresses.* This is the best method because it offers you the flexibility of altering your IP address assignments very easily. Windows NT DHCP servers default to this type of assignment with a default lease time of three days. Although not usually necessary, you can increase the lease time to decrease the number of renewals and lower network traffic (see the "DHCP Network Traffic" section later in this chapter).

- *Random permanent addresses.* This is accomplished by setting the lease duration to Unlimited. You should avoid this type of assignment if possible because it creates a network you cannot change. When the clients receive a TCP/IP address, they never contact the server again—preventing you from easily changing your IP address scheme or adding and changing options. If you are considering a permanent assignment, it is strongly suggested that you use a random leased assignment and set the lease time to a long period.

- *Static addresses.* This type of address is called a *reservation* in the DHCP Manager. It basically links the MAC address of a network interface card to a specific IP address assignment. This is not a good idea because it will cause chaos if you ever replace a network card.

Author's Note

The algorithm used to assign IP addresses is not truly random. It is actually a sequential algorithm that assigns the next available IP address until the pool is exhausted. However, "random" is used in this discussion to imply that a client may not receive the same IP address each time it renews its address.

The IP address and network parameters assigned by the DHCP server do not appear in the Network Configuration dialog boxes found in Control Panel. For Windows NT machines, you can type `ipconfig /all` in a command window to reveal its network parameters assigned by DHCP. With Windows 95, a graphical utility called WINIPCFG.EXE can be used.

Figure 13.3 shows the output of the `ipconfig /all` command. Notice that the IP address of the DHCP server is listed. After receiving a valid IP address, the DHCP client must periodically renew the address depending on the lease duration. After 50% of the lease duration expires, the client attempts to contact the original DHCP server. After 75% of the lease time expires, the client attempts once again to contact the original DHCP server. If 87.5% of the lease time expires, the client issues a broadcast packet (rather than a directed datagram) and attempts to contact any DHCP server.

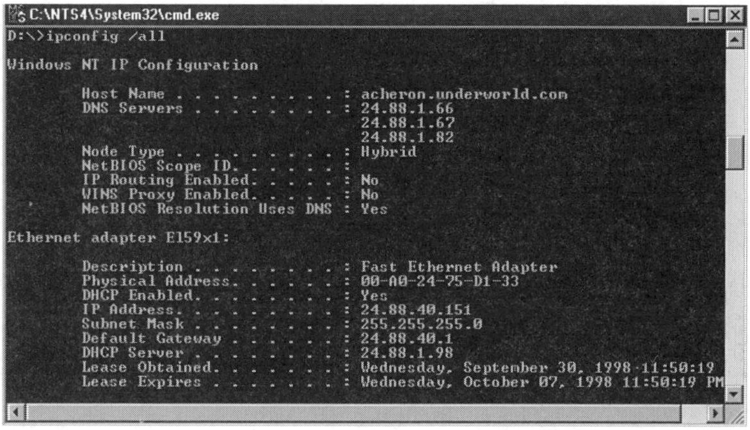

```
C:\NTS4\System32\cmd.exe                                          _ □ ✕
D:\>ipconfig /all

Windows NT IP Configuration

        Host Name . . . . . . . . . : acheron.underworld.com
        DNS Servers . . . . . . . . : 24.88.1.66
                                      24.88.1.67
                                      24.88.1.82
        Node Type . . . . . . . . . : Hybrid
        NetBIOS Scope ID. . . . . . :
        IP Routing Enabled. . . . . : No
        WINS Proxy Enabled. . . . . : No
        NetBIOS Resolution Uses DNS : Yes

Ethernet adapter E159x1:

        Description . . . . . . . . : Fast Ethernet Adapter
        Physical Address. . . . . . : 00-A0-24-75-D1-33
        DHCP Enabled. . . . . . . . : Yes
        IP Address. . . . . . . . . : 24.88.40.151
        Subnet Mask . . . . . . . . : 255.255.255.0
        Default Gateway . . . . . . : 24.88.40.1
        DHCP Server . . . . . . . . : 24.88.1.98
        Lease Obtained. . . . . . . : Wednesday, September 30, 1998 11:50:19
        Lease Expires . . . . . . . : Wednesday, October 07, 1998 11:50:19 PM
```

Figure 13.3   *The Windows NT* ipconfig *command displays the parameters assigned by the DHCP server.*

Tip

You can force a DHCP client to give its IP address back to the DHCP server by issuing an ipconfig /release *command in Windows NT. Likewise, you can issue an* ipconfig /renew *command to get an IP address from a DHCP server. These two commands can be used in logon scripts to force the renewal of an IP address and associated DHCP parameters.*

The configuration parameters related to DHCP are located in the Registry. You can find the DHCP Registry parameters in the following location:

```
HKEY_LOCAL_MACHINE\SYSTEM\CurrentControlSet\Services\DHCPServer\Parameters
```

DHCP Network Traffic

The amount of DHCP traffic on a network is related to several factors. DHCP traffic results from the following situations:

- A DHCP client initializes (four packets).

- A DHCP client machine reboots (two packets).

- A DHCP client renews its address (two packets).

- You move a DHCP client to a new subnet (six packets).

- You replace the network adapter of a DHCP client (four packets).
- The `ipconfig /release` command is issued (one packet).
- The `ipconfig /renew` command is issued (four packets).

For most networks the amount of DHCP traffic is minimal. In fact, at the 1997 TechEd conference Microsoft presented a study revealing that less than one percent of network traffic results from DHCP. The only way to decrease DHCP traffic is to increase the lease duration, forcing clients to renew their addresses less frequently. However, you must be careful not to set the lease duration too long if you have a large number of mobile clients on your network or a small address pool.

DHCP Strategies

DHCP is a wonderful tool that is highly recommended. However, there are a few issues you must consider when using DHCP:

- You must select the best type of address assignment (random leased, random permanent, or static).
- You must select a lease duration for a leased pool of addresses.
- For larger networks, you need fault tolerance to avoid a single point of failure.

The following sections help you determine the best choices and methods for accomplishing these tasks.

Leveraging the Dynamics of DHCP

To leverage the greatest benefit from DHCP you should use random leased addresses because they offer the maximum flexibility. Suppose you are using DHCP and do not currently have a DNS server. When you add a DNS server, you can use DHCP to provide the address of the DNS server to all DHCP clients by configuring a Global or Scope DHCP option. Within the specified lease duration, all DHCP clients receive the new parameter when they renew their IP addresses. To be crafty, you can lower the lease time before adding or changing a DHCP option. Thus, after the option is changed, it is propagated to the clients more quickly. Such automation is a great asset to a busy administrator.

The lease duration greatly depends on the number of IP addresses in the DHCP pool, the number of mobile users, and the frequency and duration of use by the mobile clients. When a machine shuts down, it does not release its IP address back to the DHCP pool. Therefore, the address remains unavailable until the lease duration expires and the address is returned to the pool.

Suppose you are the administrator of a sales office with a DHCP pool of 100 addresses. There are 50 addresses dynamically assigned to desktops and servers, leaving 50 available address for mobile users. The lease duration is set to seven days. Twenty salespeople attach laptops to the network on Monday and use 20 of the available addresses. On Wednesday, 15 more mobile users acquire DHCP addresses. On Friday, several salespeople are at the office for training, and 20 of the trainees decide to plug in their laptops to retrieve their corporate email during lunch. As you would expect, five of the 20 users cannot obtain DHCP addresses because the pool is exhausted. A three-day lease would have prevented the problem by returning the addresses assigned on Monday to the pool on Wednesday, making 35 leases available on Friday.

> **Tip**
>
> *You can extend the DHCP pool dynamically by changing the End Address of the DHCP pool. This makes more addresses available while leaving all the underlying leases undisturbed.*

DHCP Server Placement

Ideally, you should try to place a DHCP server on every LAN. However, in some cases this is impossible, and the clients must obtain their IP addresses from a DHCP server across a WAN.

If a DHCP server is located across a router, you must enable BOOTP forwarding on the router or use a DHCP relay agent to get the DHCP packets across it. DHCP is based on the BOOTP protocol—a broadcast protocol used to support diskless workstations. Because of its broadcast format, the DHCP packets are blocked by routers.

> **Tip**
>
> *The original Windows NT 4 DHCP server ignored BOOTP requests. However, with Service Pack 2, the DHCP server provided TCP/IP information for BOOTP clients.*

The process of enabling BOOTP forwarding on a router differs from vendor to vendor. However, the DHCP Relay Agent (see Figure 13.4) is available on Windows NT Server and accomplishes the same objective. The DHCP Relay Agent inserts its IP address into the gateway interface address (GIADDR) field of a DHCP broadcast packet that it sends to a specific DHCP server located across a router. The DHCP server uses the information in the GIADDR field to send the packet back to the requesting client through the DHCP Relay Agent.

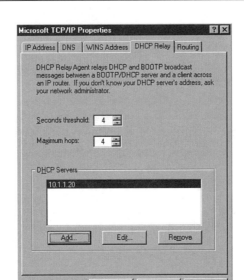

Figure 13.4 *The DHCP Relay Agent is used to forward DHCP broadcast packets to a DHCP server located beyond a router.*

You can place more than one DHCP server on the same LAN. However, you must be sure that the servers are configured with address pools that do not overlap. DHCP servers do not communicate with each other like WINS servers and DNS servers; consequently, DHCP servers are unaware of the presence of other DHCP servers.

> **Tip**
>
> *You can use DHCPLOC.EXE from the Windows NT Resource Kit to locate other DHCP servers on the local subnet.*

DHCP Fault Tolerance

You can introduce DHCP fault tolerance into your network by splitting an address pool between two DHCP servers. Microsoft recommends a 75/25 split, but you can use any percentage you feel comfortable with. Figure 13.5 illustrates a DHCP fault-tolerant network in which the failure of DHCP Server A forces the client to use DHCP Server B.

> **Tip**
>
> *In reality, you do not immediately suffer from a downed DHCP server. By design of the address renewal process, you have at least 50% of the lease duration to recover the downed server before clients lose their lease.*

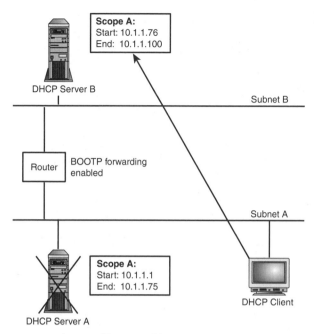

Figure 13.5   *You can split an address pool between two servers for fault tolerance.*

NetBIOS and Domain Names

NetBIOS is a command set used for file and print sharing on Microsoft networks. In Windows NT, NetBIOS is implemented as an API that can be called over any underlying protocol. NetBIOS names are 16 bytes (characters) in length. The first 15 bytes are used to store the name and the last byte is used to store a code that describes the NetBIOS name or service. The code stored in the 16th byte is often referred to as the NetBIOS suffix. To see the NetBIOS names registered by a Windows NT machine, type `nbtstat -n` in a command window.

Author's Note

> *The 15 character limitation of the computer name on a Microsoft network results from the NetBIOS limitation explained above.*

Making the distinction between a computer's NetBIOS name and domain name is important. As long as your computer is networked, it has a NetBIOS name (see Figure 13.6). The name is used by the browser to display the computer and its shared resources. If the computer uses the TCP/IP protocol, it also has a host name and a domain name, which are part of the TCP/IP properties (see Figure 13.7). The domain name is appended to the host name to form what is called a *fully qualified domain name (FQDN)*.

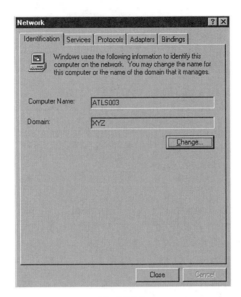

Figure 13.6   *The computer name is a NetBIOS name.*

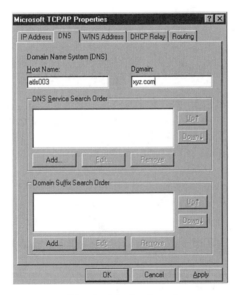

Figure 13.7   *The host name combined with the domain name constitute the FQDN for a machine.*

NetBIOS names and domain names are both used to access a machine's resources. The name that is used depends on the client application. The PING.EXE utility, for example, assumes the name used is a domain name, whereas the NET.EXE utility assumes the name is a NetBIOS name. Because computers communicate using network addresses rather than names, the names must be translated to an IP address on TCP/IP networks (see Figure 13.8).

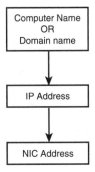

Figure 13.8 *NetBIOS and domain names must be resolved to IP addresses, and IP addresses must be resolved to network adapter addresses to communicate on a TCP/IP network.*

NetBIOS Namespace Limitations

The biggest problem with NetBIOS names is the lack of a hierarchical naming structure. NetBIOS uses what is known as a *flat namespace*, whereas domain names use a *hierarchical naming structure*. When using a centralized name resolution mechanism such as WINS within a large organization, you may encounter many problems with conflicting computer names. The hierarchical structure of DNS eliminates the potential of name conflicts.

Figure 13.9 illustrates the problem. Company XYZ has two sales offices: one in Atlanta and one in Boston. There is a computer at each office named SALES01. One of the two computers is unable to register with the WINS server because of the name conflict.

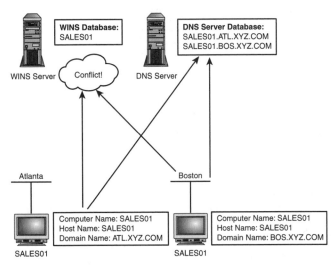

Figure 13.9 *One of the two SALES01 machines is unable to register with the WINS server, which cannot distinguish between the two.*

Name Resolution Mechanisms

Name resolution refers to the process of mapping a computer name (NetBIOS or domain name) to a network address. On a TCP/IP network, the name must be resolved to an IP address. Because a TCP/IP client has both a NetBIOS name and a domain name, confusion can easily arise. Depending on the type of name, a variety of name resolution mechanisms can be used.

Here is a list of name resolution mechanisms, in no particular order:

- *NetBIOS name cache.* Each time you resolve a name to an IP address, the name/address combination is placed in your computer's local NetBIOS name cache. For Windows NT machines, the cache has a 10-minute timeout. Your interface to the cache is the NBTSTAT.EXE command: Type `nbtstat -c` in a command window to reveal your machine's NetBIOS name cache.

- *Broadcast name resolution.* Broadcast name resolution is the most basic method for resolving a NetBIOS name. It is the equivalent of walking into a crowded room and yelling someone's name. If the person you are looking for is in the room, he or she responds.

- *LMHOSTS file.* This mechanism is a carryover from the LAN Manager days. As you may suspect, its purpose is to resolve NetBIOS names. The file is static and must be distributed to every client machine.

- *HOSTS file.* The HOSTS file is a carryover from UNIX used to resolve domain names. Much like the LMHOSTS file, it is static in nature and must be distributed to every client machine.

- *WINS server.* WINS is a robust name resolution mechanism that supports centralized, dynamic registration and resolution of NetBIOS names. WINS clients query the WINS server directly when looking for the IP address of another machine.

- *DNS server.* DNS, another robust name resolution mechanism, is used to resolve domain names to IP addresses. The resolution is performed by querying a centralized static database (instead of the dynamic database used by WINS).

WINS is the best mechanism for NetBIOS name resolution, whereas DNS is the best mechanism for domain name resolution. The other mechanisms are generally regarded as backup methods. The static HOSTS and LMHOSTS files require a lot of work because they must be updated and distributed every time a machine is added or removed or has its IP address modified. Furthermore, you cannot use HOSTS, LMHOSTS, or DNS to resolve names of DHCP clients because the DHCP client's IP addresses can change.

The order in which the resolution mechanisms are used depends on the application, the node type of the client, and the extensions enabled on the client. Applications derived from the UNIX world use domain name resolution mechanisms, whereas applications related to Microsoft file and print sharing use NetBIOS name resolution mechanisms. There are two extensions related to name resolution:

- Enable DNS for Windows Resolution

- Enable LMHOSTS Lookup

The extensions are set via Control Panel, Network, Protocols tab, TCP/IP, Properties, WINS tab. The role of the extension in the name resolution process is discussed in the "Name Resolution Order" section of this chapter.

Node Types

The *node type* determines the order in which a client uses broadcast name resolution and/or WINS name resolution. The node type is configured in the Registry and cannot be accessed via the Control Panel. By default, Windows NT clients are set to b-node; however, when you turn a computer into a WINS client by giving it the address of a WINS server, the client is automatically changed to h-node. Figure 13.10 summarizes the node types and how each affects the resolution mechanisms used.

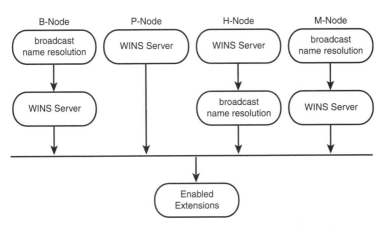

Figure 13.10   *There are four node types for Microsoft clients. The node type determines the type and order of resolution mechanisms used.*

For networks that use WINS, h-node offers the best advantage. Broadcast queries are eliminated because h-node clients query the WINS server first. And, if the WINS server becomes unavailable, the clients can resort to broadcast name resolution. Using broadcast name resolution, the clients can at least browse and attach to resources on the local subnet.

Tip

If you use DHCP to assign a WINS server to DHCP clients, you must also assign the node type. Otherwise, the DHCP clients remain config-ured to the default b-node type, using only broadcast name resolution for NetBIOS names. The option in DHCP is listed as 046.

Name Resolution Order

The order of name resolution mechanisms depends on the node type, the enabled extensions used, and whether the client program treats the name as a NetBIOS name or a domain name. For example, email clients use domain names, whereas mapping a drive to a Microsoft server uses a NetBIOS name. The node type determines whether a client issues a broadcast or sends a WINS query first. The extensions enable the use of DNS for resolution of NetBIOS names and the use of an LMHOSTS file. To present an ordered list of the name resolution mechanisms, assumptions about the extensions and client node type must be made. For the listings, it can be assumed that the clients are set to h-node and the extensions for DNS and LMHOSTS are enabled.

For a NetBIOS name, the name resolution mechanisms are used in the following order:

- NetBIOS name cache
- Primary WINS (three queries)
- Secondary WINS (three queries)
- Broadcast name resolution (three broadcasts)
- LMHOSTS
- DNS

For a domain name, the name resolution mechanisms are used in the following order:

- HOSTS
- DNS
- Primary WINS (three queries)
- Secondary WINS (three queries)
- Broadcast name resolution (three broadcasts)
- LMHOSTS

WINS Overview

Windows Internet Name Service (WINS) is a centralized, dynamic database used to register and resolve NetBIOS names. WINS runs only on Windows NT Server and not on Windows NT Workstation. You can configure clients to use WINS by adding the address of a WINS server to their TCP/IP properties. The WINS clients then make use of the WINS server to accomplish four tasks:

- *Name registration.* WINS clients register their NetBIOS information with a WINS server during the boot process. The name registration process is illustrated in Figure 13.11. In this example, the SALES01 computer registers its computer name (00 record), messenger service (03 record), and server service (20 record) with the WINS server.

- *Name renewal.* A computer's name registration is good only for the amount of time that is specified via the WINS server (four days by default). The client must issue a name refresh request periodically to the WINS server to maintain an active entry in the database.

- *Name resolution.* WINS clients send queries to a primary WINS server to discover another computer's IP address based on the target computer's NetBIOS name. If the primary WINS server is unavailable, the WINS client queries the secondary WINS server. The WINS server returns the target computer's IP address to the WINS client, and the WINS client proceeds to contact the target computer by IP address using a directed datagram.

- *Name release.* During a controlled shutdown, a WINS client sends a name release request to the WINS server to inform the server that it is going offline.

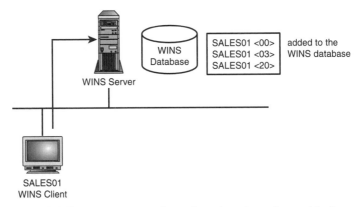

Figure 13.11 *A WINS server supports dynamic registration of a machine's computer name and NetBIOS services.*

WINS offers the following advantages:

- It reduces network traffic created during broadcast resolution.

- Because the WINS database is dynamic, no human intervention is required to register the NetBIOS names and IP addresses.

- The dynamic database used by WINS works great with DHCP clients.

- Some browser traffic is eliminated.

- Domain workstations and servers can access resources across subnets.

- Domain workstations and servers can browse across subnets.

WINS also suffers from the following disadvantages:

- All computers that register with WINS must have unique NetBIOS names in the WINS database. This creates many problems when dealing with a company merger or integrating multiple business units.

- You must configure at least two WINS servers and WINS replication to avoid a single point of failure.

- WINS replication for an enterprise network can be very complicated.

- WINS offers no ability to restrict registrations and queries.

Enterprise WINS Configuration

Enterprise WINS configuration can be challenging. You must decide how many WINS servers are needed, where to locate them, how to configure WINS replication, and how to achieve a reasonable convergence time for the namespace. There is no calculation that yields the magical number of servers or the magical configuration settings—there is only a process of iterative tuning and singular network changes you must perform until you achieve the balance you desire.

Nevertheless, there are some guidelines you can follow. According to Microsoft, a single WINS server can support up to 10,000 users, although it is doubtful that you want to load a WINS server with that many clients. The WINS server service is quite efficient and streamlined. In most enterprise networks, it is not a matter of the number of clients per WINS server, but it is a matter of correctly locating WINS servers.

WINS usually has a minimal impact on a network. WINS packets are small, ranging from 196 bytes for a name resolution packet to 214 bytes for all other packets (registration, renewal, and release). A WINS client issues WINS traffic under the following conditions:

- A *name registration request* is issued when a WINS client boots. If the client already has an entry in the database, the entry is marked active and the time-to-live (TTL) is updated. If the client is a domain workstation, a WINS query for a domain controller is also issued.

- A WINS client issues a *name refresh request* when half of the TTL expires.

- A WINS client generates *name resolution requests* when the client must access resources on any other machine.

- A WINS client communicates a *name release request* to the WINS server during a controlled shutdown. This marks the entry as inactive in the WINS database.

With the preceding list, you can see that the amount of WINS traffic on a network depends on several criteria. For example, users sharing data in a peer-networking situation generate more traffic than users in a client-server networking situation—because the peer networking forces each user to retrieve data from multiple computers, thereby forcing the resolution of multiple names.

> *Tip*
>
> *You can reduce the amount of WINS traffic on a network by leaving machines on, increasing the WINS TTL, and consolidating resources to fewer servers.*

Consider the WINS planning required to bring a small remote office of 15 computers online. The office has a server that contains most of the data needed by the end users there. However, the end users must be able to reach the corporate network for email and an inventory database. The remote network is connected with a 56K frame relay circuit.

In this case, you must decide how to best leverage the WINS server. If you simply point the clients to the WINS server, they will generate a large number of unnecessary WINS queries to access the other local computers and the local server. Implementing WINS on the server at the remote office would require WINS replication, which not only complicates the setup but also generates replication traffic over the WAN.

Perhaps the best solution is to set the clients to an m-node configuration by changing their Registry settings. This way, the clients would successfully use broadcast resolution to access all local resources and send WINS queries over the WAN only when the resources are not local.

When implementing WINS for enterprise networks, one of the primary goals is to reduce the number of WINS servers. This sometimes means clients must query WINS servers across the WAN. Depending on the balance of use between local and remote resources, the situation may be acceptable. Do not forget that everything in an enterprise network may not always be optimized and sometimes a compromise is acceptable.

WINS Replication

On any connected network with more than one WINS server, you must configure the servers to perform replication. The type of replication and replication partners that should be used are determined by the design of the WINS system.

To simplify the replication process when numerous WINS servers are involved, you should pursue a *hub and spoke configuration*. In other words, you should establish *hub WINS servers* at strategic locations and *spoke servers* to replicate with the hub server. Figure 13.12 illustrates a hub and spoke configuration for a national enterprise network. One hub server is located on the East Coast and another on the West Coast. The two hub servers replicate with each other, and the other WINS servers replicate with the hub servers.

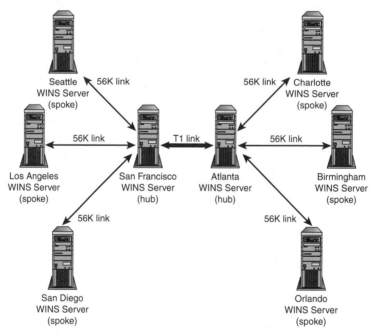

Figure 13.12   *A hub and spoke WINS configuration.*

WINS fault tolerance is limited by the ability to specify only two WINS servers: a primary and a secondary. Consider a client workstation on the Orlando network pictured in Figure 13.12, the client settings of which are illustrated in Figure 13.13. Notice that the primary WINS server is set to the

WINS server on the local LAN. The LAN-located server offers the quickest response and keeps traffic off the 56K WAN link between Atlanta and Orlando. The secondary WINS server is set to the hub server located in Atlanta. For the configuration to work properly when the Orlando WINS server fails, the Orlando WINS server and Atlanta WINS server must perform push and pull replication (which is described shortly) with each other under normal operating conditions. Thus, when the Orlando WINS server fails, the Atlanta WINS server has a complete copy of the Orlando server's database.

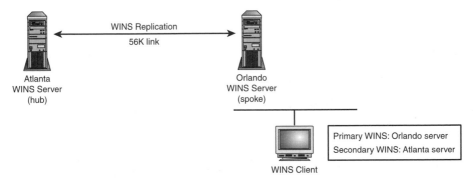

Figure 13.13   *The WINS client configuration for a hub and spoke arrangement.*

> **Tip**
>
> *In networks of two or more WINS servers, registrations owned by the secondary WINS server are an indication of problems with the primary WINS server. Either a client machine was pointed to the wrong primary WINS server or the primary WINS server was unavailable when the client machine performed a name registration.*

There are two types of WINS replication:

- Push replication
- Pull replication

A WINS server can be both a push partner and a pull partner. Additionally, a WINS server can have multiple push and pull partners. A pull partnership is based on a specified time interval: At every interval, a WINS servers pulls the new database entries from its pull partners. The new database entries are identified using the Version ID. For a push partnership, replication of entries is based on the number of updates (or number of new entries). When a WINS server reaches the specified Update Count, it notifies all push partners of the new entries.

In nearly every situation you encounter, you should use push and pull replication between two WINS servers. The pull replication allows you to calculate a definitive convergence time for the namespace, and the push replication ensures that a WINS server is not overwhelmed by a large amount of replication data.

For an enterprise WINS configuration, you must be concerned with the convergence time of the network. The convergence time of the WINS system is the amount of time it takes for a new registration to be replicated to all WINS servers. Suppose you must calculate the convergence time for the network in Figure 13.12. Assume the hub-to-hub replication interval is one hour, and the hub-to-spoke replication intervals are 30 minutes. The longest path through the network is from an East Coast spoke server to a West Coast spoke. Such a path yields a convergence time of 30 minutes plus one hour plus 30 minutes—which equals two hours.

Configuring Intervals and Timeouts

The Configuration selection found on the Server menu in WINS Manager reveals what may seem to be an awkward menu of timers. The intervals and timers describe how a WINS server approaches the removal of database entries. There are four states to a WINS entry:

- During the time a computer is powered on, its record is marked *Active* in the WINS database.

- When the computer goes through a controlled shutdown, its records are marked *Released*.

- From there, the record enters an *Extinct* state.

- Eventually, the records are removed by a process known as *scavenging*.

Figure 13.14 outlines the process. The corresponding WINS time intervals are listed between each transition.

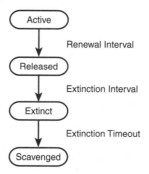

Figure 13.14   *WINS records go through many states before being removed from the database.*

Figure 13.15 illustrates the WINS configuration options containing the interval settings outlined in Figure 13.14.

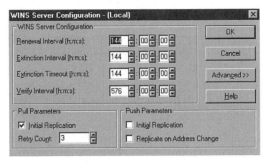

Figure 13.15 *The WINS Server Configuration dialog box contains several timing intervals that can be changed to improve performance on large networks.*

There are four primary configuration options you must consider:

- *Renewal Interval.* This interval specifies the TTL for all WINS registrations owned by the WINS server. WINS clients issue name refresh requests when half of the TTL expires. If the WINS client does not refresh its NetBIOS information within the renewal interval, its records are moved to a released state.

- *Extinction Interval.* This value specifies the amount of time an entry remains released before being declared extinct. The value depends on the renewal interval and the maximum replication time if the WINS server has replication partners. The value should be set to the renewal interval or twice the maximum replication interval, whichever is lower.

- *Extinction Timeout.* This value specifies the amount of time extinct entries remain in the database before they are scavenged (removed) by the WINS server. The value depends on the renewal interval and the maximum replication time between the WINS server and any replication partners. The value should be between one and four days.

- *Verify Interval.* Entries replicated from other WINS servers must be verified based on this interval. The value depends on the extinction interval, with a minimum of 24 days.

Introduction to DNS

Domain Name System (DNS) is a set of protocols and services used to resolve domain names to IP addresses. DNS was first implemented on BSD UNIX to alleviate the singular administration of distributed HOSTS files.

Author's Note

DNS is not a primary need on a network consisting only of Microsoft operating systems; Microsoft file and print services are accessed using NetBIOS names and WINS, not DNS. However, if your network is connected to the Internet or uses email, you must have a DNS server. In such cases, a UNIX or Microsoft DNS server is typically used to resolve a handful of names for Web servers, email servers, and news servers.

The DNS hierarchical namespace allows the name resolution service to be distributed among multiple servers, each having an authority over a specific set of names. Figure 13.16 illustrates the DNS namespace and some of the top-level domains.

At the top of the namespace are the *root servers*. At present there are 13 root servers, which contain the addresses of servers that are responsible for first-level domains such as .com, .edu, .gov, .mil, and so on. When a commercial organization registers its domain name with the InterNIC, the InterNIC adds the domain name to the databases on all DNS servers authoritative for the .com domain. Then the .com DNS servers return the address of the company's DNS server to all clients who query for a machine or domain in your company's namespace.

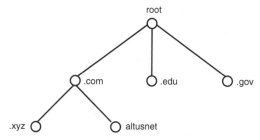

Figure 13.16 *DNS is composed of a hierarchical namespace.*

Configuring a DNS server requires you to manually enter all the domain name and IP address combinations into the static database of the DNS server. Domain names are restricted to the following character sets:

- a–z

- A–Z

- 0–9

- — (dash)

> **Troubleshooting Tip**
>
> *Notice that slashes and underscores are not allowed. You may also want to avoid dashes because they cause problems with ODBC clients.*

> **Tip**
>
> *To prepare for Windows 2000 and the use of DNS namespace, you should make sure all your NetBIOS computer names use only those characters that are allowed by DNS. This will make the transition much easier.*

Unlike WINS servers, DNS servers are specifically configured to be primary or secondary DNS servers. The primary maintains the master copy of the database. Whenever you change entries on the primary database, you must increment the serial number of the file and stop and restart the primary and any secondary nameservers. The newer serial number forces the secondary servers to download the new zone file from the primary nameserver. The process of replicating the DNS database from the primary to the secondary server is called a *zone transfer*.

> **Author's Note**
>
> *In addition to primary and secondary DNS servers, there are also caching-only servers, forwarders, slaves, and stub DNS servers. These types of DNS servers are beyond the scope of this book; they are better left to a book devoted to DNS implementation. One such book that offers excellent coverage of DNS is* Windows NT DNS *by Michael Masterson, Herman Knief, Scott Vinick, and Eric Roul. It is one of the best DNS books I have read to date.*

There are two types of resolution a DNS client can perform:

- *A forward lookup.* This occurs when the DNS client knows the domain name and asks the DNS server for the matching IP address.

- *A reverse lookup.* This occurs when the DNS client knows the IP address and asks the DNS server for the matching domain name.

A Sample Query

DNS clients issue queries to nameservers. The client software that allows a computer to be a DNS client is called a *resolver*. The resolver takes care of the following tasks:

- Querying a nameserver

- Interpreting responses from the nameserver

- Returning information to programs that use the resolver

There are three types of queries a client can issue to a nameserver:

- A recursive query
- An iterative query
- An inverse query

For a recursive query, the nameserver must respond with the requested data or an error. The DNS client (resolver) normally sends this type of query to a DNS server.

For an iterative query, the nameserver can return the best answer it has to the client. Iterative queries are normally issued between two nameservers. Figure 13.17 summarizes the queries and resolution process. The DNS client in the example issues a recursive query for www.microsoft.com to its primary nameserver, which first checks its cache. Assuming there is no entry for www.microsoft.com, microsoft.com, or .com in the cache, the primary nameserver sends an iterative query to a root server. The root server has no knowledge of the exact IP address of www.microsoft.com in its database. However, it does have the IP address of a nameserver authoritative for the .com namespace. Thus, the IP address of the .com nameserver is returned to the primary nameserver. The primary nameserver then issues an iterative query to the .com nameserver. As you may guess, it returns the IP address of the microsoft.com authoritative nameserver. Finally, the microsoft.com nameserver is contacted, and it has the IP address of the WWW host in its database. The target IP address is returned to the primary nameserver, and the primary nameserver returns the address to the DNS client.

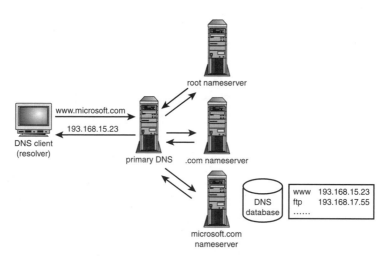

Figure 13.17 *A DNS client generates a recursive DNS query to its primary nameserver, which issues a series of iterative queries to other nameservers to satisfy the original request.*

Notice the number of DNS queries generated. To reduce the number of DNS queries, each DNS server caches the results of each query for a specified amount of time.

Microsoft or UNIX DNS

Berkeley Internet Name Domain (BIND) is the protocol used by DNS. There are several versions of BIND available; in general, the later versions of BIND are developed for UNIX and then ported to Windows NT by third-party companies. Thus, if you want to keep up with the latest BIND, a UNIX DNS server should prove best.

Author's Note

Instead of using the graphical DNS included with Windows NT 4, I prefer to use BIND 4.9.5 available from `http://software.com`. *The Windows NT DNS server is based on an earlier version of BIND and lacks much of the functionality offered by BIND 4.9.5. The latter version of BIND increases network security through its ability to limit zone transfers. In addition, the BIND 4.9.5 product operates like the UNIX implementation of BIND. Consequently, it is much easier to update and administer than the Microsoft DNS server.*

The Microsoft DNS does offer a particular advantage over UNIX DNS servers: a feature referred to as *dynamic DNS* in Windows NT 4. You can configure the zones of the DNS server in Windows NT 4 to use a WINS server for forward and reverse lookup. This allows you to use DHCP to assign client addresses and to use a DNS server to resolve the client domain names if you register the clients with WINS. The system works reasonably well, but the reverse lookup functionality is limited to the subnet on which the DNS server resides. This is because the DNS server performs a reverse lookup by issuing a *NetBIOS node status request*—a broadcast packet that is blocked by routers.

DNS and Windows 2000

The version of DNS included with Windows NT 4 is limited compared to the latest versions available for UNIX. Windows 2000 contains a much newer DNS server based on BIND version 8, which supports dynamic updates, enhanced security features, and SRV records.

SRV records (service locator records) are used to identify service providers. On a Windows 2000 network, they are used to locate and identify domain controllers. The records are also used to store information related to Kerberos two-way transitive trusts.

You can configure the Windows 2000 DHCP server to send updates to the DNS server. This configuration allows clients to obtain a dynamic TCP/IP address and register the address with the DNS server.

Using the Windows 2000 DNS server, you are able to completely eliminate WINS and NetBIOS. When you first install a Windows 2000 domain controller, it defaults to mixed mode. After converting your down-level domain controllers, you can change the domain controllers to native mode. The switch to native mode enables Windows 2000 features such as transitive Kerberos trusts and multimaster replication.

Author's Note

Information on the features of BIND version 8 can be obtained from RFC 2136, which contains information on dynamic DNS updates and RFC 2137, which contains information related to secure dynamic DNS updates. For information on the latest revision to BIND 8, visit http://www.isc.org.

Tip

DNS will play a key role in the transition to IPv6. During the transition period, clients will run both IP stacks—IPv4 and IPv6. The DNS server will be responsible for determining the TCP/IP stack used for an incoming request and returning an answer to the query using the proper IP version.

DNS and Firewalls

A firewall usually forces you to split your DNS services into an external DNS database (to resolve outside queries) and an internal DNS database (to resolve inside queries). Figure 13.18 illustrates the scenario.

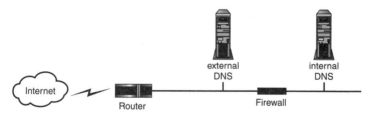

Figure 13.18 *A firewall usually forces you to maintain both an external DNS and an internal DNS.*

You typically need to publish the following entries in your external DNS server database:

- Your Web server(s)

- Your FTP server(s)

- Your email server(s)

- The address of your external router (optional)

- The address of your external firewall interface (optional)

Tip

Your external DNS server can be located inside a firewall. In such a situation, you must map port 53 (used for DNS queries) to the external DNS server located on the inside of the firewall.

Appendix **A**

Working with Performance Monitor

Performance Monitor is an invaluable tool for measuring the performance of Windows NT and BackOffice products. The utility was originally intended for use by developers, but it was later added to the release of Windows NT. Performance Monitor includes many built-in objects (called *core objects*) and allows vendors to add objects (called *extended objects*). Products such as Microsoft Exchange and SQL Server add numerous objects to Performance Monitor.

You can use Performance Monitor to

- Load-balance servers

- Gather estimates for capacity planning

- Detect and troubleshoot bottlenecks

Measuring System Performance

Following are the four primary system resources you should monitor, along with typical questions that monitoring should answer:

- *Disk.* When will you run out of disk space? Is the pagefile sufficiently large? What is the average percentage of the pagefile in use? How well does the system with a RAID 5 controller perform compared to the non-RAID system?

- *Memory.* Does the server need more memory? What process is using the most memory? Are there any programs with a memory leak? What is the memory impact of connecting 100 MS Exchange users compared to connecting 30?

- *Processor.* Is the new multithreaded application efficiently using the second processor? How many processes are running on the system under normal operating conditions? Is there any process that is monopolizing the system?

- *Network.* Is the network card dropping packets? Is the upgrade to switched Ethernet offering any significant performance advantage? Does the in-house program work better with a TCP or a UDP transport? What is the level of broadcast traffic on the network?

All these questions can be answered quickly and easily using Performance Monitor.

Tip

When using Performance Monitor, it is important to remember that you should be concerned with averages, not peaks or dips. If the processor utilization reaches 100% for a few seconds, you should not worry. If it consistently runs at 90%, however, perhaps you should seriously consider investing in a multiprocessor system, moving applications, or changing to a different processor architecture.

Getting Started

The first step in performance monitoring is to enable counters for the network and hard disk. By default, the counters for the disk subsystem are not enabled. You must set the counters to activate upon startup to measure logical and physical disk activity. To do this, you must open a command window and type `diskperf -y`. A reboot of the machine is then required to activate the counters.

Tip

If you use Windows NT RAID capabilities and have a striped disk set, you must use `diskperf -yE` to enable the disk counters. You should also be aware that the logical disk counters are not correct because the system sees two or more disks in a stripe set as a single logical disk.

The next step is to enable the TCP/IP counters and the network segment counter. To enable these counters you must invoke the Network applet in the Control Panel. Go to the Services tab and add the SNMP Service and the Network Monitor Agent. The SNMP Service adds the ICMP, IP, Network Interface, TCP, and UDP object; the Network Monitor Agent adds the Network Segment object. After making these changes to the system, you must restart the machine.

> **Tip**
>
> *After adding the SNMP service, you need to reapply the latest Service Pack. Otherwise, you get an SNMP error when you restart the machine.*

Now you are ready to use Performance Monitor. Performance Monitor is located in the Administrative Tools group on both Windows NT Workstation and Windows NT Server. All system resources appear as an *object*—a system resource that you can measure—in Performance Monitor. Table A.1 lists core objects built into Performance Monitor.

Table A.1   Core Objects in Performance Monitor

Object Name	Description
Cache	A portion of RAM that holds recently used data
LogicalDisk	Disk partitions and other logical views of the hard disk
Memory	RAM
Objects	Certain system software objects
Paging File	A portion of the hard disk used to supplement RAM
PhysicalDisk	Hard disk
Process	Counters for all running programs
Processor	A hardware device that executes program instructions
Redirector	A file system that diverts file requests to network servers
System	Counters that monitor the overall system
Thread	A portion of code that can be executed as a single unit

For each object there is an associated set of *counters*—units of measure for the object. Counters for the Memory Object include the following:

% Committed Bytes In Use	Available Bytes
Cache Bytes	Cache Bytes Peak
Cache Faults/sec	Commit Limit
Committed Bytes	Demand Zero Faults/sec
Free System Page Table Entries	Page Faults/sec
Page Reads/sec	Page Writes/sec
Pages Input/sec	Pages Output/sec
Pages/sec	Pool Nonpaged Allocs
Pool Nonpaged Bytes	Pool Paged Allocs
Pool Paged Bytes	Pool Paged Resident Bytes
System Cache Resident Bytes	System Code Resident Bytes
System Code Total Bytes	System Driver Resident Bytes
System Driver Total Bytes	Transition Faults/sec
Write Copies/Sec	

To get a description of each counter, you can click the Explain button in the
Add To Chart dialog box (see Figure A.1). When you do this, the dialog box
extends vertically to include a Counter Definition text box containing a
description of the selected counter. In Figure A.1, notice that you can monitor
the performance of remote computers. Also, the Instance list box is used to
display more than one instance of an object. For example, you can use the
Instance list box to monitor each processor separately on a multiple-processor
system.

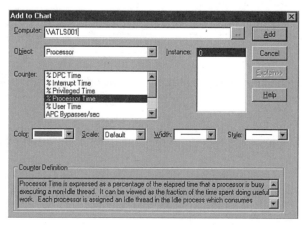

Figure A.1   *The Explain button provides a brief description of each counter.*

Working with Views

Performance Monitor has four views: Chart, Report, Log, and Alert. Each
view offers a different presentation of the data. They are described in the following sections.

Chart View

Chart view, the default view for Performance Monitor, displays the value of a
counter over a period of time. A multiplier is used to scale the value to a range
between 0 and 100. Figure A.2 illustrates a chart view in Performance
Monitor.

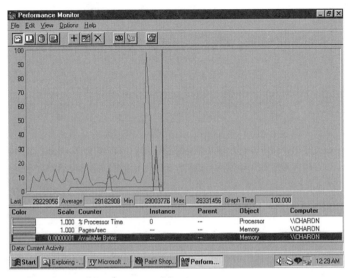

Figure A.2   *Chart view of Performance Monitor.*

Report View

Report view displays a column listing of counters and values. The values for each counter are periodically updated, and you can set the frequency of updates using the Options menu. You cannot see how the values change over time (like you can with Chart view), but you can quickly view numerous counters and a snapshot of their values. Figure A.3 illustrates a report view in Performance Monitor.

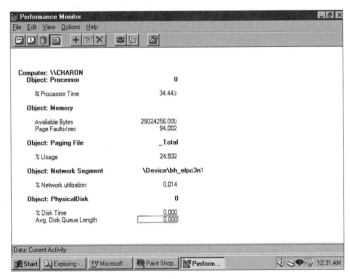

Figure A.3   *Report view of Performance Monitor.*

Log View

You can use *Log view* to set up the logging of data to a file. You can select only the objects you want to log—not the specific counters. When you select an object, all the counters for the object are logged. Performance Monitor can replay the log file after its collection.

When using the Log view, you must be concerned with the size of the log file and how quickly it grows. Depending on the number of objects you monitor and the frequency of updates, the log file can grow very quickly. You should always test the growth of the log file by sampling for a short period of time (a few minutes). Figure A.4 shows an example of configuring a log file in Log view.

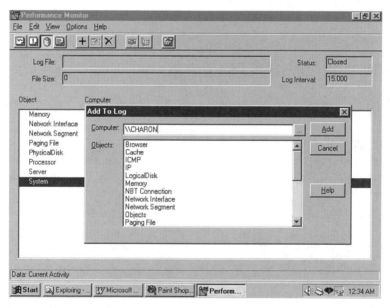

Figure A.4   *Log view of Performance Monitor.*

Tip

You can use MONITOR.EXE from the Windows NT Resource Kit to automatically log performance data when you are away from the office. The setup works great for monitoring the performance of nightly backups when you are out of the office.

Alert View

Alert view is used to configure the alerts for one or more counters. For each counter, you can specify a threshold value and run a program when the counter value rises above or sinks below the threshold value. Figure A.5 illustrates the configuration of an alert in Performance Monitor.

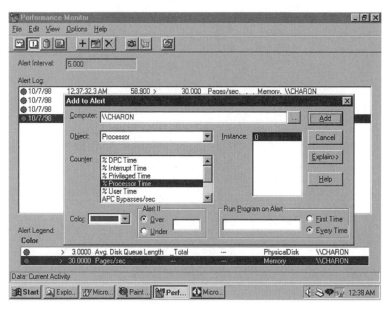

Figure A.5   *Alert view of Performance Monitor.*

Saving Views and Counters

Performance Monitor allows you to save your views and counters into a .PMW file. You can create the file by selecting Save Workspace from the File menu. Note that the file saves counters and views but not the data you have collected. If you want to save data, you must save the report or chart to a tab- or comma-separated text file. You can easily import either file type into most spreadsheet programs and perform a more-detailed analysis.

Deciding What to Monitor

It is easy to be overwhelmed by the number of counters available in Performance Monitor. If you are not careful, you can add too many counters and obscure the collection of data. Your selection of counters depends on your intended use of Performance Monitor. The following sections present general guidelines for deciding what to monitor.

Monitoring Basic System Resources

For basic system monitoring, you need to consider only those counters related to memory, the hard disk, the processor, and the network. Table A.2 presents a list of counters you would use for a basic measurement of system performance.

Table A.2   Objects and Counters for Basic Performance Monitoring

Object	Counter	Threshold
Processor	% Processor Time	More than 75%
Memory	Pages/sec	More than 20 pages/sec
	Available Bytes	Less than 4MB
Paging File	Committed Bytes	More than the amount of physical RAM
Physical Disk	%Disk Time	More than 65%
	Avg. Disk Queue Length	More than two
Network Segment	%Utilization	Depends on the network topology and number of network protocols

> **Tip**
>
> *If the system has more than one processor, you must use the System: %Total Processor Time counter to see the overall processing time.*

Isolating a Processor Bottleneck

If you want to isolate a processor bottleneck, perform the following steps:

1. Switch to Chart view and change the Gallery option from Graph to Histogram.

2. Invoke the Add to Chart dialog box and select the Processes object, the % Processor Time counter, and all instances except _Total (see Figure A.6).

3. After clicking OK, a histogram bar is used to represent the processor time used by each process. You should notice very high bars for one or more of the processes on the system. Select one of the taller bars to discover the process that is using an excessive amount of processor time.

4. If the process is related to services, stop the appropriate services until the % Processor Time noticeably decreases.

> **Author's Note**
>
> *Many antivirus and card service programs for laptops run background processes that require an excessive amount of processor time. Unless the process is critical to your daily use of the machine, I suggest stopping the*

process and starting it only when needed. For example, you may want to manually scan for viruses rather than running a service to constantly scan files that are opened or downloaded.

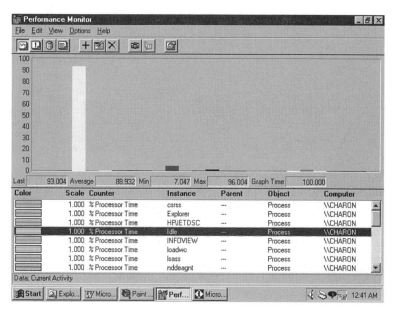

Figure A.6   *The Histogram option is used to isolate a processor bottleneck.*

From Here

You should establish a baseline for your network. A *baseline*, a collection of data under normal operating conditions, typically contains basic performance counters related to processor, disk, memory, and network resources. After establishing an initial baseline, you should continue to collect data on a weekly, biweekly, or monthly basis. The baseline data provides you with useful information that allows you to compare performance statistics as network and server changes are made. The captured data also gives you a solid reference that you can use to substantiate budget requests for new equipment and upgrades.

You should always attempt to collect data remotely because the Performance Monitor application itself affects the results, especially when used in Chart view. For large enterprise networks, you should dedicate at least one NT workstation to the task of monitoring the performance of other systems. Happy monitoring!

Appendix **B**

Working with Network Monitor

Network Monitor is a software utility available with Windows NT Server and Microsoft's Systems Management Server (SMS). You can use Network Monitor to gauge network performance; discover common network problems; and troubleshoot network services such as DNS, WINS, DHCP, RAS, and so on. For example, you can use Network Monitor to identify network servers or services that generate a large amount of broadcast traffic on your network, or you can use it to troubleshoot application problems. For example, Network Monitor can be used to troubleshoot configuration problems with Microsoft Outlook and Microsoft Exchange.

There are two versions of Network Monitor:

- Windows NT version
- SMS version

The Windows NT version ships with Windows NT Server and has many limitations compared to the SMS version. The most significant limitation of the Windows NT Network Monitor is that you can only monitor traffic to and from the machine on which the application is installed. The SMS Network Monitor allows you to monitor traffic between any two machines on the LAN and allows remote capture of data from Network Monitor Agents. (Network Monitor Agents can be installed on Windows NT Workstation, Windows NT Server, and Windows 95.) The SMS Network Monitor also allows you to edit and retransmit frames on the network.

Tip

If you use the SMS Network Monitor, you should load the Network Monitor Agent on every workstation and server. Then you can use the SMS Network Monitor from your workstation and capture sessions between any machines on the network.

Network Monitor operates by placing the network card in promiscuous mode. In other words, it tells the network adapter to accept all frames and place them into a capture buffer, which exists in RAM. As soon as frames are in the capture buffer, you can use a display filter to show only the data you need rather than the entire capture buffer.

> **Tip**
>
> *If all machines are on a switched Ethernet segment, you must install the Network Monitor Agent on LAN machines to get a complete capture of traffic to and from the machines. Otherwise, you get only a portion of the traffic that really exists on the network.*

Installing Network Monitor

To install the Windows NT Network Monitor, open the Network applet in the Control Panel, select the Services tab, and click Add. The Select Network Service dialog box displays a list of all uninstalled network services for the machine (see Figure B.1). The list contains two selections related to the Network Monitor: Network Monitor Agent and Network Monitor Tools and Agent. Only with Network Monitor Tools and Agent do you get the Network Monitor utility. If you are already using the SMS version of Network Monitor, you can select Network Monitor Agent to perform a remote capture.

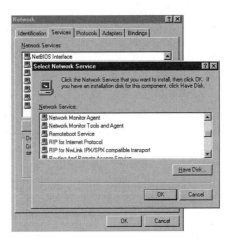

Figure B.1   *Network Monitor is installed via the Network applet in the Control Panel.*

Using Network Monitor

Network Monitor is located in the Administrative Tools group. When you open Network Monitor, it displays the following four window panes (see Figure B.2):

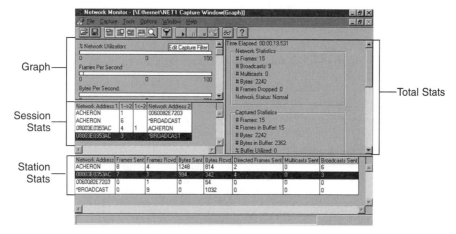

Figure B.2 *Four window panes compose the Network Monitor interface.*

- The Graph window pane gives a representation of all activity taking place on the network; it is a great place to get a summary of the network utilization and the broadcast traffic on the network.

- The Session Stats window pane displays statistics about individual sessions taking place on the network.

- The Station Stats window pane presents statistics about the sessions opened by the computer running Network Monitor.

- The Total Stats window pane gives summary statistics about the network activity detected since the capture process.

Before you begin a capture with Network Monitor, you should increase the buffer size. By default, the capture buffer is set to 1MB. You should increase the buffer to at least 5MB for most networks. The required buffer size is directly proportional to the amount of traffic on the network and the duration of the capture. You can use a capture filter to limit the capture to specific frames and avoid overflowing the capture buffer. If capturing data for an hour or more, you likely need at least a 10MB capture buffer.

> ### Troubleshooting Tip
>
> *The capture buffer exists in RAM. A large setting for the size of the capture buffer requires the same amount of free RAM. If the RAM is unavailable, the Network Monitor will drop frames.*

Capturing Frames

A capture is initiated by selecting Start from the Capture menu. You can then select Stop or Stop and View to end the capture. You can pause the capture by selecting Pause, and you can resume it by selecting Continue.

However, instead of using the Capture menu, you should familiarize yourself with the toolbar buttons. Unlike most toolbars that contain several useless buttons, the Network Monitor toolbar is very handy.

Viewing the Captured Data

You can view the data by selecting Stop and View from the Capture menu. If you select Stop, you must select Display Captured Data or press F12. The capture window (see Figure B.3) displays the contents of the capture buffer in chronological order in a *Summary pane*. The left column adds a frame number starting at 1. You can double-click on any frame and invoke two additional window panes: the *Detail pane* and the *Hex pane*.

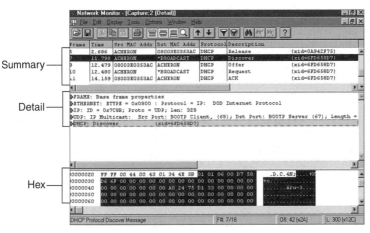

Figure B.3 *The capture window has three panes: Summary, Detail, and Hex.*

In the Detail window pane you can expand each frame to show all the protocols used to encapsulate and transport the data. The Hex window pane shows the data transmitted in the frame in both hexadecimal and ASCII text. For packets that contain clear text passwords, such as all POP3 email clients, you can see the password in the ASCII text (see Figure B.4).

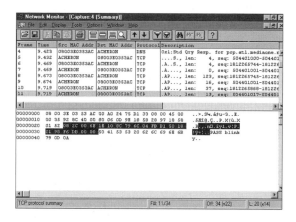

Figure B.4   *The Hex window pane of this capture displays a user's POP3 password in clear text.*

Using Filters

Network Monitor has two types of filters you can use:

- Capture filter
- Display filter

A *capture filter* limits the frames that are captured, allowing you to use a smaller capture buffer. A *display filter*, on the other hand, captures all frames to the capture buffer but limits the frames displayed in the capture window. Both filters use a logical statement to filter the frames.

Figure B.5 shows the Capture Filter dialog box. You can edit the SAP/ETYPE line to filter based on specific protocols. The Address Pairs section filters based on sessions between specific machines, and the Pattern Matches section limits Network Monitor to capturing only those frames containing a specific hex or ASCII pattern.

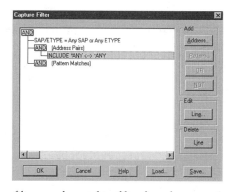

Figure B.5   *A capture filter can be used to filter based on protocol, network address, or frame content.*

Capturing from Remote Agents

You must use the SMS version of Network Monitor to capture from Network Monitor Agents. The following steps explain how to connect to a remote Network Monitor Agent:

1. Select Networks on the Capture menu.

2. In the Select Capture Network dialog box, choose the REMOTE Node Name.

3. Click Connect, and the Connect To Network Monitoring Agent dialog box appears (see Figure B.6).

4. In the Agent Name text box, specify the name of the agent to which you are trying to connect.

5. Click Connect. If the Network Monitor Agent on the remote computer is password-protected, you are prompted for a password.

6. Select Start on the Capture menu to begin capturing from the agent.

Figure B.6   *The SMS Network Monitor can connect to remote agents located across switches and routers.*

Saving Capture Files

You can save the capture buffer to a .CAP file and open it later for analysis. In the Save Data As... dialog box, you can select Filtered to save only those frames that meet the specifications of the current display filter (see Figure B.7). You can also save a range of frames by entering the beginning and ending frame numbers into the From and To text boxes.

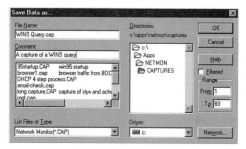

Figure B.7   *The Save Data As… dialog box has many options that allow you to save a subset of the frames you have captured.*

Appendix **C**

Changing IP Addressing Schemes

Most Windows NT networks use TCP/IP as a primary communication protocol. Throughout this book there have been references to several Windows NT design issues that are closely related to TCP/IP network design. For example, you should locate a master domain backup domain controller (BDC) on every subnet in each resource domain.

A good domain design requires a good underlying TCP/IP network design. In this appendix you will find guidelines for allocating IP addresses and subnets. You will also find useful information on how you can use DHCP to help make a smooth transition to a new IP addressing scheme.

Background

The *Internet Network Information Center (InterNIC)* is responsible for assigning IP addresses. Years ago, if your company wanted to communicate over the Internet, you would contact the InterNIC and obtain a series of addresses to use on your network. However, times have changed, and you now must express your needs to your communications carrier. Since the advent of numerous Internet service providers (ISPs), the InterNIC started assigning large blocks of addresses to the ISPs and made them responsible for delegating the address space to commercial clients.

The process of assigning large blocks of address space to ISPs goes against the original address classes set up by the InterNIC. The new method of assigning blocks of address space is referred to as *Classless InterDomain Routing (CIDR)*. CIDR allows the primary routers of the Internet to operate more efficiently because they have fewer entries in their routing tables. In other words, it is much easier for the routers to send information to and from a small number of ISPs than it is to send information to and from millions of businesses. An example of a CIDR block of addresses is given in Figure C.1.

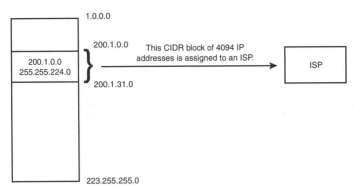

Figure C.1 *CIDR blocks of addresses simplify the routing tables of Internet routers— making the routing process more efficient.*

So how does CIDR affect you and your company? If your company has reserved an address class and plans to connect to the Internet, it is unlikely that you can use your previously assigned address space—with good reason. If your company were allowed to use your previously assigned address space, the primary Internet routers would require an additional entry to tell everyone how to reach your address space. Consequently, you are likely to use a set of addresses assigned to you by your chosen communications carrier.

This is where you encounter another problem: a lack of addresses. Most carriers want to give you only 6, 14, or 30 real IP addresses. If you are a customer with a hundred or more clients, you are forced to seek a better solution. This is where products such as Microsoft's Proxy Server and Network Address Translators (NATs) enter the picture.

By using a proxy server, you can assign private IP addresses on your network and use an Internet IP address to make HTTP requests on behalf of the clients with the private addresses. NAT takes the idea one step further by substituting a real IP address for the private IP address in the outgoing packets and altering the responses to route them to the correct private IP address. A *private IP address* is used here as an arbitrary addressing scheme for your network that is not unique to the addresses found on the Internet. Figure C.2 illustrates an example of using private IP addresses on the company network.

The following addresses have been allocated for assignment on private networks:

Start Address		End Address
10.0.0.0	to	10.255.255.255
172.16.0.0	to	172.31.255.255
192.168.0.0	to	192.168.255.255

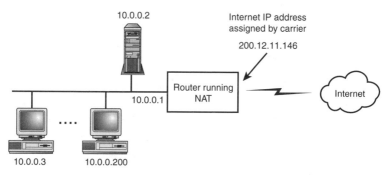

Figure C.2   *A private address scheme is used on the internal network and mapped to a real IP address using a NAT.*

Designing a Good IP Address Scheme

You can choose any address scheme you want on your internal network, so you should choose the scheme that gives you the greatest flexibility. Fortunately, the choice is easy. The 10.0.0.0 scheme gives you maximum flexibility because you can control 24 bits of the address space. The control of the 24 bits allows you to subnet the address space and give portions of it to other offices and remote sites.

A well-designed address scheme should provide you with flexibility and expansion while sufficiently describing the computers and devices on your network. Suppose you have three site locations—New York, Atlanta, and Los Angeles—with 200 or fewer machines at each site. Table C.1 provides a layout of the address ranges you could delegate to each site location, and Table C.2 divides the range given to each city into specific categories.

Table C.1   Address Ranges

IP Address	City
10.1.10.x–10.1.11.x	New York City
10.1.12.x–10.1.19.x	Future New York state sites
10.1.20.x–10.1.21.x	Atlanta
10.1.22.x–10.1.29.x	Future Georgia sites
10.1.30.x–10.1.31.x	Los Angeles
10.1.32.x–10.1.39.x	Future California sites

Table C.2   City Configuration

Address Range	Type	Purpose	Number of IPs
10.x.x.1– 10.x.x.10	Static	Router ports	10
10.x.x.11– 10.x.x.60	Static	Servers	50
10.x.x.61– 10.x.x.75	Static	Admin. workstations	15
10.x.x.76– 10.x.x.110	Static	Network devices	35
10.x.x.111– 10.x.x+1.154	Dynamic	DHCP pool	300
10.x.x+1.155– 10.x.x+1.254	Static	Network printers	100

Troubleshooting Tip

You must be careful not to make the address space too restrictive. For example, allocating a portion of the space based on an operating system is not a good idea because you will likely upgrade operating systems every few years.

The Address Change Implementation

This section illustrates how to implement an IP address change. The next section explains the variations you may encounter in applying the example to your network.

Suppose your current addressing scheme is based on 194.15.12.0. You have six servers, eight printers, and 120 clients. The clients are set up for DHCP and ATLS002, an NT server running DHCP. All printers have JetDirect cards with static IP addresses. Figure C.3 illustrates the network, and Table C.3 summarizes the current IP assignments.

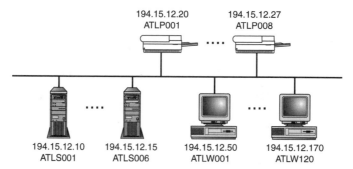

Figure C.3   *The old network uses a 194.15.12.0 scheme for all machines.*

Table C.3   Old IP Address Scheme

Computer/ Network Device	Description	Address/ Address Range
ATLS001	NT PDC running WINS, DNS	194.15.12.10
ATLS002	NT BDC running WINS, DNS, DHCP	194.15.12.11
ATLS003	NT Exchange Server	194.15.12.12
ATLS004	NT SQL Server	194.15.12.13
ATLS005	Novell 4.11 Server	194.15.12.14
ATLS006	UNIX Server	194.15.12.15
ATLP001	HP LaserJet 4MP (accounting)	194.15.12.20
ATLP002	HP LaserJet 4000 (accounting)	194.15.12.21
ATLP003	HP LaserJet IIISi (design)	194.15.12.22
ATLP004	HP LaserJet 4 (engineering)	194.15.12.23
ATLP005	HP LaserJet 4000 (data processing)	194.15.12.24
ATLP006	HP LaserJet 4000 (distribution)	194.15.12.25
ATLP007	HP LaserJet 6M (sales)	194.15.12.26
ATLP008	HP LaserJet 4000 (sales)	194.15.12.27
ATLW001–ATLW120	Client workstations assigned by a DHCP server	194.15.12.50– 194.15.12.200

The new IP address scheme will be based on the 10.0.0.0. The UNIX server's IP address cannot be changed because several clients run a manufacturing application that accesses the UNIX machine based on IP address. Figure C.4 illustrates the network, and Table C.4 summarizes the new IP address scheme.

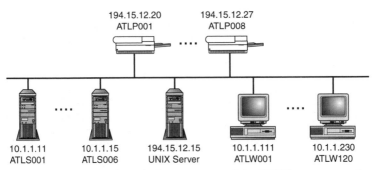

Figure C.4 *The new network, with the exception of the UNIX server, uses the*
10.0.0.0 IP scheme.

Table C.4   New IP Address Scheme

Computer/ Network Device	Description	Address/ Address Range
ATLS001	NT PDC running WINS, DNS	10.1.1.11
ATLS002	NT BDC running WINS, DNS, DHCP	10.1.1.12
ATLS003	NT Exchange Server	10.1.1.13
ATLS004	NT SQL Server	10.1.1.14
ATLS005	Novell 4.11 Server	10.1.1.15
ATLS006	UNIX Server	194.15.12.15
ATLP001	HP LaserJet 4MP (accounting)	10.1.2.155
ATLP002	HP LaserJet 4000 (accounting)	10.1.2.156
ATLP003	HP LaserJet IIISi (design)	10.1.2.157
ATLP004	HP LaserJet 4 (engineering)	10.1.2.158
ATLP005	HP LaserJet 4000 (data processing)	10.1.2.159
ATLP006	HP LaserJet 4000 (distribution)	10.1.2.160
ATLP007	HP LaserJet 6M (sales)	10.1.2.161
ATLP008	HP LaserJet 4000 (sales)	10.1.2.162
ATLW001– ATLW120	Client workstations assigned by a DHCP server	10.1.1.111– 10.1.2.154

Changing to the new scheme is a multistep process. Steps 1 and 2 must be
completed prior to the changeover date; steps 3 and 4 are completed the day of
the changeover (usually in the evening after everyone has left the office); and
steps 5 and 6 are follow-up steps. Following is a summary of each step.

Step 1: Lower DHCP Lease Times

Clients typically renew their DHCP lease after half the lease time expires. If
you use the default three-day lease time, clients will renew their IP addresses
after 36 hours. If you change the DHCP pool, some clients may not get the

new IP addresses for up to 36 hours. During the interim, clients with the new IP addresses will not be able to contact the clients with the old IP addresses unless you use a router. Because you plan to change the IP addressing during the evening hours, you want all clients to have their new IP addresses by the following morning. Thus, the lease time should be set to 10 hours.

Over the next 36 hours, all clients will renew their IP addresses and receive the 10-hour lease time. Because the renewal time is lower, there is an increased amount of traffic on the network. Given the size of this small network, the traffic increase will not result in any noticeable degradation in network performance.

Step 2: Install a Temporary Router

You can use a hardware router or turn an NT machine into a router for this step. But let's assume that you do not have a hardware router and you must use an NT machine. Here are the steps you should take to set up the NT machine:

1. Assign two IP addresses to the machine:

   IP address 1:   194.15.12.1
   Subnet mask: 255.255.255.0
   IP address 2:   10.1.1.1
   Subnet mask: 255.255.254.0

2. Enable IP routing.

3. Restart the machine.

Step 3: Change the DHCP Pool

The present DHCP scope is deactivated. A scope with the following properties is added and activated:

   Start Address: 10.1.1.111
   End Address: 10.1.2.154
   Subnet Mask: 255.255.254.0
   Lease Duration: 10 hours

The DHCP options are modified or added as follows:

DHCP Global Options

   006 DNS Servers = 10.1.1.11, 10.1.11.12
   044 WINS/NBNS Servers = 10.1.1.11, 10.1.11.12
   046 WINS/NBT Node Type = 0x8

DHCP Scope Options

   003 Router = 10.1.1.1

Step 4: Change the Statically Assigned IP Addresses

This can be a time-consuming task. You must go to each server (except the UNIX server) and change the IP address, subnet mask, default gateway, WINS server, and DNS server address as indicated in Table C.2. For all servers except the UNIX server, the default gateway is set to 10.1.1.1. For the UNIX server, you must change the DNS server address and set the default gateway to 194.15.12.1.

Step 5: Monitor and Test the Network

After the change to the DHCP pool, the clients will receive a DHCP NAK (negative acknowledgment) when attempting to renew their leases for the old IP addresses. The NAKs can be monitored using the Event Viewer Application Log on the DHCP server. By the following morning, all clients should receive the new IP addresses. In some cases, people turn off their machines when leaving work; when the machines are started the following morning, they will follow the same renewal process as the others and receive the new addresses.

Step 6: Increase the DHCP Lease Time

After all clients receive the new IP addresses from the DHCP server, it is safe to increase the lease interval. For this network, the default lease time is sufficient, so the lease duration of the scope should be set to three days.

Applying the Example to Your Network

For your network, you should consider some of the following issues:

- What is your current DHCP lease time?

- How long will it take you to change all hardcoded IP addresses?

- Are there any hardcoded IP addresses you cannot change?

- Will you need a temporary router to give you time to change all static IP addresses?

Depending on the size of your network, setting the DHCP lease time too low can result in performance degradation. You may want to experiment with the DHCP lease times to make sure the change has minimal impact on the network.

Some networks use security software that requires static IP addressing of all client machines. Because such networks do not use DHCP, changing the IP addressing is a huge task. And because changing the IP addresses of all clients is a time-consuming task, a temporary router is usually required.

Appendix **D**

Changing Naming Conventions

What's in a name? On a Microsoft network NetBIOS computer, names are used to access shared folders and printers on each machine. All computers should be named according to a reasonable naming convention; random or creative naming ultimately leads to confusion and conflict.

While your choice of names may be trivial for a small network, the adoption of a naming convention is a necessity on a large enterprise network. The name must be descriptive and unique. It also must be a reasonable number of characters.

Selecting a Naming Convention

Selecting a domain name is perhaps one of the biggest decisions you can make as a network or system administrator. The domain name is critical because all workstations and servers in the domain use it—and it is not easily changed. In addition to a domain name, you must also select a name for each of the following:

- Workstation
- Server
- Printer
- Network device
- Workgroup (for Windows 95 and Workgroups for Windows)
- Microsoft Exchange organization
- Microsoft Exchange site
- Microsoft SMS site
- Windows NT user account
- Windows NT group account

With all these required names, you must decide on a good convention that can be used throughout your company. All too often companies allow different locations to independently administer computer names, domain names, printer names, and so on. Although this makes everyone happy and prevents conflicts between administrators, it can be a real source of aggravation when consolidating domains or enterprise services such as WINS and DNS.

For example, suppose a company has two sales offices. At each office the administrator decides to name the workstations SALESXX, where XX corresponds to a workstation number. Now suppose the company introduces a global WINS server for all locations. Immediately there are conflicting registrations because there are identical computer names at each location.

> **Tip**
>
> *Windows 2000 helps you avoid this particular naming problem by allowing you to eliminate WINS and use DNS for name resolution. The hierarchical structure of DNS ensures there is no conflict for two machines with the same host name. For more information on DNS, see Chapter 13, "Enterprise Services: DHCP, WINS, and DNS."*

A naming convention should always apply globally within an organization. The exact convention you should use depends on the geography and organization of your business. In most cases, codes are developed to describe the device, the location of the device, or the department where the device is located. Additionally, a numerical code is usually appended.

For example, ATLS003, used throughout this book, uses a three-letter city code (ATL, for Atlanta), a one-letter device code (S, for server), and a three-digit numerical code (003, for server number three). You can be more specific by establishing specific device codes for database servers, messaging servers, print servers, and so on. However, you must be cautious, because in many cases a device may fall into multiple categories. For instance, a server may simultaneously act as a file, print, and database server.

Names and Security Identifiers

In Windows NT, a domain is not only defined by a NetBIOS name but also a security identifier (SID). ACLs and other security features use the SID, not the NetBIOS name, to identify the domain. When you change the NetBIOS name, the underlying SID remains the same. SIDs are completely unique; duplicate SIDs are impossible. If you reinstall Windows NT as a primary domain controller (PDC), a new domain SID is generated.

Changing a Windows NT Domain Name

You must use caution when changing a domain name. There is no absolute guarantee that all services will be operational under the new domain name. It is important to note that Microsoft does not guarantee that third-party software will work after a domain name change.

Carefully follow these steps for a successful domain name change:

1. Break all trusts.

2. Stop all application-related services, such as email and database services.

3. Change the domain name on the PDC. This triggers a warning stating that you will have to change the domain name on all workstations and servers and re-establish any trusts (see Figure D.1).

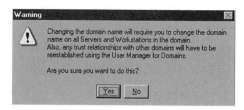

Figure D.1   *Any change to the domain name must be completed on all Windows NT computers in the domain.*

4. Restart the PDC so that the <1B> record for the new domain is registered with WINS.

5. If using WINS, force a replication from the PDC's primary WINS to all other WINS servers.

6. On each BDC, change the domain name and restart.

7. Force WINS replication.

8. Re-establish all trusts.

9. Open the Services applet in the Control Panel and re-enter the service account and password for each application-related service.

> *Tip*
>
> *The Service Control Manager database stores the service accounts in text format rather than SIDs. Thus, you must re-enter the service account information and password after changing the domain name.*

10. Restart all application-related services.

11. Change the domain name on each member server and workstation.

> **Tip**
>
> *You can use NETDOM.EXE from the Windows NT Resource Kit Supplement 2 to change the domain name remotely.*

12. Change all Windows 95 and WfW clients to a workgroup name that is the same as the new domain name.

Known Issues

If you are running SQL Server with integrated security, you will have to reset the Default Domain field in the SQL Security Manager. If you are running Microsoft Exchange, you must use Exchange Administrator to change the default domain to the new domain name. Also, all security on public folders is lost. It is recommended that you use PFADMIN.EXE from the Exchange Server Resource Kit to export the public folder security settings to a text file to make reconstruction of the permissions easier.

Changing the Windows NT Workstation Names

All Windows NT domain workstations and servers have a computer account in the domain SAM. Because you are not allowed to rename this account, you must delete it using Server Manager and create a new one by joining the domain with the new NetBIOS computer name. As a result, you must remove the computer from the domain, change the computer name, and join it back to the domain. The specific steps are as follows:

1. Invoke Server Manager. Delete the current computer account.

2. Change the computer from a domain to a workgroup with the same name. This change requires you to restart.

3. Change the name of the workstation and restart.

4. Change the workstation from a workgroup to a domain. This change requires you to create a computer account in the domain SAM.

Index

Symbols

$ (dollar sign), hiding home
directories, 164

A

abilities, 140-141
  configuring, 143
  domain controllers, 141
  see also permissions
access control lists, see ACLs
accessing
  domains, 14, 44-45
  files, 182
    permissions, 183-185
    shares, 9-10
  folders, 182
  Internet
    domains, 73
    troubleshooting, 132
  resources, 119-121
    trusts, 188
    permissions, 49-50
    Windows 2000, 121
    sharing, 50
account domains, 67
Account Policy, configuring, 127-129
accounts
  abilities, 140-141, 143
  built-in, 124, 136-137

groups, 135-136
  built-in local, 138
  trust relationships, affect on,
    144-145
  implementing, strategies,
    148-150, 152
  local, 136
  naming conventions, 146
  policies
    configuring, 124
    lockouts, 129
  rights, 140-141, 143
  templates
    troubleshooting, 165
    underscoring, 147
  unused, 147
  user, 135-136
    moving to new domain, 100-103
    policies, 173-176
    profiles, 169-171
    resource permissions, modifying,
      104-105
    roaming profiles, modifying, 172
    Windows NT, 8
  user-defined, 138
    global group, 140
    global user, 139
    local, 138
    local group, 139
Acknowledge packets (DHCP), 219
ACLs (Access Control Lists), 181
  complete trust model, 66
  group access, 190-191
  inheritance, 186

Q-R